Zen Living

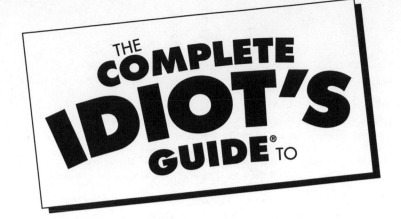

THE COMPLETE IDIOT'S GUIDE® TO

Zen Living

Second Edition

by Gary R. McClain, Ph.D., and Eve Adamson

A member of Penguin Group (USA) Inc.

ALPHA BOOKS

Published by the Penguin Group

Penguin Group (USA) Inc., 375 Hudson Street, New York, New York 10014, U.S.A.

Penguin Group (Canada), 10 Alcorn Avenue, Toronto, Ontario, Canada M4V 3B2 (a division of Pearson Penguin Canada Inc.)

Penguin Books Ltd, 80 Strand, London WC2R 0RL, England

Penguin Ireland, 25 St Stephen's Green, Dublin 2, Ireland (a division of Penguin Books Ltd)

Penguin Group (Australia), 250 Camberwell Road, Camberwell, Victoria 3124, Australia (a division of Pearson Australia Group Pty Ltd)

Penguin Books India Pvt Ltd, 11 Community Centre, Panchsheel Park, New Delhi—10 017, India

Penguin Group (NZ), cnr Airborne and Rosedale Roads, Albany, Auckland 1310, New Zealand (a division of Pearson New Zealand Ltd)

Penguin Books (South Africa) (Pty) Ltd, 24 Sturdee Avenue, Rosebank, Johannesburg 2196, South Africa

Penguin Books Ltd, Registered Offices: 80 Strand, London WC2R 0RL, England

Copyright © 2004 by Amaranth Illuminare

International Standard Book Number: 1-59257-243-X
Library of Congress Catalog Card Number: 2004108622

08   07   06   8   7   6   5   4

Interpretation of the printing code: The rightmost number of the first series of numbers is the year of the book's printing; the rightmost number of the second series of numbers is the number of the book's printing. For example, a printing code of 04-1 shows that the first printing occurred in 2004.

Printed in the United States of America

Note: This publication contains the opinions and ideas of its authors. It is intended to provide helpful and informative material on the subject matter covered. It is sold with the understanding that the authors, book producer, and publisher are not engaged in rendering professional services in the book. If the reader requires personal assistance or advice, a competent professional should be consulted.

The authors, book producer, and publisher specifically disclaim any responsibility for any liability, loss, or risk, personal or otherwise, which is incurred as a consequence, directly or indirectly, of the use and application of any of the contents of this book.

Most Alpha books are available at special quantity discounts for bulk purchases for sales promotions, premiums, fund-raising, or educational use. Special books, or book excerpts, can also be created to fit specific needs.

For details, write: Special Markets, Alpha Books, 375 Hudson Street, New York, NY 10014.

Publisher: *Marie Butler-Knight*
Product Manager: *Phil Kitchel*
Senior Managing Editor: *Jennifer Chisholm*
Senior Acquisitions Editor: *Randy Ladenheim-Gil*
Book Producer: *Lee Ann Chearney/Amaranth Illuminare*
Development Editor: *Christy Wagner*
Senior Production Editor: *Billy Fields*
Copy Editor: *Nancy Wagner*
Illustrator: *Chris Eliopoulous*
Cover/Book Designer: *Trina Wurst*
Indexer: *Julie Bess*
Layout: *Ayanna Lacey*
Proofreading: *Donna Martin*

To my father, Dale McClain.

Contents at a Glance

Appendixes

Contents

Foreword

As a busy physician, I experienced the irony in being asked to write the foreword to the first edition of *The Complete Idiot's Guide to Zen Living*. After all, I spend my very un-Zenlike days going at double speed, my head crammed with facts and my body tight with the frustrations of dealing with insurance companies and full schedules. But every once in a while, I stop in the hallways of my office, listen to the sounds of my work life, inhale deeply, and enjoy, just for a few seconds, the great slice of life that it represents. These moments, I now know, are Zen moments.

Modern medicine is rapidly documenting just how healthy the regular practice of Zen and other meditative systems are. In one recent study, relaxation techniques lowered blood pressure, cholesterol, and stress hormone levels in a group of men. In another survey, meditation led to a lessening of chronic back pain in long-time sufferers. Relaxation exercises are associated with greater longevity in the elderly, with a better sense of well-being in cancer patients, and with improved exercise tolerance in athletes.

But certainly, Zen and other systems that teach relaxation are not merely for people with diseases. The greatest reason to pursue a Zen lifestyle is for preventive medicine purposes. My medical practice integrates family practice and acupuncture with nutritional and mind-body medicine. All day long in my office, patients tell me how little time they have to care for their health. Our modern lives are nonstop busy, and this means constant stress. Stress causes wear and tear on our bodies and exhaustion of our minds. This is because hormones are secreted by the adrenal and other glands in response to stress. These hormones (cortisol, adrenaline, and others) raise blood pressure and blood sugar; weaken the immune system; irritate the blood vessels, leading to hardening of the arteries; and deplete serotonin, resulting in depression. Over the years, this unrelenting stress will lead to the loss of health and happiness. Zen relaxation counteracts this chronic situation. Relaxation lowers these hormone levels, preventing their ravaging effects. Even more, relaxation promotes the production of hormones that protect the body cells from breakdown, boosts well-being, encourages restful sleep, and aids in proper digestion.

Anyone who leads a busy life could use this book. In clear, simple terms, Gary McClain, Ph.D., and Eve Adamson describe the ideas behind Zen, the scope of its practice, and how to incorporate it into your life. As you will learn in the book, Zen is a centuries-old relaxation technique that is easy to learn and to practice. But it is much more than a meditation system. Practicing Zen at home, at work, and in between offers a way of counteracting the wear and tear of daily stress. Zen provides a way of living in the moment, in every moment. What makes Zen so unique is that it does not have to be a religion, but, in fact, is more of a lifestyle. There are Zen ways of being with people and Zen ways of being by yourself. Zen does not require you to learn foreign languages, dress differently, or attend religious ceremonies. It requires you to *notice* your life, to experience who you are and what you are doing in a full and conscious manner. The results will be a healthy body and a mind free to enjoy what life might offer.

Glenn S. Rothfeld, M.D., M.Ac.

Dr. Rothfeld is medical director of WholeHealth New England, a complementary medicine center in Arlington, Massachusetts. He is also clinical assistant professor of family medicine and community health at Tufts University School of Medicine in Boston, where he developed one of the nation's first courses on alternative medicine. Dr. Rothfeld has been at the forefront of integrative and alternative medicine for more than 20 years. In addition to his training in family medicine, Dr. Rothfeld is trained in acupuncture, nutritional medicine, and herbal medicine. He is the co-author of several popular books, including *Thyroid Balance* (Adams Media), *Ginkgo Biloba* (Dell), *Folic Acid and the Amazing B Vitamins* (Berkley), and *The Acupuncture Response* (Contemporary).

Introduction

You can't teach Zen. Just ask a Zen master. You can't explain it or draw a diagram of it or transfer it via Vulcan mind-meld to anybody else, and if you could, wouldn't we all be enlightened by now? And yet, Zen is simple: It is simply being, right here, right now. We believe the search for self-knowledge and the ability to pay attention and really live is a universal one. Therefore, rather than creating another Zen manual that details this ancient and venerable tradition in all its complexity of sects and various cultural manifestations, we have done our best to illuminate the ways in which Zen resonates for Western culture—for you, right here, right now, living in America and standing in a bookstore reading the introduction to this book. Our goal is to assist those seeking greater self-knowledge, happiness, inner contentment, and peace in finding a valid contemporary Western way to embrace Zen living and all it offers your very consciousness.

You'll find this book is full of real-life examples mixed in with the most ancient Zen stories. And you might even notice that, Western or Eastern, American or Japanese or Chinese or Vietnamese or Korean, anecdotes about Gary or Eve or Bodhidharma or Dogen or Joshu or the Buddha himself, all our stories and all our suggestions are meant to be read lightly—not grasped, not held as sacred, not revered. Rather, consider them with a smile, a wink, or even a belly laugh. We won't exactly tell you to kill the Buddha should you meet him on the road (as the saying goes), but you might want to give him a knowing nudge with your elbow. It's what we like to do. We know he would get the joke.

Zen and its many illuminations, contradictions, and enigmas can confuse, please, frustrate, amuse, and eventually enlighten any heart from any culture. It can help you deal with your existence on this planet with fearless determination and a real sense that you are living in your present moment in the very best way you possibly can, because the past is gone and tomorrow never really comes. We hope this book will guide you toward the enlightenment that is waiting inside your own heart.

What You Will Learn in This Book

This book is divided into six parts, each tackling a different angle of living Zen in your life.

Part 1, "Dharma 101," will explain what Zen is, exactly. We'll give you a brief introduction to what Zen can do for you, and then we'll tell you how Zen evolved, from its ancient Indian origins to twenty-first–century America.

Part 2, "The Future Is the Past Is Now: Being Zen," is about truth. *Dharma* is the Sanskrit word for "truth," as taught by the Buddha. But what is truth for you, and how can you get more of it into your life? In this part, we'll talk about a Zen approach to everyday life, even when bad things happen. We'll also introduce the concept of enlightenment.

Part 3, "1-2-3 Zazen: Zen Techniques for Zen Living," will give you some right-now, get-started techniques for living a more Zenlike existence, such as meditation, breathing, mindfulness, and the practice of koans. We'll also talk about some Zenlike lifestyle choices.

Part 4, "Personal Zen," is all about you. Who are you? Who is the real you? Zen can help you gain self-knowledge, and it can bolster your romantic, friendship, and family relationships, too. Plagued by desire, fear, worry? Zen's got you covered.

Part 5, "Zen in the Workplace," is all about you and your job. Can Zen make you more successful? In a way—read and find out how! Zen can also improve your on-the-job relationships and the way you handle work-related stress.

Part 6, "Home Is Where the Zen Is," helps you integrate Zen techniques and attitudes (which are really just the attitudes of the real you) into your home environment, your creative expression, and your appreciation for the arts. We'll end by discussing what comes after mindfulness. What do you see? Love, kindness, and compassion. Here's how to put that into practice and, finally, how to discover just how Zen you want to be—and just how Zen you already are.

Following these parts, you will find three appendixes that cover further Zen readings, a glossary of Zen terms, and an explanation of the 10 Bulls illustrations.

Zen Extras in a Box

Throughout each chapter in this book, we'll add four types of extra information, neatly packaged in boxes, for your further enlightenment:

Nirvana Notes

These boxes offer tips, techniques, and good old-fashioned Zen advice for more effective Zen living.

Monkey Mind!

These boxes supply you with things to watch out for, be careful of, or avoid. These are the "heads-up" boxes.

Zen-Speak

These boxes define words we use in the text that you might not know. Some are Japanese, Chinese, or Sanskrit words. Some are plain old English but refer to technical or other areas that might not be common knowledge.

One Hand Clapping

These boxes contain ancient and modern Zen wisdom from around the world, as well as other information that adds to or expands upon each chapter.

Acknowledgments

Thanks to friends—especially Deborah—who support me even when I am out of the flow and am temporarily thrashing around in the water. Thanks to my personal trainer, Max, who reminds me to breathe. And thanks to Lee Ann and Eve, for being such excellent collaborators.

—Gary R. McClain, Ph.D.

Thanks to my father—Zen master in a Presbyterian disguise—and to my mother, who never stands in the way of whatever I need to be or do, even if she thinks it's odd. Thanks to Lee Ann, for being a pillar and for being a friend. Thanks to Ben, for being my muse (all that seeing, all that poetry …). And thanks to my children, Angus and Emmett, who remind me every day to live in the moment, and who, by their very existence, make life worth mindfulness.

—Eve Adamson

Special Thanks to the Technical Editor

The Complete Idiot's Guide to Zen Living, First Edition, was reviewed by an expert who provided invaluable insight to help ensure that this book tells you everything you need to know about bringing Eastern Zen to your hectic, stressed-out Western lifestyle—that is, Zen living. In its pages, you'll learn how to live mindfully and enjoy life's vicissitudes with a Zen smile unseen in the West since Leonardo da Vinci painted the *Mona Lisa*. Our special thanks are extended to Gail Carr Feldman, Ph.D.

Gail Carr Feldman, Ph.D., is a clinical psychologist, author, and public speaker. Gail has appeared on radio and television programs across the country, including *Larry King Live*, and is the author of *Releasing the Goddess Within* (with Katherine A. Gleason) and *Releasing the Mother Goddess* (with Eve Adamson). She has a passion for travel and has spoken in Greece, Puerto Rico, and Australia on higher creativity and the transcendent life. She credits her two grown daughters with bringing her inspiration and some of the wisdom that has flowered from sitting zazen in the lotus position over the last 30 years of being a mom. She is learning the Zen of the "empty nest," a.k.a. a clean and uncluttered living space, now that one daughter is married and teaching massage therapy and the other daughter is working as a journalist in Guatemala. Gail lives on the high desert of Albuquerque and enjoys hiking and skiing (and being one with) the New Mexico mountains.

Trademarks

Part 1

Dharma 101

You've heard the word *Zen*, and you've wondered what it's all about. In Part 1, we'll give you the lowdown: what Zen can do for your mind, your body, your spirit, and your life. Zen means living right here, right now. Simple? Deceptively so! We'll introduce you to the ideas and show you how a few simple adjustments in your attitude can make your life simpler, happier, and more real.

Next we'll trace Zen's origins and its evolution to twenty-first–century America, from the Buddha in India to China, Japan, Vietnam, Tibet, Korea, and finally, the United States. Zen has changed, evolved, and blossomed into a uniquely Western incarnation. American Zen makes a lot of sense for those of us struggling to find meaning in today's sometimes frightening and usually stressful world. Zen provides the answers, both to the questions you have about yourself and the questions and confusion you might sometimes feel in a world where you seem to have no control. Those answers have been right inside you all along.

Spring Cleaning for Your Life

In This Chapter

◆ Does anybody need Zen these days?

◆ What is Zen, anyway?

◆ What Zen has to do with you, right here, right now

◆ Zen in a post–September 11 world

◆ How Zen can make your life better

This book is about Zen living, but not the kind that takes place in a monastery or in a cave or even, necessarily, in Japan. This book is about Zen living for you.

"Who, me?" you might ask, glancing behind you. "I'm no Zen master." Don't be so sure! Just because you don't wear *Matrix*-style black robes or spend your days chanting or sitting in silent meditation or contemplating the nature of reality doesn't mean you can't live a more Zenlike life. Anyone can do it. It's easy. You just have to begin.

Begin what? Decluttering. Rethinking. Stepping back and taking a look at what's really going on. Living Zen is like spring cleaning the life you already have, getting all the junk out of the way, and carting it off to that universal recycling center so you can really get down to the business of living.

Zen can do more than help you live a calmer, more organized life. It can also help you see through confusion and infuse your life with a sense of peace and rightness. Zen can even help you understand the fear, anxiety, worry, hurt, and all those other feelings that tend to plague you in this uncertain and sometimes unstable world.

Zen can help you, not deny those feelings, but rise above them like soap bubbles to look down at them and see them for what they are: feelings, nothing more, nothing less. There they are. Just look at them. And then Zen can teach you how to let go of those feelings when you are done feeling them, rather than holding on for dear life to things that are only figments of your brain. Now that's a handy life skill!

Why Zen?

Life has become very complicated, hasn't it? The world changes, sometimes in ways that hardly seem positive. People worry about security, politics, money, relationships, and status. Everyone seems so busy; it is almost as if one tries to distract himself from himself. The fine art of multitasking is no longer reserved for computers. We all do it, every day. We talk on cordless phones and cellular phones while typing e-mails and sending faxes. We schedule meetings on our PDA while attending meetings via the Internet. Then we check our caller ID and voicemail to see what calls we missed. We pay our bills online, chat online, and keep track of our schedules electronically. We listen to our MP3 players while running on a treadmill, take our laptop computers on the road, even send instant messages to the people living upstairs in our own homes because we are too busy to walk up the stairs! (Yes, we really know people who do this. Maybe you are one of them!)

But what about free time? What about relationships? Our lives are fully scheduled with activities, plans, even conversations we think we *should* have. Or maybe your free time is spent collapsed on the couch, staring blankly at the television, letting the screen fill your mind with a stream of images you can barely recall an hour after you've shut off the set. What else can you do after such an exhausting week?

Partners, children, and friends fit in somewhere—or not. We may cling obsessively to our personal relationships, hoping our loved ones will provide the anchor, the sense of self we can't seem to find within us, hoping they will love us, or hoping that if they don't, we can keep busy enough not to notice or to feel too lonely. And then there's always Internet dating, right? This can be nice and safe and anonymous for as long as you want it to be; you can fill that photo on a computer screen with all your hopes and dreams without the annoying necessity of actually meeting and finding out the other person's faults, annoying habits, needs, etc.

Meanwhile, we watch the 6 o'clock news or follow the lead stories on news websites and wonder if we will all be okay, if the world is falling apart, and if we are safe. It can be a stressful world to plunge into each day!

We really don't mean to make modern life seem completely bleak. Modern life really is very exciting. We, too, have our laptop computers, our mobile phones, our e-mail accounts, our instant message friends list. We can be in touch in a second. We feel connected, at least electronically, and the entire system, precarious as it might sometimes seem, allows us to do lots of work in record time. We multitask. We feel pride in our accomplishments. Life in the electronic age, traveling down the information highway at a breakneck pace, can be thrilling. And when we get too worried about the world, we use a remote control to turn off the evening news.

Nirvana Notes

Zen might seem as if it's a solitary practice, but it doesn't exist in a vacuum. Zen relationships are just as much "Zen" as Zen meditation. A Zen approach to relationships means relishing each moment with people, really listening, accepting them for who they are, and telling the truth. (For more on Zen relationships, see Chapter 14.)

But sometimes we also feel overwhelmed, stressed, too busy, disorganized, isolated, lonely, and frightened. We're just like you.

So what does all this have to do with Zen? What can Zen do for you, for us, for any of us? Just because it doesn't have the word *cyber* in front of it doesn't mean Zen isn't more relevant today than it ever has been. Zen can teach us something exceptionally important for finding peace, contentment, and happiness in the twenty-first century—or any century. Zen teaches us to relinquish control.

Yikes! Relinquish control? Let go of the steering wheel? Set the great ocean liner that is our life adrift, untended and without a captain? Impossible! Or is it?

It certainly is not. Zen can teach you to let go in a way that frees you, not from your duties as captain of the ship, but from the effort, the strain, and the burden of trying to manipulate that giant, seaweed-clogged rudder against the inevitable waves and tides. Your ship can run beautifully by itself. Just keep an eye out for icebergs, and you'll be fine. You'll see.

What Is Zen?

Zen is not complicated. It doesn't involve any special knowledge. It doesn't involve any equipment. Zen is anti-equipment in that it helps you clean out the attic that is you and drop off all the stuff you don't need—your worries, fears, opinions, preconceptions, attachments—at that recycling bin.

Zen-Speak _____

Zen is the Japanese word for "meditation," not in the sense of the contemplation of something, but as a mode of existing (whether sitting, walking, or otherwise going about your day) without any goal or ulterior motive. Alan Watts, in his *The Way of Zen*, calls it "unified or one-pointed awareness." *Dhyana* in Sanskrit and *Ch'an* in Chinese, the term *Zen* originated with Buddhism in India.

Zen is for anyone, no matter his or her religious beliefs, country of origin, or lifestyle. Living Zen is simple. Although many say Zen defies all definitions, we would define it with one simple, short word: *now*.

"Now? What about it?" you ask.

Exactly.

Monkey Mind! _____

What's so bad about thinking? Nothing at all. Yet becoming so engaged with your thoughts that you forget to live in the moment or allowing your thoughts to cause you suffering are surefire ways to miss the truth bus. How can you fully manifest each moment of your precious existence if you are letting your thoughts or feelings torture you?

If you are thoroughly confused, don't worry. Zen is already beginning to work its magic on you. Zen is a practice full of surprises—enough to fill volumes. Yet despite the wealth of guidance, inspiration, and philosophical suppositions Zen has inspired throughout history, it still comes down to this: now, right now.

Humans are programmed to think, interpret, analyze, examine, and define—and then think some more. We can't help it! It is one of the side effects of having such big, complex brains. Our lives are so busy and complicated that we have to think to keep everything in order. If we don't think, we are in big trouble. Thinking makes us who we are.

We're not going to tell you to stop thinking, so turn that mental chatter down to a dull roar and listen up: Zen is not about obliterating your thoughts, your feelings, your personality, or any other aspect of you. On the contrary, Zen helps you declutter yourself so you can think more easily, see more clearly, understand more readily, and know yourself more intimately.

That sounds pretty good, doesn't it? We think so.

But first, here is something else to throw into the mix: Zen isn't about end results.

"Huh? Then what's the point?"

There is no point to Zen.

"What? No point? Then why am I wasting my time?"

We Westerners are very goal-oriented, aren't we? When we have a problem, we want to fix it … now! We go to school to get a job. We get a job to make money. We make money to buy stuff. We work harder to make more money to buy more stuff. We worry about our stuff, and we want something to fix it … now! We worry about each other, and we want to fix each other … now! We worry about the world, and we want someone to fix it … now!

It is easy to get seduced into thinking that everything should have a goal and that we can change, fix, correct, and rectify everything we don't like in the world. And what if we can't? At least we can be worried, angry, or anxious about someone else doing it for us! How else would we ever get anywhere? How would we get ahead? How would we feel secure enough to get through the day? How else would everything finally be okay?

One Hand Clapping

One day, Baso, a Zen monk, was sitting in zazen (meditation). His teacher passed by and asked him what he was doing. Baso replied, "I want to become a Buddha." The teacher immediately picked up a tile and began to polish it vigorously. "What are you doing?" Baso asked. "I'm polishing this tile to make it a mirror," replied the teacher. "What? How can polishing a tile make it a mirror?" asked Baso. "How can zazen make you a Buddha?" the teacher answered. Just as Baso mistakenly believed the point or goal of zazen was to become a Buddha, so we may mistakenly believe Zen, or zazen, has a goal. Zen itself is the already-achieved goal. This moment is your life, so wake up and start living it.

In Zen, you don't get anywhere. You don't get ahead. You don't get in there and fix stuff, and you certainly don't make anybody else do it, either. Most important, in Zen, everything already *is* okay, because in Zen, the present moment is all that matters. Live, right now. That's all. Live without judgment, without emotional striving, without preconception. Just live. Right now. Be.

That doesn't mean you don't plan or try to make your life work or change the things you can change. But it does mean waking up to the present moment and really living it rather than hovering in the past, worrying about the future, or criticizing yourself for "doing it all wrong."

Plus, Zen living has some great side effects. Although Zen isn't really Zen if you practice it specifically to achieve some benefit (being goal-less as it is), there are undeniable benefits to living Zen. Let's look at some of them.

Mental Clutter Control

If your desk looks anything like Gary's or Eve's desk, you have a nice example right in front of you of a cluttered mind. Consider *zazen* your professional organizer. Zazen is sitting, Zen sitting. It is the one technique used in Zen, and it isn't complicated. You sit—simple yet challenging, simple yet exceptionally useful. Although it doesn't sign permission slips or finish reports or do the dishes for you, zazen helps purge your brain of all the stuff that is keeping you from doing what you need to do.

Oh, and one more thing about that messy desk metaphor: Gary used to criticize himself for his messy desk at home and also for his messy desk at his office. Eve has a home office but doesn't like to let people in there for fear they will see how disorganized her work space appears. But you know what? True Zen is anti-metaphorical. Does your messy desk signify your disordered mind? No. We've just imposed that comparison. A messy desk just means you have a messy desk. If it worries you, clean it. If it doesn't, then you have no problem. Now you're getting into Zen mode!

Zen-Speak

Zazen is the Japanese word for "sitting meditation." *Za* means "to sit," and *zen* means "meditation." The Chinese word for zazen is *T'so-chuan*.

Finding Yourself

Zen is free to everyone, regardless of what country he lives in or what his condition in life is. And although it doesn't provide a professional to help you interpret yourself, practicing Zen does provide you a space in which you can learn to see and know yourself more clearly, completely free from interpretation. Your zazen time is your time to be with yourself, not actively thinking, "Who am I?" or "What am I doing?" or "Where have I gone wrong?" but to just be, just you, with no confusion or complicated issues.

Zen gives you that opportunity to find yourself—the real you, not the you you try to be at work or at home or in your relationships, not the you people tell you is you, not the you you tell yourself you can someday become, but the *you* of right now.

And that is really the only you there is, the only you there ever will be. Your external circumstances, appearance, and reputation will probably change as the years go by, but as long as you exist, you will always exist only in the present moment. You, now. That's all. Kind of a relief, isn't it?

One Hand Clapping

What is Zen? Zen means doing anything perfectly, making mistakes perfectly, being defeated perfectly, hesitating perfectly, doing anything perfectly or imperfectly, perfectly. What is the meaning of this perfectly? How does it differ from perfectly? Perfectly is in the will; perfectly is in the activity. Perfectly means that at each moment of the activity there is no egoism in it …. Our pain is not only our own pain; it is the pain of the universe. The joy of the universe is also our joy. Our failure and misjudgment is that of nature, which never hopes or despairs, but keeps on trying.

—From *Zen and Zen Classics* by R. H. Blyth

Paying Attention

One of Zen's most dramatic benefits is that it teaches you to pay attention. Living life on automatic pilot might seem more efficient at times, but it is certainly less beautiful. Learning to live in the moment, to be present in the now, means paying attention to everything you do as if you've never done it before. Everything is new and wonderful: doing laundry, talking to a friend, sweating through your exercise routine, filing, walking your dog, petting your cat, sitting through a staff meeting, tasting your morning toast and coffee, completing a project, and so on. Zen teaches you to pay attention to every detail, immersing yourself in your activity to such a degree that you become the activity. You might surprise yourself at what you are able to accomplish when you pay attention.

Peace at Last

It's a funny thing, giving up control and letting life spin out the way it will anyway. When you stop thinking you can control everything that happens in the world, in your country, in your city, in your neighborhood, even in your own house, life comes into focus. You start to see exactly what you can control (your own mind) and what you can't (other people). You start to recognize that the world is a complicated, chaotic, changeable place full of complicated, chaotic, changeable people, and you start to recognize yourself as one of them.

Then you start to see how it all flows like a great river and how everything and everyone, including you, is a part of that river. You start to see how letting yourself go with the flow of the river is a lot easier than trying to control the shapes of all those other waves, ripples, and currents. And at last, when you start to see how you can just let it go and live your life, you will begin to feel an inner calm, peace, and sense of security. You really can find peace at last, no matter what goes on around you. Now is all that matters, and you—the inner you, the real you, the essential you—will always be there, will always be perfect, and will always be just fine.

What Westerners Can Learn from an Ancient Eastern Religion

Zen might seem a little foreign to you—it sounds so otherworldly or at least other-culture-ly. But just because Zen is an ancient Eastern religion that originated in India and traveled to China, Korea, and Japan doesn't mean it isn't fully real and organic to you. British Zen scholar R. H. Blyth, in his *Zen and Zen Classics*, writes:

> Zen arises spontaneously, naturally, out of the human heart. It is not a special revelation to any person, class, or nation. Thus, to say it came from India to China and from China to Japan is nonsense. One might as well say that the air we breathe in one country comes from another.

That's not to say there isn't a fascinating history attached to Zen's arrival in the Western world (see Chapter 2). But Zen's antiquity simply doesn't affect its truth. We can learn a lot from living Zen, as much as anyone ever did in any country, in any century. We can learn to be, to relish life, to live each moment perfectly. We can learn a few other things helpful to our lives, too. The lessons in the following sections include all these things.

Moderation in All Things

The Buddha himself, Siddhartha Gautama (see Chapter 2), proclaimed the importance of the Middle Way. After living a privileged life of luxury, then spending years being an extremely deprived ascetic, the Buddha discovered that moderation is the only way to find true balance and the best way to live fully and with a complete and mindful awareness.

Zen-Speak

Asceticism is the practice of self-deprivation or self-denial, which can include doing without possessions, undergoing extreme fasting, going without sleep, begging, and even inflicting self-pain.

This concept means making a conscious effort not to overconsume, overindulge, live inconsiderately, or hurt others. It also means refraining from *asceticism* or subjecting oneself to other extremes of deprivation and self-denial. Find moderation in all things, as they say. These are words true for Buddha and words to live by today.

Buddha sits in meditation under the bodhi tree.

Cut the Chaos

Living in the moment, without attaching oneself to regrets about yesterday or worries about tomorrow, goes a long way toward cutting through the chaos of everyday life. Have you ever noticed that the more hectic your life becomes, the more you start to misplace things (your car keys, your planner, that crucial computer file) or forget things (the new employee's name, that dentist appointment, picking your son up from soccer)? You may even get clumsier (tripping over your own feet, dropping that water glass, accidentally tossing the salad all over the kitchen floor).

Chaos breeds chaos. Zen stops the cycle. Suddenly you remember exactly where you need to be and exactly where you put your car keys. Your mind is centered and clear, like an organized desk, and all that information is much easier to access.

Know Thyself

A person with self-knowledge is a wise person, and knowing the self is the first step toward knowing all humankind. Zen living means recognizing that all is one just as each living thing is an individual. Zen exists on the edge of this contradiction: Each thing is diverse, and all things are one.

Knowing the self is helpful, then, on two levels: Who are you, that person who is completely unique and different from anyone else before? And who are you, that person who is, in essence, the same as the whole world? Both types of wisdom can be helpful in all walks of life.

Serenity Today

Whether or not you ever attain something akin to *nirvana* (enlightenment), living Zen can bring a level of serenity into your life that you might never know without it.

You can feel more calm, tranquil, relaxed, and peaceful today because Zen is today. It works right now. It will work better the more you do it, sure. But it starts working the moment you embrace it. So what are you waiting for?

Zen-Speak

Nirvana is the Sanskrit word for "enlightenment," the state achieved by the Buddha (and many since) upon the true realization and recognition of the unity of all things. Some approaches to Zen stress nirvana as a kind of goal, although it is far from an end result. Rather, nirvana is thought to be a state that launches an enlightened life into continued spiritual growth.

Zen Living in an Uncertain World

People like to characterize different decades, different centuries, and eventually, probably even different millennia. How will they someday characterize the twenty-first century? Many have already entered their predictions.

Doomsday proselytizers aside, some people believe that as the twenty-first century progresses, human-kind will move toward a more generally enlightened state, with more equality, more peace, more tolerance, more openness, and more demonstrated love for all sentient beings.

We have had a rocky start to the twenty-first century. For all of us, the events of September 11, 2001, changed the world in ways we continue to explore and cope with. But we have also learned that nobody *knows* what will happen next, so why should we waste our precious present moments worrying about it and waiting for the other shoe to drop? Instead, living in the present moment will help us squeeze every last wonderful drop of being from every wonderful moment of our life. Isn't that's a much nicer way to contribute to human progress? We think so!

Nirvana Notes

Ambition can be Zenlike or un-Zenlike. Ambition to live mindfully and succeed ultimately in the present moment is Zenlike. Ambition to get ahead of others, gain more material possessions, and achieve status at the expense of compassion is counter-productive to Zen living. Ironically, Zen living can be more effective in personal as well as career success than a less-compassionate but more ambitious approach.

You Have No Future

Zen has nothing to do with the future. Living Zen means you have no future. That doesn't mean you should scrap all your investments, your kids' college fund, and your 10-year career plan. You still have to stay mindful of your life as a whole as well as your life right now. Yet looking at it another way, right now is your only life. Ten years from now, when your career plan is in full fruition, you will still be living in the right now. You have to make now count for everything. You have no future; you have power over this moment only; your future is happening now. By recognizing this, you will have power over what you don't have. (Ponder that one for a while!)

You Have Already Succeeded

Because you have no future and because your future is now, you have already succeeded. The 10-year plan is great, but it is like a map. A map has many roads, and you might encounter detours or country roads that aren't on the map. You never know what will arise in the present moment.

Except you do know what will arise: you. Here you are, in the now, living, being. You are the one and only consistent factor in the story of your life. A story is supposed to have a beginning, a middle, and an end. In Zen, you are the beginning, the middle, and the end. You live your entire life story every moment, so you have nowhere to go. You are already there. The story finishes each second, then starts again. Here you are, living. The end.

This Is Zen: Right Here, Right Now

There you have it, the essence of Zen: right here, right now. "If it's that simple, how are you going to write any more about it?" you might ask. Because like everything else about Zen, appearances are deceiving. Zen is simple, but living it can be monstrously complicated for human beings, who are so attached to their thoughts and emotions, that they readily engage them, allow them to control their lives, and live at their mercy.

Learning how to live your Zen is like learning anything worthwhile. It takes practice to get into new habits, and eventually, new habits help you break into a new awareness. Then Zen really will seem like a breeze.

The Least You Need to Know

◆ Modern life is complicated; Zen living is simple.

◆ Zen living means living fully in the present moment.

◆ By practicing Zen you can spring clean your brain, get to know yourself again, and learn how to pay attention.

◆ Zen is as simple as sitting and experiencing without attachment, attitude, or opinion, and it has been so since ancient times.

◆ Zen living helps you learn moderation, minimize chaos, get organized, cultivate self-knowledge, and feel serene.

Chapter 2

A Brief History of Zen Buddhism

In This Chapter

- ◆ How a man became the Buddha
- ◆ Some basic principles of Buddhism
- ◆ How Buddhism in India turned into Ch'an in China
- ◆ How Ch'an in China evolved into Zen in Japan, Son in Korea, and Thien in Vietnam
- ◆ What a Zen teacher can (and can't) do for you

Westerners, when first learning about Zen, or any other sect of Buddhism, have a disadvantage. In the East, every child grows up knowing all about the life of the Buddha, if not all the details of the evolution of Buddhism. In the West, we might have seen a movie or two about the Buddha or perhaps read *Siddhartha* by Herman Hesse in high school, but other than that, most of us don't know much unless we have gone out and sought the information.

But knowing how Zen came about and how it evolved into its present incarnation is more than interesting. What the Buddha, and others after him, learned through experience can help each of us live in a more Zenlike way in our daily practice.

If you really hate history, don't worry—we won't pile a bunch of dates and dry facts on you. We'll try to make this as relevant as possible for your life right now. (And a little historical knowledge never hurt anyone!)

A Man Named Siddhartha

So who was this Buddha guy anyway? Was he some kind of god, like Krishna, or some kind of incarnation of God, like Jesus? Was he some kind of prophet, like Mohammed or Moses? No, the Buddha was just a guy, a rich guy, in the beginning; a poor guy, later on. And more important, he was a guy with a lot of drive toward the spiritual. But still, he was just a guy.

A lot of mythology surrounds the Buddha, and, of course, there is much we don't know for sure. People transmitted the details of the Buddha's life orally for centuries before anyone ever wrote anything down, so historical accuracy is less of a sure thing than getting the basic idea. But let's look at the story as it is generally told.

One Hand Clapping

Like any story that is thousands of years old, the story of the life of Buddha has certain mythological elements. One story says Buddha's mother conceived him after being pierced in the side by an elephant's tusk. Another relates how, immediately after being born, Buddha stood up and took seven steps. As a lotus blossom appeared in each footprint, the baby then raised his hand and announced his intention to become enlightened.

Who Was Buddha?

Approximately five centuries before the birth of Jesus Christ, a prince was born of India's warrior class. His parents named him Siddhartha Gautama (sometimes spelled Siddhattha Gotama). Siddhartha's well-intentioned father desired a military career for his son and decided to isolate his son from any and all contact with the outside world. If Siddhartha never suffered, his father might have reasoned, he would never have reason to pursue spiritual matters and endure the hardships of a spiritual life. He would stay the course set out for him and become a great leader.

The pampered and privileged prince grew up, married, and had a child. But he was naturally curious about the world outside the royal enclave. It is even said that Siddhartha's father commanded the servants to remove all withered flowers from the garden before Siddhartha walked in it so he would never see that flowers died. You can imagine how limited his view of life must have been!

The story goes that, in an attempt to learn about life, Siddhartha ventured out in disguise, without the knowledge of his father or other family members. He wanted to know what it was like out there, where not everyone was privileged, where people weren't princes. He walked among the common people on four separate nights, and on each night, he learned something startling.

On his first journey, he saw someone who was very old. Siddhartha asked his servant, "What is wrong with that man? Why is he so stooped and wrinkled?" The servant answered, "The man is old, master. All humans must grow old." Surprised, Siddhartha returned to his palace. Old? He hadn't known of such a thing.

On the second journey, Siddhartha encountered a sick man lying on the side of the road. Again, he asked his servant, "Why is that man lying on the side of the road that way?" The servant replied, "That man has a disease. All men are susceptible to such disease, pain, and suffering." "You mean, I could fall prey to a disease?" Siddhartha asked. "Yes, master," replied the servant. Amazed, Siddhartha returned home.

 **Nirvana Notes** _____

The classic novel *Siddhartha* by Hermann Hesse presents a more detailed but fictionalized (as opposed to mythologized) account of how Siddhartha became a Buddha. Hesse based the book on historical knowledge and legend, adding his own ideas about how it might have happened. If you didn't read it in high school (or even if you did), we suggest your picking it up. It's a quick read and can give you a better understanding of where and why Buddhism, and eventually Zen, began.

On the third night, during his wanderings, Siddhartha saw a dead body. "Why doesn't that man move?" asked Siddhartha. "What is wrong with him?" "He is dead, master," said the servant. "Eventually, all men must die." "I will die?" inquired Siddhartha of his servant.

One can only wonder if the servant was terrified to reveal such answers to his privileged but ignorant master or if the servant took some pleasure in being the one to give Siddhartha his dose of reality. "Yes, master. Even you will die, someday."

On the last night, Siddhartha ventured out yet again and saw a wandering ascetic searching for spiritual truth, traveling with his begging bowl in poverty, a look of serenity on his face. "What is that man doing?" asked Siddhartha. His servant informed him, "That man is seeking the meaning of life and the answer to suffering. He wanders, fasts, begs for his food, has no possessions, meditates, and inquires into the nature of truth."

The father's plan had backfired. By sheltering Siddhartha from suffering, he made his son's eventual encounter with the human condition all the more shocking. Siddhartha vowed that he would find the answers. He left his wife, his son, and his privileged life within the castle walls and set out on his own spiritual quest.

Man Becomes Buddha

Siddhartha searched for six years. He tried being a wandering ascetic and nearly starved himself to death in a desperate attempt to apprehend truth. He followed several different religions, mastered them, and moved on. Eventually he decided asceticism wasn't the answer, and he embraced the path of moderation. Still, he was dissatisfied.

Then one day, Siddhartha sat meditating under a bodhi tree (a fig tree). He vowed that he would not arise until he had apprehended the truth of existence and the nature of the unborn mind. All night he sat. According to the story, during the first half of the night, Siddhartha realized how *karma*, or the universal law of cause and effect, functioned. During the second half of the night, he recognized the great unity of all things, the nature of suffering, and how to end suffering. By dawn, he had achieved nirvana. He was enlightened. He was a Buddha, an "enlightened one."

 Zen-Speak

Karma (also called kamma) is a Sanskrit term for the universal law of cause and effect. Everything one does will be balanced by an opposing or balancing reaction, either in this life or the next, as the universe seeks ultimate equilibrium. Karma isn't punishment for bad behavior or reward for good behavior. In Buddhism, no one punishes or rewards an individual. Instead, karma plunges a person into the midst of a complex network of universal being and can grant him the awareness that, sooner or later, everything he does has a consequence.

Transmission of Dharma

Of course, life doesn't end after enlightenment. Siddhartha was only in his 30s when he attained nirvana. For about 40 more years, he traveled around, teaching the truth he had discovered, something Buddhists refer to as *dharma*. This truth was organized into certain principles, which we will explain later in this chapter (see the following "The Three Treasures," "The Four Noble Truths," and "The Eightfold Path" sections). One of the effects of the Buddha's enlightenment was a deep compassion for all living things and the wish for all to recognize their own Buddha nature. These feelings compelled him to spend his life helping others achieve enlightenment.

When the Buddha died (supposedly from eating poisoned food), he told his followers that they should consider the dharma their teacher. From that point on, the principles of Buddhism have been passed from teacher to student all over the world. Let's look at them.

Zen-Speak

Dharma means the teachings of the Buddha. It has also come to be known as a word for the truth about all existence, as realized by those who attain enlightenment. This is, of course, what the Buddha was pointing to through his teachings.

Counting Coup

The principles of Buddhism are conveniently grouped into various categories, each named in part according to the number of principles it includes. Don't worry. This isn't like math. It's more like good advice in little parcels.

The Three Treasures

In Buddhism, the three treasures are the three things in which every Buddhist can take refuge and find relief. They are …

- The Buddha himself and the notion that everyone has Buddha nature.

- The Buddha's teachings, or dharma, and the recognition that the teachings reflect ultimate truth.

- The Buddhist community, or *sangha*, which can mean, on a small scale, the people with whom one practices meditation and shares like-mindedness, and

Zen-Speak

Sangha is the community, either of Buddhists or other like-minded individuals, who practice meditating together. On a wider scale, sangha is the community of all sentient beings, who are essentially one.

on a larger scale, all sentient beings, who are all unique yet all one, as waves in an ocean are all part of the ocean.

The Four Noble Truths

The Four Noble Truths are the heart of the dharma. They cover the primary problem which humans encounter, why they encounter it, and how to overcome it. We'll talk about them in more detail later, as they are relevant. Here, we'll just sketch them out for you:

- The first noble truth is that living means experiencing *dukkha*. Dukkha is the Sanskrit word for discontent, dissatisfaction, suffering, and fear, whether from something tangible or something we can't quite put a finger on. It is the condition of human existence, the feeling that something just isn't right. Sometimes the *something* is obvious. We get hurt, physically or emotionally. We lose something we love, a person, possession, job, or house. Other times, we simply feel a deep dissatisfaction. "Why aren't I happy? Why aren't I ever satisfied with what I have? Why aren't I like other people? What is missing in my life? What's wrong with me?" That's dukkha. If you're human, you know what we mean.

Zen-Speak

Dukkha is the word for suffering or, more generally, that deep feeling of discomfort, dissatisfaction, restlessness, unfulfilled desire, and want that so often characterizes human existence.

- The second noble truth tells us why we have dukkha. Suffering is caused by desire. Desire is wanting something we don't have, wishing something were some way it isn't, or being otherwise generally dissatisfied with the way things are. Desire also holds the belief that things would be better, we would be happier, or life would be sweeter if only this were the case, if only that would happen, or if only something were different than the way it is now.

- The third noble truth says we can eliminate suffering. How? By eliminating desire. If we remove the cause, the effect will stop. That doesn't mean we give up living, working, having relationships, feeling compassion and joy, and appreciating life. It just means we give up that futile grasping, painful longing, that feeling that we have to have something we don't have. We already have everything we need.

- Just give up desire? Easier said than done, you might say! The fourth noble truth tells us how: The way to eliminating desire is by adhering to the Eightfold Path. These eight steps (see the following section, "The Eightfold Path") to living the Middle Way, as the Buddha suggested, help put us on the path to living that will ease our desires and, thereby, ease our suffering, bringing more joy into our life. In Buddhism, enlightenment is the culmination of this practice, but we'll talk about that later.

One Hand Clapping

Another set of Buddhist precepts is the 16 Bodhisattva Precepts. The long-practicing Zen practitioner formally commits to these precepts in an official ceremony. These precepts, which embody the spirit and values of Buddhism, are: (1) be one with the Buddha; (2) be one with the dharma; (3) be one with the sangha; (4) don't do evil; (5) do good; (6) do good for others; (7) don't kill; (8) don't steal; (9) don't misuse sex; (10) don't lie; 11) don't become intoxicated; (12) don't put other people down; (13) don't blame anyone or consider yourself above anyone; (14) don't be stingy; (15) don't become angry; and (16) don't put down the Buddha, the dharma, or the sangha.

The Eightfold Path

The Eightfold Path is the substance of the fourth noble truth and consists of guidelines for purposeful living that will help pave the way to the release from suffering. These are not exactly rules or commandments but are more a framework for living that will make life easier and more conducive to the elimination of suffering.

- **Right understanding** means recognizing that life is impermanent, suffering is linked to desire, and desire is linked to the false notion that we are lacking something. Right understanding has also been described as recognizing the truth of karma and the unity of all beings.

- **Right thought** means thinking kindly and refusing to engage in cruel, mean, covetous, or otherwise nasty thoughts. What we think is what we are.

- **Right speech** means refusing to lie, talk meanly, gossip, command everyone's attention, or inflame people. According to Buddhism, right speech should be wise, kind, and minimal. One should talk when necessary but not be a chatterbox. (Those of us who can't help being chatterboxes are working on cultivating the power of silence!)

- **Right action** generally means following the Five Precepts, or Buddhist morals. These are nonviolence or refusal to kill purposefully; refusal to steal, which covers shoplifting, plagiarizing, even stealing attention away from someone; control of the senses and appetites from overeating to lust; talking sincerely and honestly; and refusal to alter the mind with intoxicants. That last precept doesn't mean we can't enjoy a nice glass of wine with our meal. It just means stopping short of getting schnockered.

◆ **Right livelihood** is an interesting one. It means choosing an occupation that is not harmful or unjust, but instead is honest, upright, and furthering of love and compassion in the world. The professions traditionally frowned upon by Buddhists as not being those of right livelihood include trade in weapons, people, sex, drugs, alcohol, or poison. Also included are professions that involve killing, such as a soldier, hunter, or even fisherman (you might have guessed by now that Buddhists are, traditionally, vegetarians in many countries, though not in all). In our current world, we might have mixed feelings about this one—isn't it right to fight for our country to protect our homeland? We say that right livelihood is more about the reasons behind what we do. When we feel, upon self-examination, that what we do in our life is harming our soul or the world, then it is not practicing right livelihood. If we feel, on the other hand, that what we do in our life is bringing good to the world and enriching our own soul with "rightness," then it *is* right livelihood. Remember, right livelihood does not mean telling other people they are doing it wrong. All we have to look at is ourselves.

◆ **Right effort** means making a conscious attempt to cultivate positive qualities, thoughts, and actions in ourselves while also working to prevent or eliminate negative qualities, thoughts, and tendencies. We could call this self-discipline.

◆ **Right mindfulness** means working on being mindful all the time. Being mindful means being constantly aware of our feelings, our surroundings, what our own body is doing, what thoughts and ideas we are experiencing, and what is happening around us. According to Buddhism, everybody has a Sixth Sense (no, not the ability to see dead people). It is mind, or awareness. Zen mind is waking up and living rather than going through the motions as if we were asleep.

◆ **Right concentration** means working on achieving a one-pointed mind. If we are doing something, we should concentrate wholly on what we are doing. This isn't easy, but we can achieve it through the discipline that comes from lots of meditation practice. The better our mind gets at totally immersing itself in what we are doing (no matter how mundane), the less we will be plagued by distractions, desires, and fragmentation, and the more fulfilling our daily existence will become.

Although there are more numbered lists, enumerated differently here and there and variously emphasized by different Buddhist traditions, we think that's enough morality for now. You can always read more about them on your own (check out the resource list in Appendix A).

From India to China to Japan

With some idea of the substance of Buddhist philosophy, let's look at how Buddhism spread around the world. The Buddha lived in India, where the dominant religion is now Hinduism. How did Buddhism get to Asia? Through the effort of one man named Bodhidharma.

Bodhidharma Goes to China

How did Buddhism jump from India to China? Bodhidharma is a much-legendized figure who traveled to China to spread the word of Buddhism. No one knows for sure exactly why he traveled such a distance, but Bodhidharma gets the credit for single-handedly bringing Zen to Asia. He was like a Zen missionary.

Bodhidharma is usually represented as a scowling figure with a long, hooked nose and was known as the blue-eyed demon because his Aryan appearance and blue eyes were an oddity in China. Soon after arriving in China, Bodhidharma met with Emperor Wu of Liang, whom he didn't impress. Interested in the concept of Buddhism, the emperor poured his resources into the building of many Buddhist temples but called Bodhidharma before him to ask him what spiritual benefit he would gain from all the Buddhist temples he had built.

"None," answered the strange-looking man.

"None? Then what have I done it all for?" asked the emperor. "What is the point?"

"To lose yourself," said Bodhidharma. The emperor didn't like this answer. (Emperors generally aren't good at letting go of their egos.) He sent Bodhidharma away.

Undeterred, Bodhidharma traveled to a monastery where, the story goes, he sat facing the wall of a cave and meditated for nine years. Another detail which we imagine is probably the stuff of legend rather than reality is that Bodhidharma cut off his eyelids so he would stay awake during meditation. (Getting enough sleep before meditating is, in our opinion, a slightly more agreeable option.)

One Hand Clapping

One Zen koan, or story, tells of a man hanging by his teeth from a tree branch dangling over the edge of a cliff. A man approaches him and says, "Why did Bodhidharma travel from India to China?" If the man refuses to answer, he will fail the test. If he answers, he will fall to his death. What should he do? The answer to this koan (and all koans) lies beyond logic and must be perceived on a deeper level. In Jack Kerouac's novel *Dharma Bums,* the main character, Ray Smith, asks this question of a cook in a restaurant, who replies, "I don't care." The characters agree that this was the "perfect answer." (That's Zen!)

Bodhidharma was known as the first patriarch of Buddhism. He chose a successor, who chose a successor, and so on, to transmit the dharma. Buddhism had six patriarchs, after which the lineage was abandoned, probably largely for political reasons.

The Sixth Patriarch

The sixth patriarch, Hui-neng (called E'no in Japan), was the most influential individual on Buddhism's manifestation in China. He was an uneducated woodcutter who demonstrated a profound propensity for enlightenment. The story goes that the other, more educated priests didn't appreciate his being chosen as sixth patriarch over them, even though he clearly demonstrated superior understanding, according to the fifth patriarch (whose job it was to pick his successor). Recognizing that his life was in danger, Hui-neng fled without first choosing a successor. (Politics are everywhere, aren't they?)

After becoming transplanted in China, Buddhism didn't stay just as it had been in India. Through the centuries, Buddhism mingled with China's *Taoism,* which brought what had been a relatively complex and esoteric discipline (Buddhism) into ordinary life. Taoism emphasizes escaping desire through effortless action, simplicity, and mindfulness in daily life—all qualities important to Zen. As in any religion, however, many disagreed about the details, and Buddhism began to split into a number of different sects.

One of these sects was called Ch'an (the Chinese word for Zen). When communism and other political forces began to dissipate the strength of Buddhism in China, Ch'an had already spread to Japan (where it is called Zen), Vietnam (where it is called Thien), and Korea (where it is called Son). In all these places and in all its various cultural manifestations, Zen has become firmly entrenched and still flourishes today.

Soto and Rinzai

In the West, two different schools of Zen Buddhism have a wide following: *Soto* and *Rinzai*. These two schools had their beginnings in ninth-century China, where they were known as Lin-chi (or Rinzai in Japanese) and Ts'ao-tung (or Soto in Japanese). Zen master Eisai brought Lin-chi and Zen master Dogen brought Ts'ao-tung to Japan during the twelfth or thirteenth century.

Soto Zen emphasizes silent sitting, while Rinzai is more likely to emphasize the meditation on *koans*, illogical scenarios and questions meant to push the mind closer to enlightenment. Some describe Soto as quieter, softer, and more solitary, and Rinzai as louder, more aggressive, and more interactive. However, exceptions exist to every rule, and these distinctions don't always apply.

Zen-Speak

Taoism is a Chinese philosophy and religious system emphasizing effortless action, simplicity, mindfulness, and following the Tao (sometimes translated as "the Way"). Taoism's beginnings are attributed to historical figures Lao tzu, who wrote the *Tao Te Ching,* and Chuang Tzu, who wrote the *Chuang Tzu.* Both texts explore and explain Taoism and were written around the third or fourth century B.C.E. In China, Buddhist and Taoist thought mingled to create the Asian form of Buddhism known today. (You can also read more about Taoism in *The Complete Idiot's Guide to Taoism.*)

Soto (Ts'ao-tung in Chinese, brought to Japan by Zen master Dogen) and **Rinzai** (Lin-chi in Chinese, brought to Japan by Zen master Eisai) are the two most prominent sects of Zen Buddhism. Soto emphasizes silent sitting meditation, while Rinzai emphasizes the practice of koans. Koan meditation isn't unheard of in Soto Zen, however, and in Rinzai, silent sitting meditation is also part of practice.

From China to the World

Ch'an's spread to Japan changed it further, adding a formal element characteristic of the Japanese people. Rituals, observances, and refinement became part of the Zen tradition and so did (paradoxically) the total break from ritual and observance.

Japan also contributed to the Zen approach to art, which involves a more direct, pure expression of experience free from metaphor, figurative language, technique, and artifice. Zen

Zen-Speak

Koans are illogical scenarios or questions meant to be considered until the mind makes a leap past logic to understand the koan at a higher level. The most famous koan in the West is the "one hand clapping" koan: You can hear the sound of two hands when they clap together. What is the sound of one hand clapping?

calligraphy, poetry, the tea ceremony, and other artistic endeavors reached their fruition in Japan, and many artists still embrace Zen as integral to the practice of their art.

Today, Buddhism is hardly practiced in the land of its origin, where Hinduism is now the religion of choice. Luckily, Buddhism not only enjoys a strong and healthy following in Southeast Asia but also has become a popular and important practice for many Westerners. And so, thousands of years from its conception, Zen endures.

From Master to Master

In the Zen tradition, Zen can't be learned from a book, and the dharma, or Buddha's teachings, weren't even written down until centuries after the Buddha died. Dharma was transmitted from master to master and taught by master to student. Although Zen is essentially something each student must discover internally, many believe that without the guidance of a teacher, such efforts will be fruitless. Of course, the Buddha didn't have a teacher. Or one might say life was his teacher (it can be yours as well).

Nirvana Notes

Finding a Zen teacher can be difficult if you don't live in a big city, but you can still organize a group to practice sitting meditation together. Put an ad in the paper or get a group of friends together and meet once a week (or more or less often) for meditation. A teacher may find you.

Today, many embrace the Zen teacher/Zen student relationship while others prefer to forge ahead without it. A Zen teacher cannot hand out enlightenment, but he or she can help direct our path in a more productive direction.

Finger-Pointing at the Moon

Imagine truth is the moon, and you are watching the moon's reflection in a stream. The water is moving, bubbling, flowing over rocks, and murky in some places, causing the moon's reflection to be confused, distorted, and nothing like the actual moon in appearance.

This is like a mind desperately following every thought, emotion, and feeling. When the water becomes perfectly still, when thoughts and emotions are no longer roiling the river of your mind, the moon's reflection looks just like the moon. The truth might be so clear, you might even think to look up at the actual moon. Oh! There it is! Why was I looking down into the water, anyway?

A teacher cannot make a stream stop flowing, but a teacher can help you find the techniques to calm the water. When the water is still, you can better understand that, ultimately, the teacher is pointing to the moon. The teacher's pointing finger isn't the moon, so don't look at the pointing finger (in other words, don't look to your teacher to hand you the answers). Look where the finger is pointing.

Triggering Enlightenment

Throughout Zen history many stories tell about teachers triggering enlightenment in their students. This only happens when the student is ready, of course. The story goes that Hui-neng, the sixth patriarch, attained enlightenment upon hearing his teacher (the fifth patriarch) recite the *Diamond Sutra*.

Zen-Speak

A **sutra** is a Buddhist scripture, and the **Diamond Sutra** is one of Buddha's teachings (written down many years after the words were actually spoken) that expounds on the diamond-hard edge of emptiness that can finally cut through delusion, leading to enlightenment. In many Zen communities, students recite, chant, and/or study and contemplate the Diamond Sutra and other sutras such as the Heart Sutra and the Platform Sutra.

Whether you choose to study Zen with a teacher or alone, the real work of Zen is an internal process of "breaking and entering" the Zen mind within. Everyone has it, but it can be difficult to find. After you can access your Zen mind, you'll be amazed at how obvious that great big moon up there really is.

The Least You Need to Know

- The Buddha was a man named Siddhartha Gautama, born of the warrior class in India in about 500 B.C.E. Siddhartha attained enlightenment after abandoning his privileged life and searching for truth for six years.

- Buddhism's Four Noble Truths are that life is full of suffering, suffering is due to desires and attachments, suffering can be eliminated by eliminating desires and attachments, and the way to do this is by following the Eightfold Path.

- The Eightfold Path includes right understanding, right thought, right speech, right action, right livelihood, right effort, right mindfulness, and right concentration.

- ◆ Buddhism spread from India to China, where it developed into many sects, eventually spreading to Japan, Korea, Vietnam, and the United States.

- ◆ A Zen teacher can't hand you enlightenment but can point the way.

Chapter 3

Zen in America

In This Chapter

- ◆ Why is Zen so "cool"?

- ◆ The evolution of Zen in America

- ◆ Who's who in American Zen

- ◆ Zen in pop culture: feminism, psychology, and the entertainment industry

- ◆ What about the Buddhism part?

Zen is hot. It's hip. It's the cutting edge. It's the wave of the future. It's totally cool. It is a term so frequently used in popular culture that it has become part of the vocabulary of the masses. You can hear remarks such as these almost anywhere. "That movie was so Zen." "That's a very Zen look for you." "What a Zen thing to say!" "Last night at the pool table, I was in the zone. I couldn't miss a shot! It was like Zen and the art of pool!"

When did an ancient Eastern religion become so fashionable, and why are Americans so enthralled with the Zen concept?

In 1893, Soyen Shaku appeared at the World Parliament of Religions in Chicago and introduced Zen to America, but it wasn't until the late 1940s, with the publication of the writings of D. T. Suzuki (whom Shaku helped bring to America), that Americans caught the Zen fever.

Since that time, Zen has enjoyed a unique and utterly Western evolution in America, making American Zen its very own brand of Zen, just as Zen has enjoyed unique manifestations in Japan, Korea, and Vietnam.

Why do Americans love Zen so much? Lots of reasons. Zen is particularly suited to the temperaments, lifestyles, philosophies, and inclinations of Americans. Only in America would Zen become cool, where being different, enigmatic, rebellious, and just a little bit off the beaten track has long been considered *the* way to be.

Why We Love Zen

Americans have an interesting relationship with religion. Some of us embrace it, some of us reject it, and some of us ignore it. Church and state are supposed to be separate, but religion and politics are by no means mutually exclusive and never have been. In this country, people are free to practice any religion they like—and free to be criticized for it, too. America is a showcase for just about every religious belief imaginable.

Monkey Mind! _____

It is easy to mistake "popular culture Zen" for real Zen. Zen isn't about wearing black and saying enigmatic things, spouting spiritual wisdom, or being able to perform martial arts moves that defy the laws of physics. It isn't shooting a bull's-eye with one's eyes closed or getting a hole-in-one on the golf course. Zen isn't slick or dramatic or showy. It is ordinary, going through your everyday life without fanfare, fully awake, aware, and absorbed in whatever you do. Don't miss the essence.

In a climate that can be a little like a religious free-for-all, people are looking for something different, something unique and personal that makes sense. Some people feel that the Western religions in which they were (or weren't) raised don't speak to them or quite make sense. Further, some people aren't interested in religion per se but do feel engaged by the search for meaning by a sense of spirituality. For many of these people, Zen works. Zen isn't bound by rules, punishments, "shoulds," or any external parental figure. It can involve community, ritual, and practice or just solitary practice. Zen is flexible, individual, and an inner development that brings the individual in touch with his or her own eternal nature. It also makes life much more interesting and satisfying because it doesn't look ahead, behind, or beyond for something else. It only looks within, see what lies there, and says, "Be."

Zen techniques also work well in conjunction with any other religion, Western or otherwise. Catholics, Protestants, Jews, Muslims, Unitarians, Wiccans, or persons of any other religion can practice sitting and listening for the true nature of the self. Anyone can practice Zen living for a more effective and meaningful life.

To live "Zen," one doesn't have to convert to Buddhism. He doesn't have to convert to anything. Zen is diametrically opposed to the concept of "conversion" because that means one should turn into something else. In Zen, what one is right now, in this moment, is just as it should be.

Furthermore, Americans love anything with a foreign flavor. An anti-aging lotion from France, a kimono-inspired evening dress, Italian leather shoes, German beer, tae kwon do lessons for the kids? We love 'em! Zen seems practically tailor-made for America, but that is partially because America has tailor-made Zen to suit itself.

Do-It-Yourself Zen

We are a pull-yourself-up-by-your-own-bootstraps kind of country. Traditional American values include self-reliance, independence, gumption, overachievement, and being a self-starter. We love self-help books, do-it-yourself projects, and build-it-from-nothing businesses. Maybe it's that pioneer spirit that drives us.

Zen is the original self-starting spiritual practice because you don't pray to anyone, you don't need anyone to bless you or forgive you, you don't follow any particular text, and you don't even need any equipment. You have everything you need right there in your own head, and you start by sitting.

Sitting is easy. You can do that yourself. It isn't a technique. It's just sitting.

Then you start letting go. It's a lot more work to hold on to a heavy load than to put it down. Zen helps you put down the load by clearing out your mind, making it a better place through which to perceive truth. You do it yourself, even if you have a teacher to help guide you. The work is up to you.

Zen also values the simple life: Do your daily work without making a big deal of it, dreading it, or disliking it. Let your daily work bring you joy. Don't overconsume, but use only what you need. Overconsumption fuels desire, which (as we've mentioned) causes suffering. Live close to the earth and marvel in its beauty. The simplicity and environmental movements in this country are nicely compatible with these values.

> **One Hand Clapping**
>
> Zen is full of paradoxes, and here's another one: The work of Zen is in understanding how to stop working so hard.

One Hand Clapping

An old Zen story tells of the Chinese Zen master Hyakujo, who worked every day in the gardens and on the grounds. When he was in his 80s, his students couldn't bear to watch him laboring so they hid his tools. When he was unable to find them, Hyakujo ceased eating that day, the next, and the next. Finally, the students returned the tools, and Hyakujo went back to work … and to his food. That evening, he said to his students only this: "No work, no food."

Cowboy-Style Religion

There is also something a little rebellious about Zen that Americans seem to respond to. We like the idea of the wandering Zen master, living each day as it comes, sleeping under the stars, absorbed in silent contemplation, a man of few words but enigmatically wise and suddenly quite unexpectedly humorous.

The romanticized cowboy, with little attachment to worldly possessions and a silent, stoic self-possession and wry wit holds a similar fascination for Americans. Zen offers the secret to many of these same qualities.

In some ways, cowboys are also the American version of the "everyman" (or "everyperson"). In Asia, Zen is primarily the business of monks and nuns, but in America, Zen is for the average guy or gal on the street. Zen communities of "regular people" getting together to meditate, even to do other things together such as work for peace and social justice, exist and thrive outside the confines of a monastery or other rigorously organized system are a common manifestation in America. Zen is for anyone. We like that.

Monkey Mind! _____

Some books on Zen can make you feel as if Zen is only for people who already understand it. Forget that! Trying to understand is not Zen. Shunryu Suzuki may have said it best (in *Zen Mind, Beginner's Mind*):

There is no need to remember what I say; there is no need to understand what I say. You understand; you have full understanding within yourself. There is no problem.

Illogical Logic

Those among us who fancy ourselves "thinkers" are particularly challenged by Zen's illogical brand of logic. Its cryptic koans and baffling stories can be nothing short of hilarious, sometimes irresistibly engaging, and sometimes both. Unpuzzling Zen is a challenge and a joy, an approach to life that says, "Hey, don't take yourself so seriously—after all, what is 'self' anyway?"

Although some people find Zen anti-intellectual, it is actually a system meant to move through the intellect and then past it into a sort of post-intellectual understanding of truth, which is free from ego, pretension, and one-upmanship. Approaching Zen intellectually is one way to approach it, but not the only way. Zen challenges and ultimately defies the intellect in a surprising and deeply satisfying way.

One Hand Clapping

Zuigan called out to himself every day: "Master." Then he answered himself: "Yes, sir." And after that he added: "Become sober." Again he answered: "Yes, sir." "And after that," he continued, "do not be deceived by others." "Yes sir; yes sir," he answered.

This koan from the collection of koans called *The Gateless Gate* plays with the idea of the ego and the self. Consider in meditation whether the monk, in having such conversations with himself, was deluded or really on to something.

This Is Living!

Another attraction of Zen is its approach to life: Live it! In a world that can be unpredictable, this notion appeals to many people. All we have is right now, and even if we all live to be 100, the concept is still true: All we have is right now.

Our culture is full of sayings and epigrams to express this notion: *Seize the day, live in the moment, wake up and smell the coffee, don't forget to smell the flowers, just do it!* If we can live in a way that helps us live more vibrantly and be more present in each present moment, wouldn't we want to know all about it?

Another koan from *The Gateless Gate* expresses this concept:

A monk told Joshu: "I have just entered the monastery. Please teach me."

Joshu asked: "Have you eaten your rice porridge?"

The monk replied: "I have eaten."

Joshu said: "Then you had better wash your bowl."

At that moment, the monk was enlightened.

Finding beauty in the ordinary and the ordinary in beauty is Zen living in action. We should experience each moment mindfully (fully and with our full mind), without attachment, striving, grasping, or involvement, but with fully involved appreciation for the essence of the moment. How lovely it is to wash the dishes. How spectacular, to drive down the highway. How exquisite, simply to sit and be yourself.

Nirvana Notes

Zen meditation isn't difficult, but posture is important. You can't do zazen lying down or slumping over. Holding your body with your spine straight, your head squarely above your shoulders, and your legs crossed puts you in control of your body, rather than the other way around. You already are like the Buddha if you just sit in this position. For more on how to meditate, see Chapter 9.

Desperately Seeking Enlightenment

Zen has come to America in waves through the work of several notable people whose various approaches to Zen have caught on and significantly influenced our culture's notions about and practice of Zen. Although the last 50 years have seen many, many influential and fascinating Zen masters, teachers, and students, we'll mention just a few of the most well-known.

D. T. Suzuki

Daisetz Teitaro Suzuki (1870–1966) is usually credited with enlightening America to the existence of the Zen version of Buddhism. In his many writings, he emphasized and expounded upon the meaning of and path to enlightenment.

Living in America and married to an American woman, D. T. Suzuki had a unique perspective from which he could integrate two cultures and find a way to live a Zenlike life in a country with little perception of the ways of Zen. He made it his life's work to bring modes of Eastern thought to the West as well as suggest ways Western thought might be beneficial to the East and, eventually, to transcend all distinctions and divisions between the two.

Suzuki was concerned with becoming a world citizen. He made Zen accessible to everyone, no matter one's country, beliefs, or perceptions.

Nirvana Notes _____

A familiar and very Zenlike concept is to walk a mile in another person's shoes. Whenever you catch yourself making "us and them" distinctions (kids today are so ..., my parents always ..., my boss can never ...), spend a moment "being" the other person. Find yourself in him or her. Doing this might change your perspective and help you find tolerance, even compassion, toward someone you thought you didn't understand.

Shunryu Suzuki

People interested in Zen but who have only read one book on the subject have probably read *Zen Mind, Beginner's Mind* by Shunryu Suzuki (1905–1971). A practitioner of Soto Zen, Suzuki emphasized living life with a "beginner's mind" as if everything was new and for the first time.

Suzuki's little book, which expounds upon right practice, right attitude, and right understanding, has become a guiding light for many American practitioners of Zen. It explains how to do zazen and also talks the reader through what it means to have a "Zen mind."

Although only in this country for the last 12 years of his life, Shunryu Suzuki made a profound impact on the American practice of Soto Zen.

One Hand Clapping

So to be a human is to be a Buddha. Buddha nature is just another name for human nature, our true human nature. Thus even though you do not do anything, you are actually doing something. You are expressing yourself. You are expressing your true nature. Your eyes will express; your voice will express; your demeanor will express. The most important thing is to express your true nature in the simplest, most adequate way and to appreciate it in the smallest existence.

—From *Zen Mind, Beginner's Mind* by Shunryu Suzuki

R. H. Blyth

Many Japanese, Tibetan, Korean, and Vietnamese Zen masters have come to the West, but Englishman R. H. Blyth (1898–1964) went to the East. While remaining staunchly Christian and Western, Blyth lived in Japan and studied Zen and Japanese literature. He wrote many works on Japanese literature and on haiku, and his writings influenced many Americans, particularly writers and poets, to study and live Zen.

Because Blyth was not a Buddhist and because he was a Westerner, many Westerners can easily relate to the way he approaches and interprets Zen thought, Zen living, and Zen literature.

Dharma Bums

In the 1960s, the Beat Generation had no more vocal or representative leader than writer Jack Kerouac. Kerouac insisted that the Beat Generation was a religious generation and that he and many of his wandering artistic fellows embraced Buddhism as the path to living a fully realized life. Kerouac described himself to the media as a "strange solitary crazy Catholic mystic," but many of his novels (which are all autobiographical with names changed) describe his relationship with Buddhist philosophy and his wrestling with Zen.

One of his novels, *Dharma Bums*, tells the story of Ray Smith, a wandering man in search of truth in the company of other wanderers, including the "Zen Lunatic" and scholar of Asian literature and philosophy, Japhy Ryder (who, it is said, is actually the poet Gary Snyder). In a typical Zen conversation, Japhy and the narrator, Ray, have it out:

> "And whom am I?"
>
> "I dunno, maybe you're a Goat."
>
> "Goat?"
>
> "Maybe you're Mudface."
>
> "Who's Mudface?"
>
> "Mudface is the mud in your goatface. What would you say if someone was asked the question, 'Does a dog have the Buddha nature?' and answered 'Woof!'"
>
> "I'd say that was a lot of silly Zen Buddhism …. It's mean," I complained. "All those Zen Masters throwing young kids in the mud because they can't answer their silly word questions."
>
> "That's because they want them to realize mud is better than words, boy."

Perhaps more than his books, Jack Kerouac's life and the lives of the other members of the Beat Generation brought the concept of Buddhism in general and Zen in particular into the public consciousness. People wanted to be wandering dharma bums. They wanted to be like Kerouac or at least like the characters in his books. They wanted to know about Zen.

Of course, Zen as practiced by the Beat Generation was a lot different than Zen as practiced in Japan (or anywhere else) and much different than Zen as it is currently practiced in America. In the Beat Generation version of Zen, women existed on the fringes, and art, poetry, and intense philosophical discussions as well as alcoholic and drug binges accompanied equally intense periods of solitude, meditation, and internal searching. The Beats might have had a handle on male ecstasy, but they hardly practiced the Middle Way nor held a particularly compassionate world view.

Zen was redefined yet again for the 1960s in an irreverent and particularly American style that has since evolved significantly. (Today in America, for example, women are regarded as equal to men in the practice of Zen, and many women are Zen teachers and Zen masters.)

One Hand Clapping

"Everything is possible. I am God, I am Buddha, I am imperfect Ray Smith, all at the same time, I am empty space, I am all things. I have all the time in the world from life to life to do what is to do, to do what is done, to do the timeless doing, infinitely perfect within, why cry, why worry, perfect like mind essence and the minds of banana peels" I added, laughing ....

—From *Dharma Bums* by Jack Kerouac

Zen and the Art of Motorcycle Maintenance

Mention the word *Zen* in a crowded room, and someone inevitably will chime in about having read (or wanting to read) Robert Pirsig's book *Zen and the Art of Motorcycle Maintenance*. Even though this book begins with a disclaimer that "it should in no way be associated with that great body of factual information relating to orthodox Zen Buddhist practice," it is for many the single most significant exposure to anything with the word *Zen* in it.

Pirsig intertwines Zen concepts with psychology as he relates his autobiographical journey from Minnesota to San Francisco on a motorcycle with his young son. The journey becomes a metaphor for a spiritual journey, and Pirsig explores dualism, unity, fear, desire, attachment, and insanity along the way. Pirsig's brand of Zen (like Kerouac's) might not sound much like anything coming out of Japan. It is uniquely American and, many would argue, not Zen at all. (Then again, to defy Zen-ness is Zenlike.)

What may be the most significant and influential aspect of Pirsig's book is his incorporation of psychology into Zen. In America today, many practicing Zen teachers are also psychologists, and some have students as patients and patients as students. Many people in America approach Zen in an attempt to address their own personal psychological state, rather than, or secondary to, their spiritual state or religious needs. (We would argue these are all intertwined.)

One Hand Clapping

The craftsman isn't ever following a single line of instruction. He's making decisions as he goes along. For that reason, he'll be absorbed and attentive to what he's doing even though he doesn't deliberately contrive this. His motions and the machine are in a kind of harmony. He isn't following any set of written instructions because the nature of the material at hand determines his thoughts and motions, which simultaneously change the nature of the material at hand. The material and his thoughts are changing together in a progression of changes until his mind's at rest at the same time the material's right.

—From *Zen and the Art of Motorcycle Maintenance* by Robert Pirsig

---

Zen in Pop Culture

Zen's marriage with psychology in America has also contributed to the awareness of Zen in pop culture. Zen is everywhere, or at least its echoes are everywhere, from blockbuster movies such as *The Matrix* trilogy that include references to Zen ideas, to Zen-inspired cookbooks to Zen gardening kits and "Zen fountains" available at the local mall. Put the word *Zen* on it, and it sells. Talk about losing the self, becoming one with the universe, subverting the dominant paradigm, waking up from the sleep of the masses, or perceiving the ultimate unity and diversity of all things, and our ears prick up.

A Woman's Place in the Zendo

Zen began to gain momentum in America just as the feminist movement was finding its voice. The timing was perfect for women to embrace Zen and remake it yet again. Today, many women serve as heads of prominent Zen centers all over the United States. While women have studied Zen in Asia for centuries, they usually came either as students or as Buddhist nuns.

In America today, women are spiritual leaders of the highest magnitude in the American Zen scene. In her book *The Beginner's Guide to Zen Buddhism*, Jean Smith lists Jiyu Kennett Roshi (who died in 1996) as the first woman to found and become abbot of a Zen monastery and also mentions many female senior heads of Zen centers, such as:

- Blanche Hartman, Senior Dharma Teacher at the San Francisco Zen Center, www.sfzc.com

- Karen Sunna, head priest until 2002 at the Minnesota Zen Meditation Center, www.mnzenctr.com

- Katherine Thanas, Abbott at the Santa Cruz Zen Center, www.sczc.org/home.htm

- Yvonne Rand, head teacher at Goat-in-the-Road in Muir Beach, California, www.goatintheroad.com/index.html

- Charlotte Joko Beck, author and teacher at the Zen Center of San Diego

- Jisho Warner, teacher at the Stone Creek Zendo in California

- Pat Enkyo O'Hara, resident teacher and head priest at the Village Zendo in New York

- Bonnie Myotai Treace, Abbott and Spiritual Director of the Zen Center of New York City

There are many others, as well as many women authors of Zen books we love, including the previously mentioned Charlotte Joko Beck and also Geri Larken, whose collected dharma talks delivered at the Chicago Zen Buddhist Temple were published, by popular demand, in a book called *Stumbling Toward Enlightenment*.

Millennium Zen

Is Zen a fad? Will we tap the trend and move on? Or does Zen have a place in America in the twenty-first century?

We think the world is changing in an exciting way, even as it is changing in an uncertain and sometimes frightening way. We are becoming more global, more unified, more aware. Cultural, political, geographical, and economic differences, although still glaringly apparent, are also blurring here and there in interesting ways. People are embracing simplicity, environmental responsibility, stress management, and the quest for serenity as modes of living. Some people believe the world is waking up in an entirely new way, as we learn from our mistakes; as we watch the world react to what we do as individuals, states, and countries; and as more people become aware enough to step forward and say, "I am living right now, and I see what's going on!"

In this climate, it is easy to understand D. T. Suzuki's idea about becoming world citizens. It is also easy to imagine Zen as an accepted way of living, even a way of living we might take for granted as obviously more worthwhile, more immediate, more productive, and more real. Zen helps us wake up and see, not fall asleep and dream. That makes sense for today, just as it has always made sense.

> **CAUTION**
>
> ### Monkey Mind!
>
> Practicing Zen without practicing any religion is not only possible but also common. Many American Zen teachers prefer that their students know the basics of Buddhism, but they don't require adherence to Buddhist beliefs. Don't feel guilty if you are a "Zennist" (a practitioner of Zen who doesn't practice the religion of Buddhism) rather than a "Buddhist." Your spiritual path may or may not lead you to more religious involvement later, but forcing yourself to change your beliefs isn't congruent with Zen thinking.

Zen Master: You?

We would guess that you probably don't consider yourself a dharma bum, you don't have time to ride a motorcycle across the country, and you aren't even a member of your local Zen center. You might just be curious about Zen, or you might be looking with some seriousness for a way to improve your life. Can you really practice Zen? Is it too weird? Is it too "on the fringe"? It's one thing to tell someone at a party he looks Zenlike. It's quite another to embrace the lifestyle. Isn't it?

It isn't. In Zen, there is no lifestyle to embrace except your own. You don't need to do anything. You don't need to change in any way. You don't need to become an expert on Japanese culture or even in zendo etiquette (although we'll tell you about that, in case you are interested). You don't have to become a Buddhist. All you need to do is be, as if for the first time. Be, do, breathe, and live, right here, right now, as if each moment is a gift, because it is. But it's not a gift from anyone else but you. Your life is your gift to yourself. Accept it graciously.

The Least You Need to Know

- Zen has been popular in America since the late 1940s when D. T. Suzuki came to America and began to write about Zen for Westerners.

- Other Zen masters and aficionados have made Zen concepts popular and accessible to Westerners through the last five decades, including Shunryu Suzuki, R. H. Blyth, Jack Kerouac, and Robert Pirsig, the author of *Zen and the Art of Motorcycle Maintenance*.

◆ Feminism, psychology, and Zennism (the practice of Zen minus the practice of Buddhism) have all influenced American conceptions of Zen.

◆ You don't need to be Buddhist or any particular religion to practice Zen, but Zen can inform and enlighten any spiritual path.

Part 2

The Future Is the Past Is Now: Being Zen

What is truth? According to Zen, truth is explained through dharma, or the teachings of the Buddha. But how does that help you, knowing stuff some guy in India might or might not have said thousands of years ago? We'll explain in Part 2. The concepts the Buddha taught are simple and relevant for anyone, in ancient India or contemporary America. We'll give it to you plain and simple: the Four Noble Truths, why you are sometimes unhappy, why life is difficult, and how you can wake up and start living in contentment.

Next we'll talk about what constitutes a Zen attitude and how it can transform your daily life, even in the wake of tragedy, into something that makes sense.

Is enlightenment the point of it all? We'll wind up Part 2 by discussing the idea of enlightenment: what it is and whether such a concept is relevant today and relevant for you.

Chapter 4

What Is Truth, and How Can I Get Some?

In This Chapter

- ◆ The truth, the whole truth, and nothing but
- ◆ Ousting your dukkha
- ◆ Techniques for escaping everyday suffering
- ◆ How to know if you are awake
- ◆ Is it in you?

Oh, the eternal question, so often contemplated in poetry, philosophy, and the trendiest coffee shops: What is truth? Truth has long been the subject of contemplation by all kinds of different traditions, and Zen books and dharma talks (talks about the teachings of the Buddha) often mention the word *truth*. Buddhism is, at its heart, all about apprehending truth rather than being seduced by illusion, so for Zen, truth is one of those key concepts. In Zen, we try to discover and embrace our true nature. We look for truth within. But what is truth? Will we know it when we see it? Can we ever truly escape our subject illusions?

The poet John Keats once wrote, in an overly quoted line, "Beauty is truth, truth beauty." That's one idea, but how helpful are truth and beauty when we can't watch the evening news without getting upset or we can't make our mortgage payment? Hello, reality check! And speaking of reality, one dictionary defines truth as "reality; actuality." But what is reality? Is it what we perceive with our senses? What we remember? Or is it what we read about in the newspaper?

Truth is tricky. Is seeing believing? We all know that sense impressions can be false, as can memory, and that something in print certainly isn't necessarily true. We also might recognize that what we see and how we *feel* about what we see aren't the same thing. But separating the two is not so easy.

Is there any hope for finding truth? And if so, how do we do it, how do we perceive truth as opposed to illusion? Will this help us get rid of our desire and, therefore, banish our suffering? According to Zen, the answer is yes; there is hope for finding truth, and that hope comes through living the *dharma*.

Dharma Is as Dharma Does ... or Doesn't

In Chapter 2, we defined dharma as the teachings of the Buddha or the realizations of the Buddha upon his enlightenment. Are we saying that some guy thousands of years ago figured it all out, and all we have to do is listen to what he said? Why should we take the word of *that* guy, as opposed to anybody else in the past, present, or future?

Actually, you don't need to take anybody's word for anything.

Here's the thing about truth: You already have it. We don't have it to give to you. Neither do your parents, your children, your teachers, your mentors, or your best friends. Only you can find your truth. Truth isn't something inaccessible or unattainable, and it isn't "out there somewhere." It is inside you, right there within. It couldn't be any closer, and yet sometimes it seems it couldn't be any more elusive. All you have to do is find it. How do you do that? Try dharma.

Monkey Mind! _____

Sitting in meditation can get downright irritating, not to mention boring. It's easy to say, "Well then, if truth is within me, I don't need to meditate." But without control over your posture and regular, concentrated practice, you might never get to apprehend your inner self. You won't get the same results lying on your bed, lazily daydreaming (although that is nice to do sometimes, too).

Dharma, rather than telling you what is true, helps you discover your own inner truth for yourself. So dharma isn't exactly a synonym for truth. It is more like that finger pointing to the moon we mentioned in Chapter 2. Dharma can guide you toward truth.

To begin your inner search for truth, you can use the dharma as a sort of guidebook, your Baedeker to truth. And what does the dharma tell you to do? What are the instructions for finding truth? Okay, pay attention, because this is deceptively simple:

Do.

Do? Do what? Do anything. But do it. Whatever you do, do it, wholeheartedly, with full awareness. Even if you aren't doing something (although technically, you're always doing something, even if it is just *breathing* and *being*), do that wholeheartedly, too. *Do nothing* with all your being. Practitioners of Zen sometimes call this *doing* nothing "not-doing." It is *doing* by way of actively *not doing.*

We can give you all kinds of lists of rules, morals, or sensible attitudes to try to adopt, but that won't work. Zen doesn't demand that you do anything different from what you are already doing (although meditation in zazen will be very helpful in living your Zen—more on that in Chapter 9). It simply means that you do what you do, really do it, without dreading it, resenting it, or even getting a particular wild thrill from it. Do your duty. Do your job. Do your housework. Eat your meals. Play with your kids. Walk your dog. Make your bed. Love your partner. Do all those things with mindful awareness, fully doing, fully being, and you will be living the dharma.

I Can't Get No Satisfaction

That sounds easy, right? But anybody who tries "just doing" will soon realize how difficult it really is. Why is it so hard? Why is it so difficult to just *do?* Because we, as humans, are full of dukkha. Remember dukkha from Chapter 2, that very human feeling of dissatisfaction, discontent, restlessness, unhappiness, and suffering? We've got it, and it makes simple, unadulterated *doing* exceptionally difficult. Dukkha isn't easy to ignore. It keeps hounding us, following us around like a stray dog or an old debt. We can't get rid of it by ignoring it, and we can't get rid of it by letting it get to us. So what can we do?

Dukkha It Out

Dukkha makes us misperceive reality. We get so caught up in our own heads that we have no idea what is really going on. For example, imagine you are in the grocery store picking up milk, bread, and a few other basics. As you stand in the cereal aisle trying to decide whether you'd rather feast on fruit rings or oat squares this week, someone behind you says, "Hey, get out of the way! You're blocking the aisle, you idiot!"

Nirvana Notes

Sometimes dukkha, or dissatisfaction and suffering, is easier to recognize if you name it. Whenever you recognize dukkha in your life—an unfulfilled desire that plagues you, an adamant opinion you hold but aren't sure why, an obsession, a destructive habit, anything that causes you pain or bad feelings—write it down. Keep a dukkha list. When you start seeing the same few items reappearing, you'll

You turn to see an irate fellow grocery store customer bump your grocery cart roughly and storm past. "Oh!" you say to the person's back. "Sorry."

Suddenly, cereal is the last thing on your mind. The nerve of that person! So your cart was in the way. You didn't put it there on purpose. He could have just said, "Excuse me." He didn't have to be so rude. And he certainly didn't have to call you an idiot.

Depending on who you are and how you tend to react to such things, you might start to get really, really angry or really, really insecure or both. How dare someone treat you that way! Is there something wrong with you? Do you look like a victim? Do you look obnoxious? Do you look like the kind of person who blocks grocery aisles on purpose, just to get a chuckle out of inconveniencing people? Do you look like an idiot?

Or maybe there is something wrong with that person who called you an idiot. Why would someone talk to you that way? Obviously that guy is deeply disturbed, right? Obviously he has major personal problems: anger issues, communication issues, and a severe lack of people skills. He is probably a sociopath. Obviously that guy needs to be taught a lesson.

Maybe you live the scenario over and over, recreating it and imagining the responses you could have made, different ways it could have happened, how you might have taught the person a lesson, reasserted your rights, or made the person feel as bad as you feel now. It might spoil your whole day. It might even keep you up at night. What is wrong with that rude person? What is wrong with you? You are letting dukkha get to you, that's what's wrong with you. If you fight with dukkha, or follow it, or engage it, or show it any sign at all that it bothers, disturbs, or upsets you, it will get worse. And as for the other guy, whatever is wrong with him isn't within your control.

But let's imagine the situation played out a different way. There you are, browsing for cereal, when you hear that same voice: "Hey, get out of the way! You're blocking the aisle, you idiot." *Crash!* goes the grocery cart against yours.

You turn. You see what has happened. You move your cart out of the way, then turn your full attention back to the cereal. The end.

What? Who could do that? Who could let such a rude person get by with behavior like that?

Someone practicing Zen living, that's who.

One Hand Clapping

An old Zen story tells of a man whose wife, on her deathbed, begged him never to go to another woman. A few months after her death, the man fell in love and became engaged. Immediately, he was haunted by his first wife's ghost. Every evening she chided him for disloyalty, describing gifts the man had given his fiancée and repeating details from their conversations. She must be real! At last the man visited an old Zen master, who suggested, "Take a handful of soybeans and demand this ghost tell you how many beans you hold." That night, when confronted with the question, the ghost disappeared without answering and never returned. The ghost didn't know the answer because the man didn't know the answer. She was an illusion! We, too, can become similarly convinced of the reality of things we have created in our minds, when they really are only ghosts of our attachments, guilt, and desires.

Here's the thing: In the first scenario, the rude person got away with it anyway, and you spent the next who-knows-how-many hours of your life suffering because you couldn't let go of the incident. You imagined all sorts of things to explain the behavior of somebody else—something over which you have absolutely no control.

Let's say that again:

You have absolutely no control over the behavior of others.

If you can't control it, let it go. Go back to your cereal. And we suggest the oat squares.

Douse Your Dukkha with Dharma

Once again, we can see where Zen's difficulty lies. It is much easier to let go of something than to let it hound you. On the other hand, it is perhaps ultimately difficult to let go of something rather than let it hound you. What a paradox—and how very Zen.

Of course, many of our reactions, thoughts, feelings, and emotions are simply a matter of habit. Part of Zen is learning to step out of our old habits that aren't doing us any good—because although habits might be easy and comfortable, they really do take a lot more energy than leaving them behind. According to Buddhism, the dharma holds an important key to the elimination of suffering: If you have right understanding, dukkha won't bother you. You'll perceive it, but you won't let it drive you up the wall or make you miserable. "There it is," you'll say. "There is that human suffering thing. But I've been there, done that, and don't need to do it this time."

You might even start trying to help others be free of their dukkha. Then you'll understand what it is to be a *bodhisattva*, someone who works to end the suffering and encourage the enlightenment of all sentient beings.

 Zen-Speak

A **bodhisattva** devotes his or her life to ending the suffering and aiding the enlightenment of all sentient beings. In classical Buddhism, bodhisattvas such as Kuan Yin (Kannon in Japanese) are similar to gods and goddesses, appearing occasionally to humans in need. A Buddhist who makes a formal commitment to the life of a bodhisattva will vow to follow certain bodhisattva precepts in a formal ceremony.

True or False: The Four Noble Truths

Remember the Four Noble Truths we discussed briefly in Chapter 2? They really can help you break the cycle of attaching yourself unproductively to things you can't control. They are called noble truths because they really do help point the way to a mode of existence that puts a lot more life in living and a lot more truth in perception. What more noble cause exists than helping others be free from suffering? That's exactly what these principles do. Let's remember them:

◆ To live means to experience suffering, discontent, disquiet, restlessness, and so on. Everything can't be perfect all the time. Bad things happen to everyone and nobody likes them, whether you are talking about a serious illness or a poorly cooked dinner. So you have to clean the house today instead of lying in the hammock reading a book. So you have to be alone for a while because your marriage didn't work. So you hate going to work every morning. So you have to exchange information with the person whose car you just hit. Nobody likes these things, and they make most people feel pretty bad. Being human means experiencing unpleasantness.

◆ How you handle those "bad" things (*bad* being a relative term) is what causes your suffering, not the bad thing itself. Even pain can be handled in a way that will keep you from suffering. It isn't easy, but it can be done. Attaching to "bad things," trying to control them, or letting them control you—these are the attitudes that cause suffering.

Nirvana Notes _____

If you are in pain, think about what causes your suffering. Pain hurts, sure, but suffering comes from the associations we attach to pain: "Oh, this really hurts. How will I ever get through the day? Will my work suffer? I hope no one (or someone) notices. Does this mean I'll die soon? This is certainly inconvenient! Will I feel this way forever? How terrifying! I can't stand another second!" Such thoughts, rather than the pain itself, cause dukkha.

◆ If you don't attach to your feelings, they won't hang around. Pain management techniques often advise people to enter and experience their pain rather than try to distract themselves from it. Meeting the pain, entering the pain, experiencing the pain, and moving through it—that is the Zen way to handle pain. During meditation, if you concentrate on an itch without scratching it, you can feel the itch increase in intensity, peak, and then fade away. So it is with all pain, physical, emotional, or spiritual. Don't follow it, hate it, fight it, or try to pretend it isn't there. Let it be, then let it go.

◆ How do you let it go? You let it go by learning exactly and precisely how you, personally, can let any experience happen to you. It is different for everyone, and Buddhism's Eightfold Path contains only suggestions. The best way to learn who you are, deep down, and how you handle things is to get to know yourself better through meditation, or zazen.

These noble truths can guide you to change your life by looking at who you really are. Look inside yourself and just be with yourself. Spend time with yourself—the most interesting person in the room and the only one you can ever really know completely. Letting go of attachments to feelings, sensations, events, and people isn't easy (and isn't the same as denying the feelings themselves). With practice, consistency, perseverance, and the right techniques, you can do it. It isn't easy to stop making life so hard, but you can do it.

When things get intense, when you feel stressed or sad or angry, you have ahead of you a challenge: Can you let this go? There are several ways to do this. Let's look at some specific techniques for keeping dukkha from getting in the way of your own personal apprehension of truth and who you are. None of these techniques is as easy as it sounds, but this is a starting place. If you are unhappy, restless, and discontent right now, these are things you can do to stop suffering and start living.

> ### One Hand Clapping
>
> When you need to slow down and come back to yourself, you do not need to rush home to your meditation cushion or to a meditation center in order to practice conscious breathing. You can breathe anywhere, just sitting on your chair at the office or sitting in your automobile. Even if you are at a shopping center filled with people or waiting in line at a bank, if you begin to feel depleted and need to return to yourself, you can practice conscious breathing and smiling just standing there.
>
> —From *Peace Is Every Step: The Path of Mindfulness in Everyday Life* by Thich Nhat Hanh

Sit It Out

One great technique for diffusing your attachment to a particularly disturbing or distracting feeling or thought is to sit. Just sit. Don't sit to fume, to plot revenge, to wallow, or to run through your various to-do lists to see if you forgot anything. Just sit. Sit out the intense feeling. Sit quietly and watch it.

Imagine you can enclose your distraction in a bubble. Give the feeling a name: anger at _____, stress about _____, sadness because of _____, pain in my _____ (*fill in the blanks*), or just plain anger, stress, sadness, loneliness, frustration, irritation, or confusion. Watch the bubble float around, and imagine the feelings banging around inside it. Concentrate on your breath, and when the feeling seems to have played itself out, take a deep breath and—*poof!*—imagine blowing it away.

Other thoughts and feelings will surely come up. Imagine them in bubbles, too. Watch them and name them. See them for what they are—just thoughts, just feelings, not necessarily reality or anything that makes you who you are. Humans eat and sleep, smile and cry, think and feel. It's all the same. What you eat doesn't personify you. Neither does what you think or feel. These are all passing activities, transitory states. None of it defines you, none of it has to control you. Just sit and watch, and blow those bubbles away when you are done observing them. The you who remains is something entirely different, something nontransitory, the you who stays when the bubbles drift away. Keep sitting. There you are.

Walk It Off

If your feelings or thoughts are too overwhelming when you sit, walk them off. Walking meditation (called *kinhin* in Buddhist circles) is very similar to sitting meditation, except you are in motion. Walking can help dispel the power of a strong feeling by increasing circulation in the body so you notice your body more and by changing the scenery so you are more likely to focus on your surroundings. When you become absorbed in the passing scenery and on the way your body is moving, your overwhelming stress or pain or anxiety can seem less crucial, less immediate, and less engaging.

Find Your Center

Sometimes, when you start to feel overwhelmed by dukkha, when your mind feels like it is bubbling over like an overfilled pot of boiling soup, all you have to do is stop and "take a moment." Take the pot off the burner, open the lid, and take a good look in there.

Stopping mid-activity to find your center and regroup can put a stop to a destructive cycle of increasing dukkha. Just stop what you are doing. Breathe. Step back, mentally, and look at your mind. Look at what your emotions are doing and how your thoughts are churning. Look at your mind as if you were outside of it (because you are). This stopping and stepping back can bring you right back to your center, to what is really happening in the here and now.

Zen-Speak

Kinhin is walking meditation. You can practice it individually or, in the context of a zendo, in a group with everyone walking in a circle. Kinhin is often used in alternation with zazen during long periods of meditation. In kinhin, the mind does just what it does in zazen. Only the body does something different.

Monkey Mind!

When you feel stressed or disturbed, rather than trying to find the root of the problem, it might just be best to give it up. Let it go. Don't analyze it or figure it out. You don't even need to understand it. Imagine wrapping up the disturbance (even if you don't know what it is) and mailing it, stamped "return to sender." Then forget about it.

Be Insufferable

By *insufferable*, we don't mean make yourself such that others can't tolerate you. We mean make yourself such that you can tolerate anything. In other words, let yourself be impervious to suffering.

If you can recognize the unfulfilled desire in your suffering, if you can pinpoint it exactly, you can refuse to acknowledge it. Voilà! No more suffering. Here's the key: Don't refuse to acknowledge the situation. On the contrary: Fully acknowledge the situation, but then refuse to acknowledge the *suffering* part.

For example: Your back hurts, and you wish it didn't. You bounced a check, and you wish you had more money. You haven't had a date in a long time, and you wish you could find someone you like. You don't like your job, and you wish you could be doing something more in line with your talents. What do you do with these feelings?

Acknowledge your pain. Face your financial situation. Cultivate a fulfilling relationship with yourself. Commit to your job, or commit to getting a different one. That's it, the end. You don't have to attach all those negative feelings to any situation, no matter how bleak and horrible it seems to you. That bleak and horrible part is your mind attaching "bleak" and "horrible" to life circumstances. You don't have to let suffering get in the way of your true nature or any of the precious moments of your life. Be insufferable! Who has time to waste on suffering, anyway?

Start Where You Are

In his excellent book *Wherever You Go, There You Are*, Jon Kabat-Zinn emphasizes mindfulness in the here and now. Where are you now? Don't think about where were you yesterday and what that means for today nor where you will be tomorrow and how you can start getting there today. Where are you right now?—that is the question. Kabat-Zinn writes:

> Like it or not, this moment is all we really have to work with. Yet we all too easily conduct our lives as if forgetting momentarily that we are here, where we already are, and that we are in what we are already in. In every moment, we find ourselves at the crossroad of here and now.

When you begin to feel overwhelmed, stop and look around you. Quite literally looking at where you are can help jolt your mind back to the present moment. Where am I? What is happening in my life at this moment? What am I going to do about it? Only by starting where you are can you ever get anywhere. Forget yesterday and forget tomorrow. You can't have yesterday back, and tomorrow never really comes. You only have now, and this is all you will ever have. Make it count.

Waking Up Again ... and Again

If you know someone who is fully mindful all the time, we'd like to meet him or her. Most people catch glimpses of mindfulness or little glimmers of enlightenment here and there. Then we forget. We get caught up again, distracted, engaged, and attached, then we start suffering again and remember: Oh yes! Be here, right now. Let the rest go.

That means waking up to our life and our true nature again and again and again, as many times as it takes. The better we become at foiling dukkha and living by the dharma, or the truth of our own nature, the more glimmers we'll get.

But being human, chances are that waking up and paying attention without unproductive and futile attachment and desire will be a lifelong process of beginning again. The ocean throws its waves on the shore again and again. The tide comes in again and again. The sun rises and sets again and again. You sit down to meditate again and again. And you keep waking up each morning, each moment.

Let Zen be a process and a pattern for your life. Forgetting to pay attention doesn't mean you have failed. It just means you forgot to pay attention. It doesn't mean anything beyond exactly what it is. Wake up again and begin anew. It's what we all do, and it is all we do. It is the nature of being human.

How Loud Is Your Alarm Clock?

Of course, without the right alarm clock, you might not ever wake up. Only you can know how loud you need your "alarm clock"— your personal techniques for achieving mindfulness—to be.

You can be caught in mindlessness all the time and not even know you are asleep. Mindlessness is an acceptable way to live in our culture. In the book *Mindfulness*, by Ellen J. Langer, Ph.D., Dr. Langer identifies various ways through which we learn to act mindlessly: "Early in life, we learn to categorize things, perform behaviors automatically, and see things from a single perspective."

Breaking out of these patterns isn't something that will occur without some effort. It isn't that breaking the cycle of mindlessness is particularly difficult. We just don't think to do it unless we consciously decide to think to do it. There aren't many punishments or negative consequences for living mindlessly, so we don't realize what we are missing—the great rewards and benefits of waking up. No negative stimulus forces us out of our comfortable dream, but oh, what we are missing.

We can help wake ourselves up by setting our alarm clocks to break out of old categorized distinctions we take for granted, by performing behaviors differently, and by seeing things from a different point of view.

Nirvana Notes

For one morning or afternoon, make a point to pause and really notice the world around you and inside you for one minute on the hour, every hour. Looking for more ways to wake yourself up? Work your five senses in new ways. Eat something with a strong, sour, pungent, or spicy taste. Smell all the spices in your cupboard, one at a time. Visit a toy store and look through a kaleidoscope. Change your radio station to a new one and really listen to the next three songs. Touch the underside of every piece of furniture in your house.

Maybe mindfulness comes easily to you. Maybe all you need to do is remind yourself now and then throughout the day, "Okay, now pay attention." If mindfulness isn't so easy, if you find yourself knowing you should wake up but persisting in your attachments and automatic behaviors, assumptions and desires, you might need a louder alarm clock.

Like what? Learn to foil your own expectations. Turn things on their head. Take a cold shower or a walk in the rain. Stand on your head and look at your living room upside down. Eat pizza for breakfast and cereal for dinner. Shake yourself up and open your eyes. Anything you wouldn't normally do can pop you right out of automatic pilot and into the current moment.

You don't have to live like a robot. Everything you do, no matter how ordinary, is worth doing with total attention. Determine what it takes to wake yourself up, and do it every day.

Mindless or Mindful?

"This all sounds great," you might be thinking, "but how do I know if I'm being mindless or mindful? What the heck do I know about it? Am I being mindful or mindless right now? Which is it?"

That is a good question, and one only you can answer for yourself. But here are some clues:

◆ When you are doing more than one thing at the same time (talking on the phone while washing the dishes, watching television while eating dinner, reading the newspaper while talking to your kids, listening to your MP3 player while working out on the elliptical trainer), you aren't doing either task mindfully. You can't focus fully on two things at once. Much of what you are doing is automatic. So as you read this, are you doing anything else? Is the television on?

Are you eating a snack? Are you exercising? Are you petting the cat? If so, you are not being fully mindful. (Automatic physical behaviors such as breathing and your heart beating don't count. Your body takes care of those things for you so you don't have to think about them.)

◆ How well do you remember what you were doing in the moments before you started reading this book? Are those moments vivid? Could you describe the room or area around you without looking around right now? If you were recently with someone else, what did he or she say? How were you standing or sitting? How did you feel? What color was the sky or the ceiling or the walls? If you don't really remember, you weren't in a mindful state then and you probably aren't right now.

◆ If you were to stop reading right now and decide to simply pay attention to everything inside and outside of you at this moment, would it feel a lot different than how you feel at this moment as you read this? If so, you are reading without being fully mindful.

◆ Do you remember the first item on this list, or have you already forgotten? Between the first item and this last item, did your mind wander to anything besides what you are reading on this page? If you've forgotten the first item already and have to look back up the list and if your mind has wandered as you've been reading this, you aren't reading mindfully.

Now don't start putting yourself down if you discovered you aren't being mindful right this moment. Truth be told, most of us aren't being totally mindful most of the time! As we said before, mindfulness is something that comes and goes for each of us and only comes more easily the more we practice (like anything else). Nobody we know does it all the time, during every moment of existence. Not being mindful isn't "bad." It's just "not being mindful." Mindfulness is simply something positive to work on because it gives you the most life for your moment. And don't we all want a bargain like that?

One Hand Clapping

To go beyond ordinary thought is to truly understand. If you just stay with your usual understanding of things, you will be like the frog that only swims in his small pond. Staying just within your little territory, you will never know anything about the larger world in which you live. You have to jump into the ocean. Then you can understand your small world for what it is.

—From *You Have to Say Something: Manifesting Zen Insight* by Dainin Katagiri

Seeking Stillness

Many Zen masters say that desire for enlightenment is still desire and, therefore, comes out of dukkha. Desire for release from stress, desire for stillness, desire for inner peace—these are still desires. We can't help wanting these things, of course. But to embrace a true Zen state, we need to stop desiring these things and simply step into them.

The release from stress, not to mention stillness, inner peace, even nirvana, are already inside us. We don't need to search for them anywhere. We already have them. We just need to sit and look.

Sure, there are a lot of things in the way. Sometimes you might feel as if you are in the very back row at a rock concert or a Broadway show and although you can hear what's going on and see some blurry figures moving around way up front under some spotlights, too many rows of people are in your way. Those people are all the feelings, emotions, thoughts, and suffering you experience and hold on to.

The concert or the show is still going on down there. You have what you need. It might even be in view. You are in the room with what you want. You don't need to desire what you already have. You just need to get to the front row.

In *You Have to Say Something: Manifesting Zen Insight*, Dainin Katagiri writes:

> This moment is not the idea of this moment. If you see it as a concept, it becomes frozen. But the real moment is not frozen. Whatever we may think about this moment, our practice is just to return to it. This moment is where all beings exist. Even though we have doubts and fears, even though we ask, "Why do I have to die?" no answer appears. Only this moment is real. There's no escaping this moment. All beings—including doubt and fear—drop off in this moment.

We know exactly what it is like to want, to need, to almost frantically desire a few moments of peace. How do you get to the front row of the concert or the Broadway show if you have a family to support, a job to go to, needy co-workers to tend, or a house to maintain? How do you have time for peace?

Once again, the serenity of Zen is in the doing of these very things. You don't need to lock yourself in a quiet room to live your Zen or find your peace. Peace is in the doing. Peace may be easier to find in a quiet room, but it is just as present and available (with practice)—and perhaps even more essential—in a noisy room. Be with your family, do your job, give to your co-workers, or maintain your house. Let peace pervade these activities. You aren't moving the activities out of your way; you are moving the anxiety you attach to them out of the way. Don't make life wait for when the activity of life stops, because it never stops. Time alone in meditation is great and important, but Zen living can happen around the clock. You can have your stillness and keep moving, too.

You Gotta Have Faith

Most people don't associate the term *faith* with the term *Zen*. Isn't faith for religions where you are supposed to believe in things without proof?

Actually, Zen does require a leap of faith. To be mindful, you have to believe that life is worth paying attention to. To meditate, you have to believe you are worth getting to know. To reach a state of inner peace, you have to believe that you have peace within you and that your true nature is already complete. You have to believe inner peace is possible, that you are already perfect, that you don't need to add anything to yourself, and that if you only practice and keep looking, you'll eventually have the proof.

If, at this moment, you don't believe some of these things, that's okay. If you can take them on faith, at least for a while—at least through the end of this book—you can decide for yourself. This is your journey, and this is the uncovering of your true self. You aren't the same as Gary or Eve or your parents or your friends or anyone else. Only you can find who you are and the way to Zen living for you.

In Zen Buddhism, faith in the Buddha's teachings as truth is an important component of Buddhist practice. If you don't believe that desire causes suffering, that desire can be eliminated, that all things in the universe are interconnected, or that such a thing as nirvana is possible, you can't really practice Buddhism. You can still practice Zen techniques, but you aren't a Buddhist.

We're talking about two kinds of faith and two kinds of truth. Faith in Buddhist or Christian or Jewish or Muslim principles is a matter for each spiritual seeker. We won't assume these in this book.

But we do make some assumptions. We have faith that you are already whole and complete, all on your own, and that meditation and mindfulness can help you apprehend this truth for yourself. We hope you'll bear with us and accept these principles as true—at least for now. Give them a chance.

The Least You Need to Know

◆ You already have truth inside you.

◆ Your attachment to things you can't control can get in the way of your perception of truth.

◆ Sitting meditation, walking meditation, pausing to find your center or start over, and the refusal to attach to states of mind that induce suffering can help nip dukkha in the bud.

◆ Practicing mindfulness is like waking up in your life.

◆ Faith in your abilities and in the process of Zen techniques such as meditation and mindfulness are necessary for finding your own truth.

Chapter 5

Getting an Attitude: A Zen Approach

In This Chapter

- Who's in charge here, anyway?
- The illusion of control
- If life is a boat, who's at the helm?
- Navigating with Zen
- Dispelling your expectations

It might seem that "getting an attitude" isn't very Zenlike. Isn't Zen about losing your attitude? In a sense, this is true. Losing your old attitudes, the ones that cause you suffering, is Zenlike. But losing attitudes means gaining new ones because an attitude is the state of your mind, and to be human is to have a state of mind.

Much Zen literature talks about not having any opinions or strong feelings about things, but this concept is misleading. You are human. You will have strong feelings, and you will certainly have opinions. You can't help it, and you shouldn't feel bad or guilty or wrong about having feelings and opinions. It's part of the package.

The trick is to have these opinions or feelings without attaching to them, to let them be recognized, acknowledged, fully experienced, then to let them pass away as they most certainly will. This is the Zen attitude.

But I'm in Charge Here (Aren't I?)

Isn't it nice to be in charge? The person in charge makes the rules, is respected, is a leader. He or she knows what to expect and sets the course, much like the captain of a ship. If you are in charge, you call the shots, right?

Being in charge is a comfortable position, even though it holds a lot of responsibility. Why be bossed around if you can be the boss? Everyone knows it pays to take charge of life, to take the reins, to make it happen, to be your own boss. But if it pays … what exactly does it pay? What's the salary for being your own boss?

It doesn't pay anything, because when it comes right down to the ebb and flow of your life, it simply can't be done. Being in charge is a comfortable illusion that can keep you from recognizing the power you really do have over your life. You might not be in charge, but you aren't helpless, either. Let us explain.

Nirvana Notes _____

The first step to relinquishing our illusory notion of being in charge is to recognize when we self-affirm that illusion: If I can just act like the right kind of person, maybe she will like me. If I can just get that promotion, my life will be great. If I say this the right way, I'll be accepted into that group. If I'm supportive enough/assertive enough/masculine enough/feminine enough, I'll be loved.

You Aren't in Control

We have some news for you. We won't call it bad news because it isn't bad. It just is: You aren't in control.

Now don't panic! It might be a scary thought: A life without anyone in charge? Won't there be chaos, anarchy, internal psychological rioting? That depends on your attitude. You can look at your life in a couple different ways.

You can try to be in charge, try to control everyone and everything in your life, and get upset, anxious, or angry when things don't go the way you planned, when people don't act the way you want them to, or when things go "wrong."

Or you can decide you aren't in charge and can't control anyone or anything in your life, and you can get upset, anxious, or angry at your powerlessness and helplessness in the face of an uncertain fate.

Or (aren't you glad there's a third choice?) you can recognize that the world spins without your help, that people do what they do, and that your life will run its course one way or the other. Sometimes your plans won't work out. Flights are delayed, people are late, accidents happen, and everyone makes mistakes. You can decide not to get upset, anxious, or angry about things over which you have no power, and you can choose to do your job and live your life with integrity, compassion, mindful observance, and a healthy sense of humor.

Guess which way is the Zen way!

Let's look at an example. Recently Gary was on his way from New York to Boston for a 3 P.M. meeting. He was scheduled on a 10 A.M. commuter flight. This is what Gary was thinking:

We leave at 10 A.M. so I'll be there by about 11:15. That will give me enough time for a leisurely lunch and a good stroll around town before the meeting.

Gary had everything under control and nicely planned, and he was looking forward to the day. But when Gary got to the airport, he was informed that Boston was fogged in and the flight would be delayed. After waiting for an hour, glancing at his watch every couple minutes, Gary heard another announcement. The flight was further delayed. This is what Gary was thinking:

Okay, I need to rethink this. Let me do some mental math. We'll probably need to wait in a long line on the runway. If we push away from the gate by 11:45 on the dot, I'll arrive in Boston a few minutes after 1. I can get downtown by 1:30, in plenty of time for lunch. I won't have time for the long stroll, but that's not such a big sacrifice.

Proud of how he had rearranged his plans to meet these unpredictable and changing circumstances, Gary smiled to himself. He had everything under control, the day all mapped out so the universe could peruse the plan and comply. No problem.

But then another announcement blared over the airport speaker system. Flights were so backed up they weren't even going to allow boarding until 1 P.M. at best and then the plane would take its place at the end of the line. A collective groan, broken by a few expletives, rose from the irritable crowd. Gary and his fellow New Yorkers (not famous for displaying the quality of patience) proceeded to rush the ticket counter. This is what Gary was thinking:

Unbelievable! How could this happen to me today? Okay, if they are going to keep delaying the flight, I'm going to get a seat on the next plane if it kills me. This is not according to the plan! So I'll make it work. I'll get a seat, and I'll get it now.

When Gary and his fellow passengers finally got on the plane, Gary was so anxious, he was almost shaking. His stomach was in knots, his fists were clenched, and he sat in his seat, tensed and leaning slightly forward, as if he might actually be able to push the plane forward with the sheer force of his will. Gary could feel the tension in the air, not only his own but that of those around him. This is what Gary was thinking:

We'll be off the ground by 1:30. We'll land an hour later. I'll sprint to the cab line and get to the meeting by 3. Forget lunch. I'm not hungry, anyway.

Monkey Mind!

Irritability comes in many forms and often masks other emotions we'd rather not face. The next time you feel irritable or inexplicably angry, stop, sit down, and think about what is really bothering you. If you can address the real problem, you can save yourself from a miserable day.

When the next delay was announced, Gary suddenly experienced an attitude change. You might even call it an epiphany. Calculations? Plans? Mapping out the day for the universe? It all suddenly seemed ultimately absurd. Gary realized that he had no idea when the plane was going to take off, let alone land. He recognized that he had never known. He had no real information, and he had no control.

Gary experienced a rush of relief. If he didn't have any control, all he could do was go along for the ride, maybe even relax and enjoy it. Gary had quite suddenly (in the great tradition of sudden enlightenments characteristic of Zen) adopted a Zen attitude.

Zen Exercise: Your Turn: Let It Go

Gary had a Zen exercise dropped into his lap during that airport incident, and you probably have all kinds of things happening to you that cause you stress, whether big stress or little stress. Maybe you've been stuck in traffic or late to an appointment. Or you've received a bad grade or been unfairly blamed for something, had a car accident or an ill-timed flu virus. Whatever it is, we're quite sure you know what we mean when we say that sometimes, life is stressful.

But what would happen if you let go of the situation the moment you detected stress creeping into your body? Do you think you could do it? Let's find out.

No, we're not going to rear-end your car or sneeze on you. We're going to encourage you to use your imagination. Studies in which people imagined stressful situations indicate that even the thought of stress can cause the body to activate a stress response, with increased heartbeat and respiration rate, muscles tensing, and the release of stress hormones such as adrenaline and cortisol. Let's warm up with some imaginary stress and see how you do.

First, sit comfortably where you won't be disturbed for at least 10 minutes. Now, think about a situation that really stresses you out such as that traffic jam, being late, losing your keys, burning that perfect dinner, or accidentally deleting that whole report you just wrote, the one that was so *perfect*. Envision the situation in as much detail as you can. How did it happen? Where are you? What are the circumstances? And most of all, how do you feel?

As soon as you feel yourself starting to feel stressed—muscles tensing, breath rate increasing—stop. Mentally take a step back and look at the situation. See if you can stop the stress response, not by denying the situation but by looking at it exactly as it is, without any feelings attached. Imagine that your feelings are separate from the experience (which they are), floating around overhead. Look at them buzzing around up there, all gray and worried. Now look at the actual situation. Every time you start to attach a feeling to it, notice that this is what you are doing, then release it and let the feeling float back up overhead. Visualize this while you breathe deeply, and see what happens.

Was this pretty tough? Not so hard? This is what Zen does for you—it separates the feelings from the situation so you see them as two separate things rather than hopelessly intertwined. It takes practice, but it really is possible.

Now, the next time you get into an actual stressful situation, see if you can repeat this exercise, letting the feelings float up overhead, away from the situation. Then look again. You'll see it all more clearly.

Giving Up Control (Even When No One Else Will)

Even if you know, logically, that you aren't really in control of other people, of your situation, and of the changing environments you encounter, it still is really hard to accept the idea. If you don't put on that act of being in control, what will people think?

Most people act, at least to some extent, as if they control their own lives and, in many cases, the lives of others. They lecture each other, give advice, make rules, enforce rules, enact punishments, and generally talk as if they, or the group with which they are associated, are keeping society together. Parents advise and discipline their children. Law enforcement officers enforce the laws made by lawmakers. Schools have rules; workplaces have rules; cities, counties, states, and countries have rules. It seems there are plenty of people in charge.

The question is, what exactly do all those "in-charge" people control? Each of us must pursue life, liberty, and happiness on our own. The rules we set as a society make living together easier as we each seek what we need for wholeness and self-awareness, but the finding is up to us, not anyone else. Who we are and what we make of our lives is up to us. And we can't force anyone else to find happiness or make their lives a certain way, either.

So when we say no one has control over anyone, we don't mean nobody can force us to follow the law. Sure they can. Or at least, they can enforce a punishment if we don't. They can also try to intimidate, coerce, bribe, or coax us into certain behaviors. But no one controls who we are inside and what we choose to do—not really. In the same way, we don't control who anyone else is and what anyone else does. What we do has consequences, sure. But our *doing* is up to us, just as our attitudes about our doing are up to us and no one else.

Still, you might believe that if you give up even the illusion of control, you'll be slipping behind, losing your place in line, falling down the ladder, or missing out on important opportunities to get ahead.

Giving up something you never had can only clarify your life.

The idea of giving up control may be frightening, but it becomes much easier if you realize that you aren't giving up anything at all. You are only giving up the illusion that you had something. No one can step in and take over something that never existed. You aren't going to fall behind by recognizing reality. Instead, you'll have a better grasp on what is really going on, and you can expend your energies in ways that are productive rather than futile.

Giving up the illusion of control is like jumping off that little hamster wheel and climbing out of the cage.

But because we are so used to thinking we have to be in control, fear is natural. It's based on illusion, but still natural.

Giving up the illusion of control also doesn't mean giving up rules, plans, or all the necessary things we need to do to live our life among others. It just means giving up control of our attachments to the rules, plans, and other details of life.

But still, you might be thinking, what will people think? How do we exist in the rat race without acting like a rat? Won't we be disqualified?

We doubt it. You'll probably be more likely to redefine the race for others.

Here's an example of something relatively trivial, just for the sake of illustration:

Let's say you work in an office where there's a rule you don't like: no coffee cups at your desk. Now let's say you really, really love your cup of coffee, and you work a lot better with a cup of coffee nearby. But because of a couple unfortunate spills and ruined computer equipment, the rule stands: no coffee cups at your desk.

A lot of people in the office don't like this rule one bit. They grumble and complain. They sneak their coffee cups behind typing stands and hard-drive cases. They talk about the boss, how unreasonable she is, and how stupid the rule is. They really let that rule get to them, and so do you. Darn it, you want a cup of coffee when you are in the thick of preparing that report. How else are you supposed to stay awake? If the job wasn't so boring, maybe you wouldn't need the coffee. If your boss gave you more prestige, more responsibility, or a promotion, maybe you wouldn't mind. But she hasn't, and you do mind. If only you could just have that cup of coffee at your desk, your whole job would be so much ….

Okay, time for a reality check. First off, do you see what you are doing? You are so attached to that rule that you are letting it drive you crazy! What would happen if you decided to give up your false sense of control and stop being so attached to that rule? You would enter the now, and you would have a couple choices: Accept the rule and move on, or take action to change it.

Nirvana Notes

Pet peeves are perfect examples of things we are attached to. Does it drive you crazy when someone cracks her knuckles or chews with his mouth open? What about when someone cuts you off on the freeway or criticizes your new haircut? Maybe you can't stand it when a co-worker is disrespectful or a boss is dismissive. Why waste energy being irritated by things you can't control? Irritation doesn't change anything; it just causes suffering.

But how would your co-workers react if you just decided to accept the rule? Do you imagine they will say something like, "Hey, what's wrong with Joe? I thought he was onboard with this whole coffee-cup-hate campaign!" Or might they say, "Joe must be kissing up to the big boss. He stopped complaining about the coffee-cup rule!" Or how about, "Joe, we've all banded together and decided not to talk to you or share any more information with you because you aren't upset about the whole coffee-cup thing."

Sounds pretty ridiculous, doesn't it? Chances are, one by one, people in your work-place will think to themselves, "Hmm. Joe doesn't seem to be too bothered by the coffee-cup rule anymore. Maybe it's time to move on." Or "Wait a minute. If Joe stops complaining about the coffee-cup rule, he might get that promotion before I do." But the point is: It doesn't matter what anyone else thinks or does because you can't control what anyone else thinks or does.

You really can't. They'll think what they want to think. You can jump through hoops trying to fine-tune the reactions of other people to everything you do, but what kind of a life is that? All you can control is your own reaction to the circumstances in your life. And that's plenty.

Of course, you can probably think of many examples where it would be much harder to ignore the reactions and behaviors of those around you. But the point remains the same: You can't control what anyone else thinks or does, so why expend valuable life energy trying to do the impossible?

If you spend your energies getting to know yourself, living mindfully, refusing to get caught up in petty details and "wheel-spinning" behaviors, and living your life with integrity and compassion, people will probably respect you, maybe even try to follow your example. Nevertheless, you can't force them to respect you, so why worry about it? Be who you are, respect yourself, and turn your attention to what you have to do. Life suddenly gets easier.

Imagine Your Life Is a Boat

Because we've used the metaphor already, let's think of your life, once again, as your boat. You are the captain of the boat. Maybe you even built the boat. Like Russell Crowe's character Captain Aubrey of the HMS *Surprise* in the movie *Master and Commander*, you know all the details of the boat, how it works, and its imperfections. You also know every member of the crew, including each crew member's strengths and foibles.

You have to steer a boat, of course, so it goes where you need it to go. But you don't have to steer it all the time, and you certainly don't need to take a route that goes directly against the currents and winds.

Monkey Mind!

It is all too easy to get caught up in what other people think of you. Ironically, the more worried you are about other people's opinions, the more negative those opinions tend to be. Those who don't give a thought to what others think tend to be the most revered.

Living your life like a competent captain means setting a course and steering your boat when necessary, then letting the wind and waves do most of the work. If you stand at the helm and try to force the rudder against every wave and gust of wind, you'll be miserable and probably seasick. You'll expend a whole lot of effort, and the boat will still go the way it's going to go.

That doesn't mean you go below the deck to party with the crew and completely ignore where the ship is going. That's the way to ram into an iceberg.

(Russell Crowe meets *Titanic!*) You have to pay attention to the ship's direction, and if you start to go off-course, you need to correct. At various points along the journey, you might need to turn east or south or take the long way around to take advantage of the Gulf Stream, to avoid a hurricane, or to harness a particularly persistent wind. That is paying attention.

But you don't waste your energy battling all those little waves, because the ocean is full of them and they keep on coming. Let them come. Enjoy the movement and the perpetual change. It makes the sea voyage interesting.

A famous visual representation of this wonderful metaphor is a series of four paintings made by the nineteenth-century American Hudson River School painter Thomas Cole called *The Voyage of Life*. The four paintings, *Childhood*, *Youth*, *Manhood*, and *Old Age*, explore a man piloting his boat on the river of life through each of life's passages. Painted in 1842 and popular in their day, the series is now on permanent display at the National Gallery of Art in Washington, D.C. Why not look up the images on the Internet for some inspiration!

One Hand Clapping

An old Zen story tells of two monks traveling along a road. They came upon a beautiful young girl who was unable to get across a stream. The older monk offered to help. He picked her up and carried her across. Several miles down the road, the younger monk could no longer contain himself. "Master, we aren't supposed to associate with women, yet you actually touched that beautiful woman. You picked her up!" The master answered, "I put that woman down on the other side of the stream. Are you still carrying her?" This story illustrates the difference between physical involvement with the world and mental attachment to the world.

Your New Navigation System

We're enjoying this voyage of life metaphor, so we're going to continue it. We hope you'll bear with us.

Adopting a Zen attitude is like installing a new navigation system in your ship. This new navigation system is particularly designed to work with the ocean rather than against it. Forget the whole "man conquering the sea" idea. With this new system, captain (human) and sea (life) become one.

Living Zen means opening yourself to a full awareness of your surroundings and yourself. Only then can you use the storms and winds and waves to propel you through life, rather than fight them or try to master them or even pretend they aren't there. Any good sailor knows that you must lose yourself and become one with the boat, water, and wind to achieve your goal. You cannot plot an inch-by-inch course because conditions change every second. You can only say, "I will go to X." The sailor who struggles to get there a specific way will be the last one to arrive.

In other words, things happen. Recognize it. Accept it. Use its momentum to propel you.

Letting Go of Expectations

So how do you do all this? How do you use what happens in your life rather than try to control it? First, you have to let go of it. You can do this in several ways, but the first big step is to let go of your expectations.

We are trained from an early age to develop expectations. When you were a baby, an adult fed you, kept you dry, and probably rocked you to sleep. Soon you learned to expect food, a changed diaper, a cuddle, and a lullaby at bedtime. Things were pretty good, right?

As you grew, things happened that caused you to set up all kinds of expectations. If your parents told you you were smart, you began to expect yourself to be smart. If your friends told you a certain person was mean or nice or so not cool, you came to expect mean or nice or not-cool behavior from that person. Maybe you were bitten by a dog and came to expect aggressive behavior from all dogs. Maybe a sibling teased you mercilessly, and you learned to expect teasing. Your expectations set you up for creating illusions that can mislead you, whether they seem to help you or hold you back.

Setting up patterns of expectations can be not only illusory, but limiting as well. Assuming every dog is going to bite you or your siblings will always put you down, even assuming a friend is reliable or a relationship will turn into the same marriage your parents had or the job you have now is the one you will have for the next 20 years severely limits your view of the world. Maybe some of these things will turn out to be true, but if you assume so, suddenly you've put on blinders. You won't be ready for the present moment because you are too busy looking ahead at what very well might never happen the way you think it will.

Living Zen means seeing each incident for what it is and not carrying any expectations forward to apply to any other incidents. That dog bit you, but who knows about this dog? That friend betrayed you, but this friend has nothing to do with that situation. Your siblings teased you once, but as adults, perhaps you can build a new relationship. Living without expectations really can open a whole new space for you to deal with things on their own terms, as they are this moment, without pulling up the past or trying to imprint the future.

Of course, we learn certain expectations for the purpose of survival. Caution around animals is sensible, whether you've ever been bitten or not. Total emotional dependence on a friend isn't healthy or productive. You know cars are dangerous, so you drive carefully and look both ways before crossing the street. You know rotten food can make you sick so if something smells bad or looks spoiled, you don't eat it. These examples mean you are remaining aware of your surroundings. But there is a fine line between awareness and using past knowledge in that awareness and letting your expectations for a situation rule your awareness.

Nirvana Notes _____

What do you assume? Make a list of everything you can think of, from the sun rising each morning to the behavior of a co-worker. Then, go over the list and imagine you couldn't assume each item—not that the sun won't come up or your co-worker will act suddenly out of character (these are just different assumptions), but that you can no longer take anything for granted. How could this open your mind to new awareness and possibility in your life?

Expecting things simply because they happened before isn't living Zen. It is living mindlessly. Being fully aware means taking every moment for what it is, as if it is completely new—because it truly is. What will happen today? What will happen in this moment? You don't know, but the fun part is, you get to open your eyes and find out.

The Least You Need to Know

- ◆ You aren't in charge of your life, and you can't control what people think of you.

- ◆ "Giving up" control just means recognizing your lack of control, thereby freeing your energy for more productive things (such as helping others, doing your job, meditating, etc.).

- ◆ Your life is like a boat. The captain can't control the weather, the condition of the sea, or storms. The captain can only commune with the air, boat, and sea to move the boat forward to its eventual destination.

- ◆ The first step to recognizing what you do and don't control in your life is to let go of your expectations. If you don't expect anything, everything will be a new experience.

Chapter 6

When Bad Things Happen

In This Chapter

- Tragedy is just a word
- The Zen approach to life's little setbacks
- Applying your Zen attitude adjustment
- Coping with major loss
- How to feel the big feelings
- Your zazen life preservers: sitting, breathing

We can talk all day long about adopting a Zen attitude, but the words won't mean much if we don't acknowledge that sometimes bad things happen, and sometimes horrible, tragic things happen. Do the rules change?

It probably seems to you as if adopting a Zen attitude is a lot easier when things are going well. And that's true! Tragedy tests anyone's resolve, faith, and way of being. But rather than thwarting our Zen attitude, "bad things" can help us discover just how powerful our Zen attitude really is.

Tragedy is a relative thing, so the word poses an interesting challenge. What is a tragedy? Both Gary and Eve were brought up steeped in the Judeo-Christian way of being, where people are supposed to be happy with what they have. If something happens, it is the will of a higher power.

Be thankful, because chances are, someone is always a lot worse off. Even in "tragedy," society delivers the message that we are supposed to count our blessings and accept that everything happens for a reason.

In a way, this is a Zenlike attitude—not to be satisfied with a less-than-satisfactory existence, but to find the joy of life in and the reality of where we are right now.

But what of the part about somebody else being worse off? That's supposed to make us feel better? If, as a child, you hated spinach, did being told children were starving in India make you relish each bite with joy and gratitude? The more common childhood response is, "Well, then, send the spinach to them!" Whether that comment comes out of a youthful humanitarian impulse or a simple desire to remove all traces of spinach from the continent doesn't matter. Clearly the approach doesn't really work. The tragedy of others is not a reason for us to celebrate.

But we digress. What about when tragedy happens to you or to those close to you? What happens when you are overwhelmed with fear, sadness, despair, or loss? Can you hold on to your Zen attitude, and can it help you?

When Tidal Waves Hit

In Chapter 5, we compared life to a boat. There you are, sailing along, bobbing on the waves, enjoying the brilliant blue sky, and smiling at the seabirds.

Then the sky starts to darken; there is lightning and thunder. The waves get choppier. You have the sense that somewhere far out in the ocean, something major is happening. You sense a deep pull in the ocean. It's something big. It's a tsunami.

When a tidal wave hits your boat, you're going to have to do some work to keep the boat afloat. Or maybe the boat sinks, and you have to swim to shore and build a new one. Let's look at how you can do this work with a Zenlike attitude because living Zen even through the bad times can help you through those times by keeping your vision clear and your energies directed where they can help the most.

Nirvana Notes

If you've ever had a bad day (and who hasn't), you might stop to think about what made it so bad. Did you label the day "bad" early in the morning when the coffeemaker broke? Was it your attitude that colored the rest of the day? A Zen attitude can erase bad days from your future—not events you don't enjoy, but the bad mood they might provoke.

The Little Tragedies of Life

Not every "tragedy" is of tidal-wave proportions. Some of the things that rock our boats are nasty, vicious little storms that fill the boat with water and ruin everything without sinking the boat or even damaging the structure. These are the little trage-dies of life.

We tend to name something a "tragedy" when it doesn't meet our expectations. The person with an hourly wage job and a family to support who loses that job feels a tragedy has happened. The Wall Street trader who misses out on a quarter-million-dollar bonus, even after sweating and scheming for months to orchestrate the finan-cial coup, believes that is a tragedy.

And what about that relationship you thought was perfect until your partner revealed his or her differing view? What about that torn rotator cuff, that failing grade, that crashed hard drive, that stolen purse, that ulcer, that demotion, that nasty stain, the fact that the transmission just dropped out of the bottom of your car … The list could go on and on.

One Hand Clapping

An old Zen story tells of how the words *The First Principle* over the gate of Obaku tem-ple in Kyoto, praised as a masterpiece of calligraphy, came to be. Zen master Kosen had been writing the words over and over one day while a presumptuous pupil looked over his shoulder and casually criticized each attempt, telling him the calligraphy was bad. "Master, I know you can do better than that!" the student would say. "Oh, no, master, that one is worse than the one before!" His confidence undermined, Kosen kept trying without success. After 84 tries, the student stepped out of the room for a moment and Kosen hurriedly dashed off the words an eighty-fifth time, without thought, beyond thought. When the student returned, he proclaimed, "Now this, master, is a master-piece!" The eighty-fifth, without-thought attempt is the one immortalized over Obaku Temple's gate.

Why must we experience such setbacks—painful, expensive, frustrating, and a waste of time, resources, and self-esteem—even when we've done our best, planned, devoted ourselves, worked our hardest, and applied our selfless love? Doesn't that guarantee we will get what we want?

Of course not. Every single one of these situations and every single other situation we can think of, be it disappointment or triumph, is simply an occurrence. Things hap-pen. That's all.

We aren't really in control of the outcome. Our actions might influence what happens, but a whole lot of other factors influence everything that happens, too. Things happen. Events occur. That's all.

But we will have feelings about these events. Of course we will. And being human, we need to have them. Let yourself feel your feelings. Feel the anger, the disappointment, the rejection, or the fear. Let the feelings flow through you, then let them end. Let yourself get to the other side.

Remind yourself that you aren't in control. Remind yourself that you've experienced a tragedy because you've decided to call it a tragedy. You could decide you have experienced an experience. Take away the label "tragedy," and watch your attitude transform.

Sometimes a tragedy presents an opportunity to realize we aren't in the right field or in the right company. Maybe we've chosen a relationship with the wrong partner, or car, or computer. Maybe we need a wake-up call about our health habits or risk-taking behaviors. Maybe we can, through an experience, find a way to grow into a fuller, more realized human being with greater self-knowledge.

> **CAUTION**
>
> **Monkey Mind!**
>
> Keeping a perspective about the events in your life is extremely difficult without maintaining a meditation practice. Meditation free from daily distractions lets you work on your attitude, which is simply to be without opinion, judgment, or expectation. This practice helps keep your Zen attitude in the front of your mind throughout the day.

Life hasn't promised us anything. But more important, every experience can teach us something. We won't enjoy everything that happens to us in our life, but opening ourselves to the positive possibilities inherent in every experience helps us grow.

So after that good cry, pillow-beating, or whatever it is you have to do to experience and then let go of your feelings, open yourself to the clarity inherent in the experience of "tragedy."

So whatever you tried didn't work. Fantastic! Now you know something that doesn't work. Great! Now you can try something else, and open yourself to whatever else is out there—something that might be a lot better.

And Then the Big Ones

Big tragedies are tougher. It probably seems a lot easier to put small, daily disappointments into perspective, but what about when things happen that are really bad, horrible, even unthinkable? Someone you love (or maybe you yourself) is diagnosed with a terminal disease, gets into a major accident, or drops out of your life completely for one reason or another. You lose your home, the use of your body, or everything you own. Someone integral to your life dies.

One Hand Clapping

Water is often used as a metaphor for a Zen attitude. Water flows. It doesn't "go with the flow," it *is* the flow. Water flows over rocks and cliffs, tree roots and boulders, around peninsulas and islands, through wide, deep channels, and across floodplains. Sometimes the water is deep and still; sometimes it is shallow and bubbly; sometimes it shoots into the air in dramatic sprays. Yet it always flows under or over the ground. Even when it reaches the sea, it evaporates into the sky and falls again. It carved the entire Grand Canyon slowly, tiny bit by tiny bit. It accepts, flows with, and helps create the landscape around it, not by fighting the landscape, but just by flowing through it.

How are you supposed to go on after something like this? This isn't something you can fix. This is major. This isn't something to deal with and move on. Your life has been forever altered. What does Zen have to do with the big things?

Everything. Although it is much harder to peel off that "tragedy" label from the really major experiences in life, it is possible. It's just that the part where you have to experience your feelings takes a lot longer and the feelings are usually a whole lot stronger. Why are your feelings so strong? Because of what the event means to you.

In *The Art of Happiness* by His Holiness the Dalai Lama and Howard C. Cutler, M.D., Dr. Cutler writes:

> There is no doubt that our attitude and mental outlook can strongly affect the degree to which we suffer when we are in physical pain. Let's say, for instance, that two individuals, a construction worker and a concert pianist, suffer the same finger injury. While the amount of physical pain might be the same for both individuals, the construction worker might suffer very little and in fact rejoice if the injury resulted in a month of paid vacation which he or she was in need of, whereas the same injury could result in intense suffering to the pianist who viewed playing as his or her primary source of joy in life.

Sometimes the natural human emotion associated with a major event (even when it is a "good" event) is so intense that we are afraid to experience it. We put on a happy face. We say everything is just fine. We talk in depth about how well we are handling the situation. In other words, we repress our feelings; we pretend they aren't there; we sometimes even attribute them to someone or something else.

But feeling our feelings is just as important—even more important—for major life-altering events than for the small inconveniences in life. The concert pianist has to feel that suffering so he or she can recognize it and pass through it, even learn from it.

When we've let ourselves feel, we can come out on the other side. You can. You might not believe it while in the throes of your grief, but many, many people who have experienced a major loss have come through it, learned from it, and made their lives better. Our society is full of such people, who stand out as an inspiration to others. There are people who are living with a terminal disease, who have endured the results of a major accident, or who have lost a child who say their lives are better than ever before because of what they have learned, how they have grown, and what they have finally understood about life.

People who come out on the other side of their tragedy really do learn a lot: never to take life for granted, how to embrace each moment, and how to help others. They have learned to recognize what is important, what is beautiful, and what is worth their attention. One more thing about the major events of our lives: Aren't most of our major "tragedies" a matter of loss? We lose all our money, all our possessions, our shelter, our loved ones, our health, a part of our body, etc. To truly embrace a Zen attitude is to recognize that we never owned any of these things to begin with.

We don't own anything.

Sure, according to society, we do. This is *my* house. This is *my* money. This is *my* spouse. This is *my* child. This is *my* body. To live in a society, everyone must take responsibility for certain things. We need places to live and certain possessions to hold jobs and entertain ourselves. We need money to buy food, clothes, and other things we need or want. Parents must be responsible for their children, and partners help and support each other. We take care of ourselves to stay healthy and feeling good.

But none of it is really ours. We live with others and we accumulate things, but any of it can be taken away at any moment. This concept isn't meant to be scary. It's only meant to remind us that every moment counts right now, and every person we have the good luck to know can enrich us. But if we attach ourselves to anything or anyone, even our own self, we are fooling ourselves into believing in a reality that isn't real or lasting.

When you lose something precious to you, you will mourn it. You will grieve. You might experience a huge range of emotion and feel compelled toward all kinds of behaviors. You might experience severe depression or rage. Of course you will. You are human. Let yourself feel it, and let yourself gradually come to see how this experience, like others, has happened and has taught you something. If you are angry because you thought something was yours and it was taken away, let yourself be angry. Then let yourself see that it wasn't yours. You were, simply, lucky enough to experience whatever or whomever it was for a part of your life.

Zen Exercise: Relax, Breathe, Prioritize

Strong feelings—pain, rage, depression—can sometimes seem unbearable, and hopelessness can overwhelm you. No matter what the cause, when your natural human feelings threaten to take over, remember three things: relax, breathe, and prioritize.

The next time you find yourself experiencing a strong feeling, one that seems to wash over you like a wave and envelope your entire emotional life, try this exercise:

1. First, let yourself sit with your feelings. Or lie down. Relax. Let the feelings wash over you while you aren't busy doing something else. Feel them. They are there, they are part of your present moment, so let them exist.

2. If you find you are too overwhelmed or overcome to sit still, you need to move! Go on a brisk walk or run, but stay focused on how you feel. Then, go back again and sit. Even if you think you can't sit still, sit down and try it. Sit down and be with your feelings.

3. Next, bring your attention to your breath. Let your breath take over; let it measure your feelings into manageable pieces: the inhale, the exhale. Use your breath to center and focus your awareness. Shunryu Suzuki says we are only a swinging door for the breath, that's all. Let the door swing; let yourself sink into and become your breath. Imagine you are nothing else but that breath.

4. Remind yourself that your strong feelings seem unendurable because you are attaching your own ideas, conceptions, regrets, and fears to them. Let them be. Visualize them as physical things—a crystal ball filled with sparks, perhaps, or a dark cloud flashing with lightning. Don't try to get

Monkey Mind! _____

If you are unable to rise out of a deep depression and your depressed feelings are interfering with your functioning in your work and your life, if the feelings persist for longer than two weeks, and/or if you have serious thoughts of killing yourself, please see your doctor. Serious depression can be effectively treated with medication.

into that crystal ball or that cloud. Just watch them rage. Keep breathing. Don't get into anything but your own breath. Inhale. Exhale. Take one breath at a time, one present moment at a time.

5. When you begin to feel more calm, make a short list about whatever it is you are going to do *right now*. Don't worry about how you'll deal with this problem, how you'll make it through the night, or any of the other details that threaten to invade. Maybe it is dinnertime. Your list could look something like this (you can be very basic with yourself here):

   ♦ Stand up.

   ♦ Walk into the kitchen.

   ♦ Make soup.

   Or maybe your list will look more like this:

   ♦ Stand up.

   ♦ Walk to closet.

   ♦ Put on walking shoes.

   ♦ Step out the door.

   ♦ Walk around the block one time.

   There, now you know exactly what to do next to plan and execute those regular life things you need to do—and do them.

6. If, after this exercise, your feelings are still present, let them be present next to you or above you, but only let the breathing be within you. If you feel they are passing, don't hang on to them, grasping at them, pulling them back to you. Let them go. Breathe. Do. That's how you get through the day.

   And tomorrow, too.

Keep Sitting

Through it all, even when you think you can't bear it, spending some time each day in zazen can become a valuable anchor for your soul and a sanctuary for your mind. Sitting puts those tidal waves on freeze-frame, or at least helps you see them from above for a while rather than from underneath. Even if you sit for only 2 minutes, you can stop the action and regroup, find your center, breathe, and remember where you are—right here, right now.

No matter what the weather of your life is like at this moment, sitting and focusing on the now can bring clarity and even gladness to your being. You'll remember who you are, then you'll remember how life is: ultimately interesting, ever-changing, and full of waves and sea creatures, storms and calm, and other ships, some armed with harpoons and others with white flags, each ship only what it is, rocking and shifting just like you are by the movement of the sea or the stillness of the doldrums, full of the beauty of diversity and the beauty of unity, and the lovely, intricate shifting and blending of the two.

The Least You Need to Know

◆ You aren't in charge of anyone or anything, and when you realize it, you will set yourself free to really live.

◆ Humans tend to categorize, label, and set up expectations. Cultivating a Zen attitude means simply living, experiencing, and being without categories, labels, or expectations.

◆ "Tragedy" is only "tragedy" because we label it as "tragedy." Removing the label and simply experiencing the experience can help negative feelings pass and can turn a "tragedy" into a learning opportunity.

◆ When humans experience catastrophic loss, it is more difficult to put things into perspective, but as with less serious losses, major loss is difficult because we attach our expectations and false sense of ownership, fears, and regrets to the things we have lost.

◆ Letting go of the attachments to our feelings of pain, grief, and sorrow can help us move through any experience.

What's the Point ... Nirvana?

In This Chapter

- There has to be a point, right?
- Nirvana: what is it, and do you want it?
- Other Zen perks
- Foiling math, complying with physics
- Improving the world

We've mentioned more than once that true Zen doesn't have any goals. Sometimes Zen is called "the goal-less goal." (Figure that one out; it's a kind of koan.) We know that's probably hard for you, because we know it's hard for us. No goals? Then why do it? What's the point? We want so badly for there to be a point.

Instead of gearing your life toward a goal, living Zen means living the goal in the moment, shifting the goal from future to present—in a sense, becoming one with the goal. We like to talk about what Zen can do to make this moment right now more real, fulfilling, or beautiful. That's the goal: right now.

However, saying there is no point to Zen isn't exactly the whole story. Historically, Zen masters and students have admitted that attaining nirvana is not only the point of Zen but their primary goal, their innermost desire, even as the Buddha taught that desire leads to suffering. (Nobody's perfect, not even Zen masters—and yet everyone is perfect.)

But hey, wait one second, back up the truck: What is nirvana anyway? Is it anything we need to know or care about today, or is it the stuff of Tibetan monasteries? This question is not easily answered. But let's see if we can color in the picture just enough to give you the idea without actually giving you nirvana (which we can't, of course, or else we'd gladly to do it!).

You Say *Satori*, and I Say *Nirvana*

Nirvana and *satori* are words that mean "enlightenment." Traditionally, enlighten-ment means the final, total achievement of the "state of mind" Zen works to appre-hend. It is the recognition that we are all one, that separation is an illusion, and that now is the only reality. It is the ability to release desire and finally free oneself forever from suffering. And it is more than the intellectual apprehension of these concepts: It is an inner knowing, an intuitive understanding, and a oneness with these truths. Describing nirvana and understanding what it is aren't the same as attaining it.

The subject of enlightenment and how to get it has been the source of much debate and even some dissension among different Zen and other Buddhist sects. Some feel enlightenment should happen all at once; others believe it happens a little at a time. In either case, however, the real work in reaching this goal is in learning how to stop striving for it (don't you love how Zen hits you with these ironies at every turn?).

Nirvana Notes

Many Buddhists believe that assuming the Buddha's medita-tion posture when he was enlightened is important for becoming enlightened. Many books describe how to assume this posture: Sit in the lotus posi-tion with your hands in front of your navel, your thumbs together to form an oval, your back straight and centered over your hips bones. For more on medita-tion posture, see Chapter 9.

In the preface to the series of drawings/poems called the 10 Bulls (by twelfth-century Ch'an master Kakuan; see Appendix C), Paul Reps and Nyogen Senzaki (in *Zen Flesh*, *Zen Bones*) write, "The enlight-enment for which Zen aims, for which Zen exists, comes of itself. As consciousness, one moment it does not exist, the next it does."

Yet, haven't we mentioned that having a strong desire for nirvana comes out of dukkha, or attach-ment? We know that basing your actions and efforts on dukkha isn't true Zen. Here's the Zen irony again: Wanting nirvana means you don't have it and can't have it. Having it means it doesn't even occur to you to want it.

When you experience enlightenment, enlightenment as a thing, as a concept, no longer exists. It is like saying, "Oh how I want to exist!" You just do. You exist. Why discuss it? It is everything you are. It is ineffable and indefinable. Likewise, after you are enlightened, there is no such thing as enlightenment.

Of course many texts and Zen masters try to describe enlightenment, indescribable though it may be. The Venerable Dr. H. Saddhatissa, in his little booklet called *An Introduction to Buddhism*, describes nirvana (he calls it nibbana) like this:

> The goal of Buddhist life is Nibbana, a word better known in its Sanskrit form as Nirvana. The Buddha said, "Nibbana is the highest happiness." Hence the highest aim of the Buddhist is the attainment of it. Attempts have been made by writing many books to define this exalted state. It has to be appreciated that Nibbana is something that has to be realized within oneself, rather than described, explained, or talked about, as it is not within the scope of logic, being a supermundane state.

In Sanskrit, the word *nirvana* means "blowing out," as if blowing out a flame. The symbolism refers to total satisfaction in the present moment, where all attachments to past, future, and anything else but the *now* dissolve. In *The Beginner's Guide to Zen Buddhism*, Jean Smith describes Nirvana as "the state of being where there is no grasping, no desire for things to be different from the way they are …. In those moments, we are experiencing our life as nirvana."

Monkey Mind! _____

It is easy to become frustrated with Zen's paradoxes and seeming contradictions, its advice that Zen can't be learned from books, can't be taught, and can't even be understood logically. Just remember, everything written or spoken about Zen is just the finger pointing to the moon. Zen will only happen within you, through your own work. Nothing matters but you in the now. That's not so complicated!

So what does this mean for us? You might be thinking, "Sure, nirvana sounds nice but not very practical." If you are sitting around in meditation all day, marveling at the intense wonder of the present moment, how are you going to get anything done?

Actually, that's not how it works at all. After the Buddha attained enlightenment, he spent the rest of his life in service to humankind. Enlightenment doesn't stop life. On the contrary: It begins life, or at least it begins life anew, because at last, the enlightened one recognizes what life really is. It is also a process. Nirvana isn't the end. It begins a gradual evolution of awakening throughout your life during which you participate fully in life with compassion and understanding, just without attachment and desire.

In the twelfth century, when Chinese Ch'an master Kakuan devised the 10 Bulls pictures we mentioned earlier, his purpose was to tell a story of a man looking for and finding a bull, which symbolizes enlightenment. These pictures have been redrawn many times by many different people, and each picture has a little Zen epithet to describe it. We include our version in Appendix C. Take a look at each stage of this experience, which is meant to represent the search for and apprehension of enlightenment.

The last picture, "In the World," illustrates the point we are trying to make here. After the bull has been captured and after both the bull and the self are transcended (in picture eight), the man goes out into the world: "My clothes are ragged and dust-laden, and I am ever blissful." The final step of enlightenment is a firm and devoted presence in the world, not a removal from it.

But it still sounds kind of "out there," doesn't it? As if should you suddenly attain nirvana, all your friends would think you had gone a little loopy? "You know, Brenda isn't the same ever since that so-called enlightenment episode. Let's not call her to go with us to the movie tonight. She's probably beyond all that—or *whatever*."

Or maybe enlightenment sounds just dandy to you. You want it. You want it bad. If you imagine enlightenment will make you spiritually, intellectually, or morally superior, you don't have the right idea, either. Zen won't make you into anything special. Zen won't make you into anything you aren't already, right here, right now.

You don't need to wear "ragged and dust-laden clothes" once you've become enlightened, and you won't want to walk around with your nose in the air, either. You don't need to drop your friends or join a monastery or stay ever-concerned with spiritual issues. You might not care quite so much about what you wear, but that's beside the point. You're still you, and you can still look good. You just won't be attached to the idea of looking good.

The point is, you are still you—even more you than you were before! This can be a little scary for people who aren't quite ready to confront themselves, but oh, how much more real, exciting, and alive your life will be when you really get to be yourself.

It is important to remember that enlightenment is not, in any way, foreign to who or what you are. It is already in you. It is you. It is the real you, unbothered and unchained. It is you, right now.

One of the currently fashionable ideas about enlightenment, taught by many modern Zen masters, is that nirvana isn't a constant thing, a "once it happens you never go back" kind of thing. Instead, it happens during moments of clarity. It isn't some strange, cultlike state where your personality changes or you become suddenly wise and utter only pithy nuggets of great meaning for the rest of your life.

Some teachers say that *kensho* is the word for those little glimmers of enlightenment, that temporary loss of self and absorption into the present moment and what you are doing, while *satori* and *nirvana* are words for a more pervasive and permanent state of enlightenment.

Zen-Speak

Kensho, satori, and *nirvana* are all words that have come to mean "enlightenment" and are often used interchangeably. Originally, the meanings differed. *Nirvana* is a Sanskrit word meaning "extinction," referring to liberation or release from the cycle of death and rebirth. *Satori* and *kensho* are Japanese words. Satori refers to enlightenment as experienced by the Buddha, a comprehension of the unity of all things. Kensho refers to those pre-enlightenment moments of self-realization that come and go.

But we think this is a matter of history and semantics and that it is just fine to experience enlightenment once in a while, a little at a time, all at once, or whatever happens to you. The more it happens, the more you learn how to live that way, right here, right now.

There's that word again, *now*. You can let all the rest go. When kensho happens, it feels great, or better than great: It feels right. And when it happens again, you think, "Oh yes! This is the way to be!" And when it happens yet again, you smile with understanding ... or pure being.

You spend your life juggling with it, trying to keep that awakened state in place as often as possible. You probably won't have it all the time. Plenty of famous, historical Zen masters had their nasty and ultimately unenlightened moments. But then you find it again, and you go on, living in the now.

Practice Zen so you can live a more enlightened life right now. That's all there is to it. The more you live in the now, the more enlightened you will become. Or maybe it will hit you all at once. In any case, it isn't something to fear, because …

Enlightenment is not, in any way, foreign to who or what you are.

You have enlightenment inside you. It just needs a bit of excavating. That's the work of Zen, and if you really, really need to use the word, that is Zen's ultimate (goal-less) goal.

One Hand Clapping

In his book *A Western Approach to Zen,* Christmas Humphreys describes the achievement of enlightenment:

> We walk into the sea, to the ankles, waist, chest; then suddenly we are swimming and the sea contains us. The clouds and earth on a sultry day become highly charged with positive and negative electricity. The build-up of force takes time but the discharge in a flash of lightning is sudden. Our eyes are shut; at last we open them and suddenly "see." Let us open them and see, not heaven but the world about us filled with, shining with, the very expression of, Zen.

Zen Perks

We mentioned briefly in a previous chapter that there were other benefits to Zen that, although not goals exactly, are certainly strong arguments for practicing Zen living. Let's look at them in more depth now because these Zen perks are so relevant to the stressed-out, busy, and sometimes isolated lives of typical Westerners.

Mental Clutter Control

There are two kinds of stress: the kind that helps and the kind that makes things worse. Have you ever noticed that sometimes, when you have a lot on your plate, you feel great? For some people, the more they have to do, the more efficient, effective, and happy they are—up to a point.

Then there is the kind of stress that has the opposite effect. This kind of stress can happen whether you have a lot to do or not. It happens when you accumulate too much mental clutter. You can have a to-do list with hundreds of items on it, but if you deal with them one at a time, with your full attention, then check them off and move on without giving them any more thought, you won't be stressed. On the other hand, you can have a to-do list with only one or two items, but you are so worried and so filled with trepidation that you won't get them right, that they can't possibly get done, that no one will agree with the way you do them, or that they are totally beyond your ability, your brain is all jumbled with attachments.

How can you find anything in there when it is such a mess? It's like trying to cook dinner when the kitchen is stacked high with dirty dishes, none of the pots and pans have been washed, and the dishwasher is full but you haven't run it yet.

Nirvana Notes

The best time to take a 5-minute break to sit still, be quiet, and listen to your breathing is when you think you have the least time for it. The busier you are and the more overwhelmed you feel, the more you need the clarity and decluttering of meditation.

This happened to Eve just the other morning. The kids wanted French toast, but last night she didn't clean the kitchen after dinner because she was so tired. She had a ridiculous amount of work to do, but she didn't do it. She was too busy worrying about it. "How can I finish three books and six articles by the end of the month? It can't be done. No one could do it. How can I do it all working only a few hours a day? I won't be able to get it done and then I won't get paid. I won't get any other jobs, so I'll have to give up this whole writing pipe dream and go back to the 9-to-5 world. I'll have to have a boss again, latchkey kids, after-school care, and my whole family will be so disappointed. Why did I ever think I could both work full-time and be a stay-at-home mom? It's too hard! I can't do it!"

Eve ended up spending the evening staring at a scary movie on television. She didn't really watch it. She just stared at it. Nothing got done: not the articles, not the book chapters, not the dishes. And now, this morning, the kids are clamoring for their breakfast.

Frustrated and irritated, Eve grabbed a skillet from last night's dinner, still coated in oil and bits of yellow rice, and began to scrub it around a pile of dishes in the sink. Then, suddenly, *crash!*

She had accidentally knocked over a stack of plates that were precariously perched on top of a rickety colander next to the sink. Six plates and a coffee cup shattered on the kitchen floor.

The kids stopped clamoring and stared. Eve stared. But before she could explode in frustration, her 4-year-old, Angus, said, with a worried expression: "Mommy, were those your favorite dishes in the whole world?"

And Eve laughed. There, shattered on the floor, was her cluttered mind. "No, Angus. Those weren't my favorite dishes," Eve answered. "I don't care about those dishes

Most people hate housework, but housework is the perfect opportunity to practice mindfulness. Wash the dishes, sweep the floor, or polish the windows and mirrors with total attention rather than with dread, distraction, and annoyance. It is a completely different experience.

at all." "That's good, Mommy," Angus said with relief, "because they're all broken." "All broken!" chimed in 2-year-old Emmett with a grin.

Eve couldn't help grinning, too, as she realized, like the dishes in her kitchen, how precariously perched all her worries had been. They weren't real, and they didn't matter. With one bump of the elbow, they were gone. They didn't have a hold on her at all.

Eve simply had some work to do. That's all. Mindfully, she swept up the mess, mopped the floor, made the breakfast, ran the dishwasher, and took the kids to the park. During naptime, she returned to her book chapters. She realized how much she had overexaggerated what she had to do. Sure, she was busy. Aren't we all? But she could handle it. This is a job worth doing, she told herself. Later in the day, she realized she wasn't even tired anymore.

The effect of those dishes crashing on the floor was something like the effect of puzzling out a Zen riddle, then suddenly getting it, a moment of kensho, when it all makes sense. And—*poof!*—the mental clutter was gone, at least for a while.

Harry Potter fans might remember, from *Harry Potter and the Goblet of Fire*, the fourth book in the series, that Professor Dumbledore kept in his office a pensieve, a basin filled with a bright silver liquid where he could store excess thought when he had too much on his mind. What a handy device! Unfortunately, pensieves don't exist. But in a way, they do, because we have Zen!

Our brains get cluttered. That's human nature. Zen helps declutter them by dissolving the clutter in an instant. Zen helps us let it go, and when we do, the clutter floats away like a helium balloon. (If only that worked for the dishes!)

Winking at Stress

One of the things we love about Zen is its sense of humor. Whenever we get too serious, Zen reminds us how pointless it is to be too serious. Being too serious means being too concerned about things, and in Zen, concern is replaced by compassion, striving by existing, and worry by joy.

Zen is a great way to put stress into perspective. When those dishes crashed to the floor, Eve remembered to wink at her stress. *Wink wink, nudge nudge*. You and I both know you aren't so important. That's a nice disguise, stress, but I can see right through you! Zen masters are famous for their ability to put a humorous spin on that which would seem a matter of the greatest gravity. They make jokes on their death-beds. They pose the most absurd questions. And when everyone gets too serious, the Zen master does his or her best to undermine everyone's assumptions.

If you are far-sighted, as Eve is (literally, as in the vision impairment), you know what it is like to hold something right up in front of your face and not be able to see it. Only when you hold it back a bit does it come into focus. The same goes for Zen koans, stories, and parables. They can be absurd, funny, or ridiculous. If you take them too seriously, if you attach to them, or if you examine them too closely with your intellect, you'll miss the point.

And the same goes for the things that cause you stress. If something "horrible" happens—your air-conditioning goes out in August; you forget to mail the mortgage payment; you get dumped, or snubbed, or sneezed on—Zen lets you step back a few feet, take a look at what is really going on, and then snicker a little.

If you don't attach to the things that cause you stress, they can't cause you stress. Sounds pretty simple, but it takes a lot of practice.

One Hand Clapping

In her book *Mindfulness*, Ellen J. Langer suggests that mindfulness and creativity can be more easily obtained through an open-ended approach to the so-called factual world. She writes, "In most educational settings, the 'facts' of the world are presented as unconditional truths, when they might better be seen as probability statements that are true in some contexts but not in others." In a study by Langer and Alison Piper, objects were identified to one group as "This is a hair dryer," "This is a dog's chew toy." To the other group, the objects were introduced as "This could be a hair dryer." "This could be a dog's toy." Then Langer and Piper orchestrated an urgent need for an eraser. Members of the "could be" group were the only group to suggest using the rubber chew toy as an eraser.

Making Room for More Tea

Another old Zen story tells of a man who goes to a Zen master in a monastery and asks to be trained in Zen. Hoping to impress the Zen master, the man launches into a speech about the many Buddhist texts he has read and the complex and erudite theories he has apprehended. The master invites the man to sit down for a cup of tea. The Zen master begins pouring the tea into the visitor's cup, but rather than stopping when the cup is full, he keeps pouring and pouring. Alarmed, the man exclaims, "Master! The cup is overflowing!"

Monkey Mind!

Expectations, opinions, and preconceptions aren't easy to recognize because they are so ingrained in us. We see what we expect to see, we recognize what we already know, and we pay most attention to the familiar and the things we want to see. That might be comfortable, but it leaves a whole lot of life unnoticed, unappreciated, and unused.

The Zen master stopped pouring the tea and looked at the man. "This cup is like your mind," he said. "How can you learn anything when it is already full?"

The point of this story is that our minds are already full of expectations, opinions, and preconceptions. When we first approach Zen, most of us have an idea of what it will be about, what we want from it, or what it can do for us. With all this in the way, as the story suggests, we don't have any room to receive the real truth of Zen. So first we must empty our minds of all these premade thoughts. Only then can we experience true Zen, which is to live in the now.

In other words, only when we dump out our teacup can we make room for the really *good* tea. It is easy to think that the "really good tea" must be Zen, or Zen wisdom, or all the stuff the Buddha said, but that isn't it. Zen is the dumping of the teacup. The really good tea is your life, your existence, you.

Stilling the Waters

Remember our analogy about the moon being truth, and how truth's reflection gets all jumbled when the waters of your mind are in turmoil? Zen helps still those waters. Yes, you will still experience waves, storms, all that stuff that gets your "life boat" tossing and moving forward and backward, on and off course. You will still experience weather. But because the ocean (life) gets moved around so much by external forces, you certainly don't need to be churning it up yourself with a big stick. Zen helps you still the waters of your mind from internal roiling.

How? Through mindfulness. And how do you learn mindfulness? Through meditation. In Part 3, we'll go into more detail on how to start meditating, why meditating is helpful, and what it can and can't do. We'll show you how it can help still the waters of your mind by letting you practice mindfulness in a conducive environment. Then you can carry that mindfulness into the world, so you can see the moon in the still water and suddenly realize that all you have to do is look up.

Zen's Goal-Less Goals

When it comes right down to it, Zen is full of goal-less goals, which aren't something in the future but rather something to experience now. What is there to experience? Let's look at a few basic Zen concepts Zen masters teach—sort of a "sneak preview" to enlightenment.

1 + 1 = 1

In Zen, basic math goes out the window because 1 + 1 = 1. No, that's not how we all learned it. Also, 1 + 1 + 1 + 1 = 1. You can add as many 1s as you like, and the answer will still be 1.

This is a principle traditionally described as having been realized by enlightened beings throughout the history of Buddhism. Although you can know this truth technically, enlightenment means becoming this truth, perceiving it internally, knowing it without thinking about it. Being it.

We are all one. Everyone is different, but we are all part of the same thing, all waves in an ocean, all blades of grass in a field, all air molecules in the atmosphere. Every living, breathing thing and every nonliving, nonbreathing thing are all part of a unified whole, and every part depends on every other part.

This concept might contradict basic arithmetic, but it is right in line with basic physics. You may have heard of chaos theory, a concept that became suddenly popular in the public mind a few years ago. (The concept was simplified for general consumption in the book and movie *Jurassic Park*, in case you're wondering where you might have heard of it before.)

What is chaos theory? Once upon a time, scientists believed that because everything in nature was a matter of cause and effect, if one understood the cause well enough, he could predict the effect.

But as we all know from being the victims of inaccurate weather forecasts, predictions often don't come true because, according to chaos theory, we can never really measure anything with infinite accuracy, and the complexity of systems are often such that we can never fully understand a cause. We can see the cause (a buildup of a certain kind of cloud, the trajectory of a low-pressure system), but because so many minute influences come into play—things we can never measure or even comprehend (a volcano eruption somewhere on another continent, a gust of wind knocking an iceberg into the ocean, or, to use the classic example, a butterfly fluttering its wings somewhere a thousand miles away) we can't really know if it's actually going to rain.

We can guess, and we might be right. We can even make an educated guess. But chaos theory hypothesizes, not that everything is chaotic, but that everything, while it *might* be organized, can never reliably and quantitatively be predicted or even apprehended. The world is vastly and infinitely complex. Or to put it more simply: We can never know it all.

Therefore, in such cases involving complex systems (a severe storm watch, a crashed computer, a theme park containing live dinosaurs), we can never predict an outcome with unerring accuracy.

But (and here's the Zen kicker) the basic premise—that everything is a matter of cause and effect—is still true! Chaos theory doesn't deny this. In fact, it supports it. Your daughter's coughing fit might trigger a series of events leading to a thunderstorm in Nairobi. A worm unearthed from your garden might influence a chance meeting between two people in Paris. The earth's ecosystem is so incredibly complex that we are all connected in a way that defies objective understanding. It isn't that it can't theoretically be understood if we had all the information and a really big computer. It isn't anything mystical; it's just ultimately complex.

Chaos theory completes the notion of cause and effect with the knowledge that, cause and effect or no, we can't possibly know what will happen or control what will happen in any given situation unless the cause and effect occur with very few variables in isolation (something that would rarely happen—in fact, we can't even think of an example).

In *Zen and the Brain*, James H. Austin, M.D., writes about the recognition of the interconnectedness of all things, "Interbeing is the whole BIG PICTURE. It relates this page of paper back through the pulp to the logger who fed his family by felling the tree, back through the parents who raised him, on through the wheat fields which nourished them all, to the rain clouds and soil and sunshine that made possible all these and everything else."

So if everything happens because of something else, we are all part of a great big, ultimately complex system. We are like individual cells in a giant body. Everything that happens impacts everything else (this is also the basis of karma, discussed in Chapter 2). We are all one, just as much as we are all separate. We don't live in isolation, and nothing we do or even think happens without its ripples in the great ocean. We can't predict the ripples, but we make them all the time.

Serve Others? Who's Serving Me?

Some who have achieved enlightenment devote themselves to a life of service. Some become Zen teachers; others help their fellow sentient beings in other ways not specifically related to a Zen organization.

In the West, we are taught that volunteerism is a noble thing and that those who "have" should "give back." But what about those who don't have much? In Zen, what we have is irrelevant. The only important thing is to perceive that, because we are all one, everyone and everything else around us is connected to us.

Helping other humans survive and find happiness, helping preserve the earth's natural resources, helping save others—children, animals, each other—from abuse and neglect, helping make the world a better place means improving and uplifting the great body of which we are a part. It isn't something we force ourselves to do. If we have to force it, it isn't Zen.

It simply makes sense. You take care of yourself by taking care of your environment and everyone and everything in it. By helping others, you are helping yourself because you are inextricable from all others.

That's not to say that serving others in Zen is totally selfish. It isn't a matter of helping only to help yourself, but it also isn't a matter of pure altruism. Altruism is concern for and action to improve the welfare of others without regard to the self. This isn't a Zen approach because it implies there is a separate self to disregard while serving others. The self and the others are all part of the same thing, so in serving one, you serve them all.

The Least You Need to Know

- The goal of Zen is to live your goal right now rather than look ahead to it.

- Nirvana, sometimes called satori, kensho, and enlightenment, is the freedom from attachments to thoughts, feelings, and desires, and a complete and total absorption in the present moment.

- Enlightened people recognize that everyone and everything in the universe is connected and interrelated in an intricate system.

- Enlightened people are frequently compelled to spend their lives helping others and improving their environments to make the most of each present moment.

Part 3

1-2-3 Zazen: Zen Techniques for Zen Living

Part 3 is the nuts-and-bolts part of the book. It's one thing to talk about adopting a Zen attitude, but we know it is easier said than done. The practice of some tried-and-true techniques can make the job easier. We'll talk about what it takes to get started (hint: you're already there!), then we'll answer all your questions about meditation, the heart of Zen (the word *Zen* actually means "meditation").

Next we'll sit you down and help you start meditating. We'll talk about various techniques for training your body and disciplining your mind. You'll learn how to sit, to breathe in a way that makes meditation easier, to be mindful, to do walking meditation, and to practice koans—those famous Zen riddles meant to prod the mind into a new way of thinking (or not thinking!).

We'll end with a discussion of the other aspects of your daily life and how to work Zen into every imaginable part.

Chapter 8

You've Already Started Living Zen

In This Chapter

- ◆ The secret of Zen living
- ◆ You have Zen within you
- ◆ So how do you get to it?
- ◆ On your mark, get set, go!
- ◆ Introduction to zazen

We've spent the first seven chapters of this book talking about what it means to live Zen, both historically and today. Perhaps now you are wondering where to start. How do you begin living in the now? How do you begin letting go of your attachments? How do you begin practicing mindfulness? What exactly are you supposed to do?

You've already started. You have! Right now is happening right now, and anytime you want to acknowledge it and start making the most of it, you can. There is nothing to wait for, to train for, or to hope for. You can do it right now, and in many ways, you probably already are doing it.

But you can get better at it, which is a little like on-the-job training. To some extent, mindfulness is something you simply can begin to do, but the first time you consciously begin to be mindful, you probably won't be able to sustain it for very long.

We offer some techniques to help you, because mindfulness and letting go are, we admit, much easier to talk about than to do. The most helpful technique for living your Zen is meditation, which we will cover briefly here and in more detail in Chapter 9.

But first, let's talk about some helpful, hands-on adjustments you can make to your life right now (which is, of course, what Zen is all about).

The Secret Is ... There Is No Secret

For Westerners, the word *Zen* has an air of mystery about it, something akin to the concept of the "ancient Chinese secret." But the thing about Zen is that there isn't anything secret about it. You don't spend years studying to uncover some great mystery. There is no treasure map, no secret compartment, and no special information you get only after going through some sacred ritual. Remember, Zen just means the real you in the right now. *You* are the secret, the X on the treasure map! You have it all within you.

You Already Have What You Are Looking For

This concept is a little bit difficult to grasp for Westerners raised in the Judeo-Christian tradition. Aren't we supposed to give up things to a higher power? This is one of the points on which traditional Western and traditional Eastern thought seem to differ.

However, we don't see why these ideas can't coexist. If you have a religious faith that involves a higher power, you can still look within yourself to find the gifts you have been given. You can still immerse yourself in the present moment to fully appreciate and savor the life you have been given and the world that has been created and grows and breathes and lives all around you. Buddhism doesn't say you are God. It doesn't really talk about God, leaving that for other faiths, or the individual, to contemplate. That's why Zen doesn't contradict other religions.

Nirvana Notes

If you are interested in the link between Zen and Western religion, many good books are devoted to the subject, including those that approach Christianity and other Western religions from a Zen perspective and those that approach Zen from a Christian, Jewish, or otherwise primarily Western perspective. Check your library, the Internet, and Appendix A for suggestions.

Many Christians and Jews practice Zen and find that it fits right into their personal spiritual or religious beliefs. People of many other faiths practice Zen, too. Although some Zen Buddhists might believe that Zen must be Buddhism and Buddhism must involve adherence to certain concepts (there is nothing wrong with such beliefs), we feel that those who choose to practice Zen should feel free to find a way to make Zen work for them.

Zen has much to give you, but everything it has to give is already inside you. Isn't that wonderful? Your perfection, your personal fulfillment, and your self-actualization are already there, like a seed or bulb or a tiny sprout just waiting for nourishment, encouragement, and some regular tending. That regular tending is the practice of Zen.

Duty, Discipline, and Devotion

Zen is also in the doing. We all have jobs to do: regular (or irregular) employment or school; being a parent, a daughter or son, a sibling, or a friend; and many other duties in life. Society and good health require a certain amount of personal discipline. And our lives are immeasurably enriched by practicing devotion: to a cause, to an art, to our jobs, to our beliefs, to our families, to our friends, to our Earth, and to our God or gods or goddesses.

Zen-Speak

Samsara is the Sanskrit word for everyday life in the phenomenal world. Technically, it refers to the succession of births and rebirths before the release from this cycle that comes out of the attainment of nirvana. The word is often used to refer to daily existence on Earth.

This everyday life, called *samsara*, is the real place for your Zen living to change things. These three external manifestations of human life—duty, discipline, and devotion—are the ideal arenas for practicing Zen living.

Do your duty without attachment and without resentment or obsession. Practice personal discipline so you can better maintain a sense of control, well-being, and good health for your own body and your own mind. Devote yourself with compassion to the world and the people and things in it—without attaching to them, without needing them, without desiring them, but simply by loving them.

Isn't There an Instruction Manual?

All these things sound good, but once again, you might be thinking, "Yes, yes, but how do I do it?"

Life doesn't have an instruction manual, and neither does Zen, even though there are plenty of books available that are happy to tell you how to do one or both (live life, practice Zen, live Zen). Both life and Zen are encountered through direct experience. You live, and you learn. No one can tell you how to do it, beyond offering suggestions you may or may not choose to take.

But these suggestions can help a lot when you feel as if you don't know where to go, feel that your life needs some direction or a jump-start, or it has gotten on the wrong track. If you ever feel like you don't know who you are, what you are doing, or where you are going, just remember: now. Now is everything.

If that isn't enough in the way of guidelines, you can also use the Buddha's five noble precepts as an anchor for your daily life. In the book *For a Future to Be Possible: Commentaries on the Five Wonderful Precepts*, Vietnamese Zen master Thich Nhat Hanh has simplified these into five commonsense guidelines. He has worded them in the form of vows for right living that give Zen practitioners something on which to hang their hats, so to speak. In short (and in paraphrase), they are:

- The destruction of life causes suffering, so I vow to cultivate compassion and learn how to protect the lives of people, animals, and plants, refusing to kill, to let others kill, or to condone any act of killing in action, thought, and lifestyle.

- Social injustice causes suffering, so I vow to cultivate loving kindness and work for the well-being of people, animals, and plants, refusing to steal and vowing to share my material resources.

- Sexual misconduct causes suffering, so I vow to respect my commitments and not to engage in sexual misconduct, and to work to protect others from sexual abuse and the effects of sexual misconduct.

- Words can cause suffering, so I vow to speak only with kindness and love and to listen deeply, never speaking words that could cause division and discord but working to avoid or resolve conflict.

- Unmindful consumption causes suffering, so I vow to cultivate good physical and mental health in myself and in society by only eating, drinking, consuming, and paying attention to things that result in physical, mental, and societal peace and harmony.

A tall order, yes. These precepts are things to think about. When you are ready for each one, it will happen in your life. If you are looking for a place to start, you can start with any of these and try to integrate it into your daily life. However, you might find that starting with mindfulness will make these precepts more natural and automatic.

So what about mindfulness? How can you begin to live mindfully right now? What can you do besides think to yourself, "I'm going to be mindful right now" (which doesn't always work very well, especially if you are new to the idea)? In the spirit of the instruction manual, let's look at a few techniques for bringing yourself back to now.

Your Life Just Started: Go!

We don't mean to inflict a sense of urgency on you, but your life just started. So go! Go! Go!! Right this second, your life is happening. This is it, right here, right now. This is as good as it gets. There is nothing to wait for. There is nothing to hold out for. This is it. So go!

When we say "*Go!*" all we mean is *wake up*. Bring yourself into your present moment. Cultivate your awareness. You don't have to lift a finger, but you do have to engage your brain in what might be a fairly unfamiliar way. No matter what you are doing (even if it's just lying around), wake up and recognize it, really do it, pay attention. Really lie around with full awareness. Be.

The easiest way to do this, to get going, to wake up, to become aware, to jump-start your awareness is—and this might seem counterintuitive ironically—to sit still.

> ### Monkey Mind!
>
> How many times have you felt you missed an important event just because you weren't paying attention or were too overwhelmed to really experience it? Even though they were right in the middle of the action, many people report "missing" their own weddings, births of their children, graduations, sports victories, award ceremonies, and other supposedly memorable moments because of the stress, pressure, nervousness, or anxiety such events induce. Zen living tones your mind so you don't let life pass you by. You can put aside your nerves and wake up so you don't miss a moment.

Too often, we travel through life as if watching television. We drive around and watch the world through the glass of the car window. We look out the window in our homes (once in a while) or in our offices (if we are lucky enough to have windows). We communicate through e-mail, instant messages, mobile phones, and faxes. In so many ways, our modern world puts several layers and filters between us and the actual world, the person we are speaking with, and the things we see or hear.

These filters make it very easy to slip into the automatic mode, to forget we are alive, that this is life happening right now. Practicing engaging your senses in your immediate environment, in "real time," can be a startling and enlightening way to remind yourself that you are alive and that you can wake up anytime you want to wake up.

So stop floating through life as if it were a dream, and wake up! Your life has begun. See. Hear. Smell. Touch. Taste. Let the world touch you and move you. Now is the only moment you know you have. Wake up and be there for it!

Zen Exercise: Start Your Life

Let's try it. This isn't exactly meditation just yet. We'd just like you to sit down for a minute. No really, even though you have a million things to do, just try this. It won't take long, we promise:

1. Get comfortable. You can sit on a chair or on the floor, whatever feels best, but wherever you sit, sit upright with your spine straight, not slumped back in a cushy recliner.

2. Now, try to notice every single thing you can notice with each of your five senses. Go through them one sense at a time, as follows.

3. Concentrate first on what you can see. Mentally list everything you can see from where you are sitting, no matter how big or small: a couch, a bay window, carpet fibers, dust bunnies, whatever. (You can also do this outside: sky, each cloud, a parked car, each blade of grass.) Really focus on the world as you are able to perceive it visually. If your mind starts to wander to things you should be doing or even to a mental commentary about what you see, gently guide it back to your visual investigation. An old Zen saying goes something like, "When you hear a dog bark, do you think of your own dog?" If you do, you are already making associations and your mind is wandering. If you hear a dog bark, just hear that dog bark, and leave it at that. Think "I hear a dog barking" or even just "dog barking."

4. After you think you've seen it all, focus on what you can hear. An airplane, a car passing, the air-conditioner, the refrigerator compressor, people talking, music, wind? In your mind, note everything in your environment you can perceive by hearing.

5. Next focus on everything you can smell. Food cooking? Dust? Perfume? Cleaners? Soap? Nothing? Really concentrate on the subtle aromas in the air all around you.

6. Now concentrate on everything you can feel. Notice the chair or floor beneath you, the way your clothes feel on your skin, the parts of your body touching other parts of your body, even the air against your skin.

7. We assume you aren't eating anything while you do this exercise (that would make it kind of difficult!), but finally, focus on the taste in your mouth, whatever is there. Toothpaste? The snack you just ate? Coffee? Leftover mint from that piece of gum?

The point of this exercise is to become totally immersed in the present moment and your environment. This is what mindfulness feels like. (This kind of attention to detail in your immediate environment is what will help you remember where you put your keys, too.)

Living Now

It is much easier to concentrate on being present in the present moment when you are sitting still, but Zen is also about doing this in daily life while you're moving around. Let's practice this a little, too. One of the best ways to do this is by starting with some simple task you know you have to do. Everyone has to clean, so let's start there. Let's wash the dishes.

You probably have a dishwasher. It seems these days, most people do. You might or might not use it all the time, but today, let's forget about the dishwasher. Eat a meal (mindfully); then wash your dishes by hand.

Your first reaction might already be something worth paying attention to. You might be thinking, "Wash my dishes by hand? I don't *think* so! That's why I have a dishwasher. I hate washing dishes! What a waste of time! I have better things to do. Forget this Zen business if it means washing dishes by hand."

Nirvana Notes

Zen is not about making your life more primitive, more difficult, or more labor-intensive (although manual labor is traditionally an important part of the Zen monastery or Zen retreat experience). A simpler life is more conducive to Zen living, but if the dishwasher, washing machine, central air, and new car make your life simpler (making mindfulness easier), by all means, continue to use them.

Or if you don't have a dishwasher, maybe you are thinking, "Dishwashing? Oh no! My one goal in life is to get a dishwasher. I'm always doing dishes, constantly doing dishes, and you are going to try to convince me it's fun? Yeah, right! I have better things to do!"

We would like to suggest that perhaps you don't have better things to do. Perhaps washing the dishes from your meal today is the best possible thing you could be doing. Perhaps you might also notice how much emotion you have attached to washing dishes, how attached you are to the notion that washing dishes is a negative experience. Why do you think you "hate" it? It's a simple chore. What is there to "hate" about immersing a plate in soapy water, wiping it clean, rinsing it, drying it, and putting it away? Where does that emotion come from? What does that negativity, that anxiety, that wasted energy afforded to the very thought of doing dishes have to do with this simple chore? For that matter, what does it have to do with the present moment?

We'll even go so far as to say that if washing the dishes is what you are doing at any given moment, it *is* the best possible thing you could be doing at that moment, simply because it is what you are doing.

Whether you use your dishwasher to save time (although a dishwasher uses a lot of energy, which costs money, which takes time to earn …) or do your dishes by hand every day and hate every minute of it, think about what repels you. Think about what kind of ideas, memories, or feelings you attach to this basic chore. Washing the dishes from one meal will probably take less than 15 minutes. Imagine cutting out just 15 minutes of Internet surfing or television time. Would it be time better spent? Let's find out.

Zen Exercise: Zen Doing

Here you go, let's face those dreaded dishes. You can do this. It will show you exactly what we mean about how Zen can help you separate your feelings from situations. Ready?

1. First, turn off the television, radio, or whatever else you might have running in the background to distract you from the so-called "unpleasantness."

2. Run the soapy water in the sink. Notice how the water sounds, looks, and feels. Notice how the bubbles billow up. Find a good scrubber—sponge, wash cloth, dish brush, or whatever. Look at it. Notice it. How does it feel in your hand?

3. If how you *feel* about dishwashing keeps creeping in, acknowledge it—oh yes, another negative association trying to attach itself to this action—then get back to your present moment.

4. Put the dishes into the water. Watch how they slide in or clink in and how they fit together into the sink.

5. One by one, select a dish, utensil, glass, or mug, and scrub its surfaces clean. Or wash them in whatever manner you like if you do it differently. Don't rush through it. Live it. Notice it. Try not to miss a second. Like it's your wedding day.

6. Rinse each dish clean and put it in the dish rack or on a clean folded towel. Pay attention!

7. Then, when all the dishes are clean, one by one, with the same attention, dry them and put them away.

Was that so bad? If you think it was, you were probably spending most of your time still attaching to those feelings you have about dishwashing rather than simply doing the dishwashing.

If you found the experience surprisingly pleasant, great! Or to be even more true to a Zen mind, if you found the experience to be, quite simply, an experience, that's great, too. Just think how your life could transform if you experienced every task just that way. We aren't saying you should get rid of your dishwasher. (To be honest, we don't plan to get rid of our dishwashers.) The point is to bring the same mindful reverence to any task you do throughout the day, from brushing your teeth in the morning to loading or unloading the dishwasher, driving to work, washing the car, making and eating your dinner, or brushing your teeth before bedtime.

> ### One Hand Clapping
>
> In his book *The Miracle of Mindfulness*, Thich Nhat Hanh talks about washing dishes in a Buddhist monastery, often for more than 100 monks, using only ashes, rice husks, and coconut husks for scrubbing in a pot of water heated over a fire. Hanh writes:
>
> Nowadays, one stands in a kitchen equipped with liquid soap, special scrubpads, and even running hot water which makes it all the more agreeable. It is easier to enjoy washing the dishes now. Anyone can wash them in a hurry, then sit down and enjoy a cup of tea afterwards. I can see a machine for washing clothes, although I wash my own things out by hand, but a dishwashing machine is going just a little too far!

Begin at the Beginning—Again!

Just when you think you've got this paying attention thing down, your mind wanders. Perhaps even during the course of the washing-the-dishes exercise, you felt as if your mind kept wandering, wandering, wandering away.

Even accomplished Zen monks, teachers, and masters experience this wandering mind. Human minds wander. But the great thing about existence is that every moment is the present moment, so every moment is a chance to begin again and again and again. It doesn't matter how many times you collect yourself and bring yourself back into the present moment. No magic number means Zen success. If you embrace the present moment upon your return from your mental wanderings 1, 2, 3, or 60 times a minute, you are still embracing the present moment. That is living Zen.

Zen Exercise: Begin Again

Let's try another exercise. This one will help you understand how easy it is to simply begin again when you go astray, without criticizing yourself or giving up, without attaching any feelings of failure or frustration, just beginning again.

1. Sit down comfortably and bring your attention to your breath. Feel how it moves into you, out of you, into you, out of you. "Watch" your breath by devoting your complete attention to it.

2. Pretty soon, your mind is going to wander. Without realizing it, you'll start wondering what that sound is outside, or planning tomorrow's menu, or going over again that conversation you had with your co-worker. What was it he said about .... Wait a minute! That's not paying attention to your breath!

3. Begin again. In, out. In, out. In, out. In, out. Some meditation techniques start with counting the breath, but don't even do that now. Just notice how it feels to breathe in, breathe out.

4. Suddenly you realize you might have forgotten to turn off the coffeemaker. You jump up and run into the kitchen. It's off. What are you doing? You forgot to keep breathing! You slink back to your spot and sit.

5. And you begin again. In, out. In, out. In, out. Are you late for something? What day is it? You glance at the calendar. Tuesday. Isn't that the meeting with your support group? Or is it the parent-teacher conference? You feel almost frantic thinking of someplace you have to be. You start to get up to check your planner, but you catch yourself this time. It can wait.

6. And you begin again. In, out. In, out. In, out.

This exercise is so difficult, especially for beginners, because your mind isn't used to paying attention to anything for very long and it resists! Just watch how it has you jumping up and down, scrunching up your forehead in worry; how it has your eyes wandering desperately around the room for something interesting to look at; how bored you feel; how much that spot on your back you can't quite reach itches ....

Yikes, this isn't so easy! Paying attention—even when it's—*(gulp)* boring?

Oh, yes. This is living Zen. That boredom part is hard, and you have to move on through it—acknowledge it, feel it, and let it go—before you can really understand and appreciate the beauty in those average, formerly-thought-of-as-dull moments in life and before you can master meditation. Suffering due to boredom is still attachment and so is longing for and desiring a more exciting present moment. Remember, just be. Just do.

And so you begin again. In, out. In, out. The first time, see if you can do this for 5 minutes. That's a long time to sit there and breathe. If you keep yourself on the floor without jumping up and rushing off to do something, check something, look up something, stir something, turn something, change something, or call somebody, congratulate yourself. Great start! We mean it.

You might be comforted to know that much of your frustration stems from the simple fact that you aren't in the habit of paying attention. The more you get into the habit of mindfulness, the easier it becomes, and your 60 beginning-agains-per-minute will soon become 2, 1, and even eventually cease altogether.

Monkey Mind!

If you are in the habit of not paying attention, you can get in the habit of paying attention. It isn't easy, but just like any habit, it can be broken and reformed. Try not to get frustrated and give up just because you can't change years of habit in a few days or weeks or even months. With perseverance and the cultivation of self-discipline through zazen, you can learn to live mindfully almost all the time.

Entering the Meditation Zone

This last exercise was really a premeditation exercise, so now let's talk about meditation. Meditation is at the heart of Zen. The word *Zen* means "meditation," just as the Chinese word *Ch'an* means "meditation."

But a common misconception exists about Zen. Zen isn't just meditation. Or it isn't just sitting meditation (called zazen). You could say Zen is just meditation if you mean meditation in life, as a synonym for mindfulness. But sitting meditation is just a technique of Zen, designed to help you discover what it feels like to be mindful

Nirvana Notes

Many people begin practicing zazen by counting their breaths, one for each inhale and exhale, up to 10, then back to one. Counting keeps the mind focused on something so it can begin to calm down. Eventually you won't have to count. You can just be.

under conditions that are much more conducive to mindfulness than running around doing your daily work.

Sitting in zazen isn't a rehearsal for life. In Zen, you are never rehearsing because your practice is your life. It is always now, whether you are in zazen, standing in a long line at the grocery store, or running full-speed after the tow-truck that just towed your car.

But sitting in zazen lets you pay attention with all your faculties under very basic conditions: you, sitting still. It is in zazen that you can learn to cultivate mindfulness so it can flower all over your day. It's like practicing scales when you first start learning to play the piano. The more you practice, the better you get, and even when you can play Rachmaninoff, you still spend time on those scales.

Everyday Zen Means Everyday Sitting

Ever since she co-authored *The Complete Idiot's Guide to Meditation* (now in its second edition), Eve has had many people say to her, "Oh, I can't meditate. I can't just sit there." Eve usually can't help answering, "Well, you *could* meditate. You just don't *want* to meditate."

Anyone can "just sit there." But who would want to? As we said earlier, it's boring. Many people are interested in meditation because of its purported benefits. They want to be more relaxed, manage stress better, think more clearly, feel more serene. But they don't want boring. What a waste of time, how irritating, how utterly unbearable! And they don't particularly want to face and unearth and declutter all the excess stuff rattling around in their brains. That's a lot of work.

We hate to break it to those of you who still haven't quite accepted the idea: Meditation means sitting—sitting *still*—every day for an actual period of time exceeding a couple seconds. Meditation gets boring. Meditation gets uncomfortable. Meditation can be downright miserable at times, even though that "just sitting" seems so effortless.

Our minds, like wild animals, don't want to be tamed. They don't want to follow any rules. They don't want to be mastered. They want to master us by running away and making us chase them, by teasing and tempting us with desires and attachments, by piling emotions and preconceptions onto every experience so we ponder, worry, obsess, and *suffer*. And they usually succeed! Only through sitting, sitting, sitting do we bring our minds under control.

The good part is, the more you meditate, the more you really do experience the benefits. It is all worth the effort, kind of like sit-ups or a daily brisk walk. It does, without a doubt, take effort, but it is an effort most of us are perfectly capable of making. Just about anyone can sit, like it or not. (The next chapter will tell you more.)

Shhh ...

A final point we'd like to make about meditation is that it can become a refuge, an oasis of quiet in the middle (or at the beginning or end) of your busy, noisy day. How incredibly rejuvenating it can be to just sit and be quiet for a few minutes. Wow! Quiet doesn't have to be a rare luxury. It can be a daily treat.

Meditation might get boring and it might be extremely difficult, but for those aching to capture just a few moments of peace, this is your chance. (Parents of small children may choose to meditate for this single reason alone—just ask Eve!)

One Hand Clapping

I learned that the core tool of Buddhism is meditation, with its focus on the breath. We are taught to follow our breath, in and out, in and out, watching it leave us, watching it enter us. In the watching we are calmed, and are made ready for serious spiritual work. And while there are other tools—chanting, volunteering, prostrations (bowing to the floor)—it is meditation that forms the path we stumble on and the walking stick we can grasp when the going gets unbelievably rough. Meditation is what sneaks spiritual progress into our days, finally offering the taste of bliss that is at the bottom of all our yearning.

—From *Stumbling Toward Enlightenment* by Geri Larkin

The Least You Need to Know

◆ Your life has already begun, and you can start living in the moment right now.

◆ Everything you need to live mindfully and completely is already within you.

◆ Doing your job, maintaining personal discipline, and developing devotion toward fellow sentient beings and the care of the world are ideal arenas for practicing mindfulness and letting go of attachments.

◆ Zen meditation is called zazen, and it means simple but mindful sitting to culti-vate full awareness.

◆ Meditation is difficult because the mind is in the habit of attaching to thoughts, feelings, ideas, and opinions. Everyday sitting will gradually train your mind to observe rather than attach.

Learning to Meditate

In This Chapter

◆ Your meditation questions answered

◆ Yikes, not lotus pose!

◆ How and where to sit

◆ What about your hands?

The heart of Zen is meditation, so we will spend this chapter talking about meditation in general and Zen meditation in particular. Then we'll actually get into position and give it a whirl.

Zazen, or sitting meditation, has some traditional guidelines in terms of position, so we'll demonstrate those for you. We'll also give you some additional options for sitting that might make you more comfortable. We'll offer you some meditation "warm-ups" to get you into the right frame of mind and some different techniques you can try when you are having difficulty sitting. (Sitting sounds so easy, but you'll soon see what we mean.)

Meditation FAQ

Ten million American adults now say they meditate in some form, and this number has doubled in the last ten years. Doctors recommend it as part of their treatment protocols, corporations permit it, airports have rooms for it, and the rich and famous swear by it.

Despite meditation's popularity, however, many people still have a lot of questions about meditation in general and zazen in particular. Before we launch into a full-fledged explanation of zazen and other forms of Zen meditation, let's address a few frequently asked questions.

What Is Zazen, Exactly? Do You Do It a Certain Way?

Zazen, or Zen sitting meditation, is the most well-known form of Zen meditation. It involves sitting in one of several specific positions in total, open awareness. Many books give you lots of guidelines for exactly how to sit, but in the true spirit of Zen, and although zazen has certain guidelines to it, whatever works for you is your zazen. We aren't going to say that if you don't sit in this particular way or center your mind on this or that, it isn't zazen. Zazen is simply you, sitting with full awareness.

But getting to this point, as we've mentioned, isn't easy. Zazen has a method because …

   ◆ People like to know how to do something in a way that will work rather than just guessing at it.

   ◆ People try to sit the way they believe Buddha sat when he became enlightened.

   ◆ Over the centuries, certain ways of sitting have proved to be more effective—that is, more conducive to meditation and more helpful in cultivating the self-discipline that makes mindfulness possible.

Do You Have to Meditate to Practice Zen?

Zazen really is the heart of a traditional Zen practice. Depending on whom you ask, zazen is either the best way or the only way to really understand the nature of reality, including your own true nature. Some argue that mindfulness in daily life, rather than sitting in meditation, is the heart of Zen. But the fact remains that without the sitting, you probably won't really master the mindfulness. You might get it here and there now and then, but without the personal discipline you cultivate through zazen, you probably won't develop your Zen living skills very well. Remember, even the

Buddha had to sit under a fig tree for a good 12 hours before he finally figured it all out—and he had been practicing sitting meditation regularly for 6 years.

How Does Zazen Develop Self-Discipline?

By being difficult! Self-discipline comes from doing anything that challenges patience. You won't want to sit there, being aware. Your mind is used to action, activity, stimulation, entertainment, and movement. Sitting is hard work and takes effort, as does the cultivation of any productive new habit. Finding the inner will and perseverance to develop this new habit is certainly a matter of self-discipline.

To Practice Zazen, Do You Have to Follow a Lot of Rules?

If you choose to meditate in a *zendo* (a Zen meditation hall), you might need to learn certain rules of form and practice based in whatever tradition (Soto, Rinzai) that particular zendo follows. But the rules aren't the point of zazen. Rules of form and practice help you cultivate your personal discipline, maintain a conducive meditation environment in the zendo, and make your meditation experience as successful and productive as possible.

In your at-home meditation practice, you will need far fewer "rules" such as facing the wall or walking in a certain direction around the room, but maintaining certain guidelines of form that have been time-tested over the centuries will, again, make the experience as successful and productive as possible.

Zen-Speak

A **zendo** is a Zen meditation hall. Many larger cities have zendos where people can come to practice zazen together or participate in Zen retreats. Certain rules of etiquette and form are typically practiced in a zendo. These vary according to different Zen traditions.

Why Would You Face a Wall While Meditating?

In Soto Zen, meditators typically face a wall, just as, according to legend, Bodhidharma meditated facing the wall of a cave. Facing a wall minimizes distractions. In Rinzai Zen, meditators typically sit in a circle and face the center. At home, you can face wherever you like, as long as it helps minimize distractions (in other words, don't face the television!).

Is Zazen Better Practiced Alone or in a Group?

Either way can be effective, but group zazen has a quality all its own that many Zen practitioners find invaluable. Zen meditation retreats, called *sesshins*, and zendos where people meet on a regular basis to meditate help remind you that you are part of a sangha. That is one of the three treasures of Buddhism: the community of people you meditate with, who are essentially representatives of the world community. Meditating with others reminds you that you are part of a larger whole and also helps engender compassion toward all other beings. (In case you forgot from Chapter 2, the other two treasures of Buddhism are the Buddha himself and the dharma, or the truth the Buddha taught.)

Zen-Speak

A **sesshin** is a period of intense practice (typically a week or two), with long sessions of zazen. It is often called a Zen retreat.

Is It Sacrilegious to Meditate?

Certainly not! We've already mentioned how Zen works in concert with any religious belief or system. All religious traditions employ some form of meditation. Zazen simply helps clear out your muddled mind so you can think more clearly and act with more perspective, compassion, and conviction (and with less attachment, grasping, and desire). Some might say true Zen is the absence of all beliefs, but we think that is fairly unrealistic. Humans have beliefs, opinions, thoughts, feelings, values, philosophies, even creeds. The point is to see them, to acknowledge them, but not to cling to them because they are all things of the world. Hold them lightly, and be open to whatever life brings you. (We can't help thinking a higher power would approve of such an approach.)

One Hand Clapping

In his book *You Have to Say Something*, Zen master Dainin Katagiri (1928–1990) writes:

> In Chinese, the character za is a picture of two people sitting on the earth. This means we have to sit zazen with others—not just with other people, but with all beings. You can't sit zazen alone—that is, you can't sit within an egoistic, selfish territory that is all your own. It's impossible. To sit zazen, you must open yourself to the universe. To sit zazen with all beings is for all beings to sit zazen with you.

What Is the Best Time of Day to Meditate?

That depends on you, your schedule, and your particular inclinations. Some people prefer morning; some mid-day; some evening. Meditate when you can. If you think you should only meditate in the morning but you aren't a morning person, you'll probably never do it. If you meditate when you are particularly tired, you'll probably just fall asleep. Early morning, however, is probably the most typical time to practice zazen. It is quieter, more peaceful, and more naturally serene. Morning also seems to be a more optimistic time of day because the day is just beginning. Because "Zen mind" means approaching everything as if it is new, morning also seems appropriate. You can dispel sleepiness by a brisk walk, jog, and/or a cool shower before zazen.

What Is the Difference?

The difference between meditation, mindfulness, concentration, relaxation, and visualization is as follows:

- *Meditation* is a conscious process wherein the meditator makes an effort to be fully aware without attaching to thoughts and feelings. Eventually, mental clamor settles down and awareness becomes more acute. Meditation can also refer to the practice of one-pointed awareness, focusing on a visual, aural, or other point (such as a mantra or a candle flame) until the meditator becomes one with the point of awareness. (These come to the same thing because mindfulness and one-pointed awareness eventually both lead to the awareness of the unity of all things.) Meditation is also the artificial environment created for practicing nonattachment, mindfulness, or one-pointed awareness—sitting just to meditate, walking just to meditate, and so on.

- *Mindfulness* is what we practice during meditation, but it can also be practiced during daily activity. It is the process of being fully aware of our external and internal environments.

- *Concentration* is an effort to focus on one particular thing rather than on general awareness. It is often a technique for easing into meditation, and it trains the mind so that the more it is practiced, the better the mind becomes at focusing for longer periods of time.

- *Relaxation* is a physical and/or mental process of leaving effort behind—relaxing muscles or thoughts—without a specific focus on awakened awareness. Relaxation is great for stress reduction and helps to declutter the mind, making mindfulness and concentration easier. One relaxation technique is visualization.

◆ *Visualization* is a technique wherein you imagine certain scenarios for relaxation (walking on a beach at sunset, sitting in a field of flowers, wading in a mountain stream) or for personal development (your succeeding in your job, in love, in school, and so on). It is more a tool for personal transformation than it is meditation, although some people like to use visualization for relaxation alone.

Is Meditation Uncomfortable? Do You Have to Sit on the Floor?

The answers are no and no. Sometimes, physical discomfort is something you can work through in meditation, but the point is not "no pain, no gain." Remember, the Buddha discovered asceticism wasn't the way, but moderation was. Don't recline in a cushy armchair with your feet up (you'd soon fall asleep), but don't sit on a bed of nails, either.

Zen-Speak

Shavasana is the Sanskrit word for "corpse pose." It is a meditative yoga relaxation pose that involves lying on your back on the floor in total relaxation.

Although the floor (with the proper cushions) often provides the best place to meditate, some people can't sit on the floor for whatever reason, and a chair works just fine, too. Even lying down can work, particularly for the yoga style of relaxation/meditation called *shavasana*. Technically, lying down to meditate isn't zazen, because *zazen* means "sitting meditation." However, as we said before, if lying down is the only thing that works for you, then that is your zazen.

Monkey Mind!

There is a difference between lying down for Zen meditation because it is the only option—a physical disability or illness prevents you from sitting—and choosing to lie down because you just don't feel like sitting up, are too tired, feel too lazy, and so on. It is much more difficult to stay acutely aware when lying down. You won't cultivate personal discipline, and you'll probably just fall asleep.

Is a Meditation or Zen Teacher Necessary?

That depends on who you are and how you work. Some people find much more success with a teacher. Others who would never seek out a teacher (or wouldn't at first) can make great strides meditating on their own. If you like the idea of a teacher, go for it! You'll probably learn a lot. If you don't, no problem. Read everything you can about zazen, and give it a try. Maybe you will eventually seek out a teacher, and maybe you won't. It's your path. Inquire at a nearby Zen center about meditation teachers, classes, seminars, and other meditation-related educational opportunities in your community.

Are You Supposed to Meditate with Your Eyes Open or Closed?

That depends on your personal preference. Although the traditional zazen technique is to keep eyes unfocused, directed slightly downward, and only partially closed, some people keep their eyes all the way open and others like to close them.

Can Anybody Meditate?

Absolutely! That is, anybody can meditate if he or she is willing to make the effort to meditate. You can't expect to meditate for 3 minutes and immediately incur all the benefits, but if you are willing to do the work and persevere, no matter who you are or what you perceive your limitations to be, you can meditate.

Lotus Pose? Are You Kidding?

Let's start with the basic form for zazen. In traditional zazen, you would use a large rectangular mat called a *zabuton*, then place a small round cushion, called a *zafu*, on the mat. The zafu is where you sit. For the traditional Japanese sitting pose (see the diagrams that follow) you can also purchase (or build) a meditation bench, also called a seiza bench, which is a low, angled bench for sitting with your legs folded under the bench. You don't actually have to sit directly on your legs or bend your knees quite as much if you use a seiza bench.

If you don't have this equipment (which is pretty expensive whenever we've seen it), you can use a regular exercise mat, carpet, or blanket and a couch cushion or folded bed pillow. (The Buddha didn't have to order any equipment from any New Age catalogue, so you shouldn't have to, either, unless you really want to spend the money.)

Zen-Speak

A **zabuton** is a rectangular mat or cushion typically used in a meditation hall, at retreats, or, if you purchase your own, in your home zazen practice. The **zafu** is the full, small round cushion placed on top of the mat and used as a seat during meditation.

Now you want to make a tripod so your weight is evenly distributed on each knee and on the cushion (on which you are sitting) or bench. Two positions are the most stable: the *lotus pose* and the Japanese sitting pose.

Zen-Speak

The **lotus pose** is an ancient yoga/meditation pose meant to mimic the perfection of the lotus flower, providing a stable, solid position for meditation. Sit cross-legged and place each foot on top of the opposite thigh. In the half-lotus pose, place one foot on top of the opposite thigh and the other foot under its opposite thigh.

The lotus pose is popular among Zen practitioners and is infamous for being difficult to achieve. In this pose, you sit cross-legged with each foot on top of the opposite thigh. Once you've achieved a degree of hip flexibility, the position isn't difficult at all. It's perfect for zazen because it puts your body into a very stable, solid, steady position, which makes it easier to keep your head up, your spine straight, and your concentration intact. It also twines your legs so that right becomes left and left becomes right—a satisfying metaphor for the balancing effect of zazen.

For people who practice yoga regularly or who are otherwise particularly limber, lotus pose might be a breeze. If you can't get into it, though, you are certainly not disallowed from practicing zazen. You just need to sit in a different way.

Meditating in lotus pose.

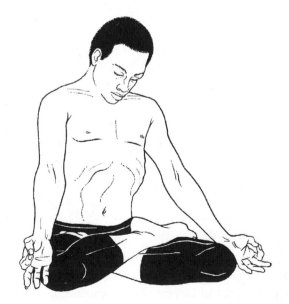

In Japan, the favored meditation position is the traditional Japanese sitting pose. For Japanese sitting pose, sit on the cushion with your knees bent and each heel and calf tucked under each thigh. (If not for the cushion, you would be sitting on your heels.) This pose gives you the same stable position with your weight on the cushion and both knees, putting less stress on your knees than crossing your legs. Just be sure not to open your feet out to the side, which can be hard on your knees. Your heels and calves should be right under your thighs.

CAUTION

Monkey Mind!

For Westerners not used to sitting in a cross-legged position (you might not have done it since childhood), it can be difficult to get your knees down onto the floor. Sitting on a cushion helps, but many people have to push their knees down to the floor again and again. Over time, your body will adjust, and your knees will stay down by themselves.

Japanese sitting pose. Feel your breath as you enter the position.

Other Ways to Sit

Sitting in the full lotus pose takes a lot of flexibility—more than some people have at first—in the hips, knees, ankles, and feet. If you aren't comfortable in lotus pose, you can use some other sitting options:

◆ **Half-lotus.** In this pose, you sit on your cushion and put one foot on top of the opposite thigh and leave the other foot under its opposite thigh. After a time, when your legs get tired, you can switch sides.

◆ **Cross-legged.** In this pose, you sit on your cushion with your legs in a regular cross-legged position, with each foot under the opposite thigh to help push your knees toward the floor. Remember, your posture will be most stable if your weight rests on your knees and the cushion rather than on your legs.

Cross-legged sitting for meditation. Remember good posture—don't slouch like the figure seated at left, and use a cushion to stabilize you, if necessary.

◆ **A chair.** Maybe you just can't muster sitting on the floor yet or aren't able to because of a physical constraint. Although it isn't traditional, you can certainly practice zazen in a chair—you are still sitting! Use a straight-backed chair to help you maintain an upright posture. If you are wheelchair-bound, that will work fine, too. Slumping makes it difficult to breathe correctly, and even if your untrained torso thinks slumping is easier and feels better, it is actually much harder on your body. Sit with your spine as straight as possible, head lifted, lower back tucked in, and feet planted squarely on the floor in front of you, in line with your knees.

Zen-Speak

Cosmic mudra is the traditional zazen hand position, in which your dominant hand cradles the other hand just below your navel with your thumbs meeting to form an oval shape.

What About Your Hands?

The most common hand position for zazen is probably the *cosmic mudra*. This hand position works no matter what sitting position you choose. Place your dominant hand (right if you are right-handed), palm facing up, just below your navel. Rest your other hand in the palm of your active hand, then bring both thumbs together to form an oval. Hold your hands in your lap so your thumbs meet just below your navel. Rest your wrists and forearms on your thighs.

Hold your upper arms out just slightly from your body, as if you are holding a raw egg in each armpit—you don't want to be so loose as to drop the egg, but you don't want to smash it, either. During meditation, if you feel your arms or hands getting tired or if they won't stay in place in your lap, bring your awareness to your hands and arms and concentrate on relaxing them. Don't press your thumbs together. The entire hand position should be light and easy.

The cosmic mudra is the most common for zazen, but you may also consider other meditation hand positions. These include resting each hand, palm up, on each knee and forming a circle with your index or middle finger and thumb (a common pose for yoga meditation) or simply resting your hands on your knees or in your lap.

Is everybody in position? Great! Now it's time to start with the breath, so let's go on to Chapter 10.

The Least You Need to Know

- Zazen is Zen sitting meditation or sitting in controlled conditions to practice mindfulness.

- Zazen has certain traditional guidelines that make meditation more effective, but in reality, other positions can be zazen if they work better for you, develop your self-discipline, and are practiced with full awareness.

- Standard zazen posture is to sit on a cushion in the lotus position, Japanese sitting pose, half-lotus, or cross-legged, but if these are uncomfortable, you can practice zazen in a chair.

- Traditionally in zazen, your hands form the cosmic mudra—one hand cupped in the other, your thumbs meeting to form an oval just below your navel.

Chapter 10

Breath, and Other Paths to Mindfulness

In This Chapter

- Follow your breath for focus
- Count your breath to tame your mind
- Managing mental tantrums
- Accomplishing mindfulness with other tools

Now that you are sitting in what we hope is at least a relatively comfortable position, you might want something to do. To go suddenly into "just sitting" is tough, as we've said, and one of the best ways to begin calming and focusing your mind so you can become more aware is by paying attention to your breath.

Start With Breath

Begin by watching your breath. Don't try to do anything to it. Don't worry about doing deep breathing or any particular kind of exercise. Just pay attention to what your breath is doing.

If you find this difficult or uncomfortable, try lightly placing the tip of your tongue on the roof of your mouth and breathing through your nose.

Monkey Mind! _____

If you have allergies or asthma or find that nose breathing makes you feel tense for any reason (Eve feels suffocated trying to nose breathe when the weather is humid—don't ask her why), breathe through your mouth. Nose breathing is healthier because your nasal passages filter the air, but it isn't worth discomfort or a panic attack if you feel as if you can't breathe that way.

Keep watching your breath. Just watch. Don't worry about it ("Am I doing this right?"), criticize it ("I really should breathe more deeply"), or even praise yourself for it ("Wow, I'm really good at this!"). These elements are all attachments. Just watch it without opinion or commentary.

Nirvana Notes _____

Paying attention to your breath is useful in many situations besides zazen. If you are nervous, edgy, jumpy, over-wrought, or otherwise on edge, take a minute to follow your breath. You'll feel calmer.

In, out. In, out. What does your body do as you breathe? What moves and what stays still? How does your breath feel coming out of your nose or mouth? How does it feel on your upper lip, in your nostrils, or in your throat? What does your stomach do? Your chest? Your shoulders?

Even though you won't consciously be trying to change anything about your breath, the more you notice it, the more you might tend to breathe more slowly, calmly, and deeply. But if you don't, that's fine. Just notice.

Breathe Like It Counts

Your mind is wandering again, isn't it? We thought so, because ours wander, too. If you are having a very hard time keeping your mind on your breath, you can begin to count your breaths. This isn't really meditating but is more like concentration. You aren't just being aware, you are concentrating on the counting, but this is a nice way to anchor the wayward mind that refuses to settle down.

Let each inhale and exhale together be one. Count only to 10, then go back to 1. If you can't make it to 10 without your mind straying, count to 5 and then go back to 1. Try to focus and really pay attention to the count. Imagine each number in your head. *One* (in, out), *two* (in, out), *three* (in, out).

Even counting won't keep your mind completely focused, and again, it will wander (and wander again). When your mind wanders to something else, notice it, then keep counting. "I wonder if the lettuce is still good. A salad sounds perfect for this hot weather … oh yes, *one* (in, out), *two*." If thoughts arise (and they will), note them and keep counting. "Maybe for that article, I could start with an example about meditation … oh, I'm thinking about my article. *One* (in, out), *two*." If feelings arise (and they will), acknowledge them and keep counting. "This is easy! I'm really good at it! I must be a natural! Oh, now I'm feeling proud of myself. *One* (in, out), *two*."

And so on.

One Hand Clapping

You may remember the Greyhound Bus slogan that invited you to "Take the bus, and leave the driving to us." What a great feeling, to relax, lean back in a comfortable seat, and let your silver-haired, reliable-looking, uniformed driver take you to your destination. It's a wonderful feeling to let someone else do the driving—someone you trust to do it right. Imagine your breath to be that smiling, trustworthy, dependable Greyhound driver. Just as he always knows what he is doing, so does your breath. It is right by definition. Trusting your breath permits you the freedom to accept experience, without the need to constantly monitor whether everything is okay.

—From *The Best Guide to Meditation* by Victor N. Davich

Breathing Through Boredom

As you relax and your thoughts begin to slow, you are going to get bored. We promise you. You are going to start complaining to yourself. You aren't going to like it. How do you get past this stage when you can hardly stand to sit there? You breathe.

Now you begin to learn about the self-discipline part of zazen. You start to itch. You start to squirm. Your mind starts to bang-bang-bang for you to get up and just do something. "I can't stand it! I have to move! I have to get something done! I can't just sit here wasting my time!"

This is your mind, once again protesting a new set of rules with all the vehemence of a 2-year-old who is told "no" for the first time. Think of it as a mental temper tantrum. If you are a parent, you know the number-one rule about temper tantrums: Don't give in!

When Eve's 2-year-old, Emmett, first started throwing temper tantrums, he did so invariably because he wanted to do something he wasn't allowed to do, like climb the bookshelf, stand on the kitchen table, or run into the street. When Eve said, "No, Emmett. You aren't allowed to do that," he would scream, with all the gusto a 2-year-old can muster: "*Em*-mett *wan*-na *do* it!"

"No."

"*Emmett wanna do it!*" (Faster, scowling and insistent.)

"No."

"*Emmett wanna do it!*" (Getting high-pitched.)

"No."

Then followed a tantrum with Emmett, face crimson, shrieking, sobbing great big dramatic tears, and limbs flailing and kicking.

This is what your brain is doing when you get bored and frustrated with sitting. Your mind wants you to get up and distract yourself from awareness. It doesn't want to bother with the subtleties of awareness. It just wants to keep jumping and flitting from thought to thought, activity to activity.

But here's the thing: As soon as Eve walks out of the room, Emmett's tantrum stops. If nobody can hear him, he isn't going to waste all that effort.

Likewise, if you hold firm and stay consistent (like a good parent should!), refusing to give in to your mental impulse to scrap this whole zazen business and go have an ice-cream sundae or watch television, if you refuse to attach to your mental tantrum, it will stop. It really will! Instead of letting your mind engage you, simply be aware: "Now I'm having the feeling of boredom. Now I'm having a thought about quitting. There goes my mind, rebelling again. How interesting. *One* (in, out), *two* ...."

The trick, in other words, is to keep all your thoughts and feelings at arm's length, for perspective. Don't jump right into them and become them. See them for what they are: just thoughts. You aren't going to drop dead if you keep meditating for 5 more minutes. But you will have taken one more step toward making zazen a habit your brain can accept.

Attending a Zen retreat is a good way to establish the zazen habit faster than you might normally be able to do. When you meditate for hours a day, the first day is like hell. The second day is worse. Then, suddenly, your mind accepts what is happening and becomes serene. Just as Emmett doesn't even try to stand on the kitchen table anymore, knowing it is a futile effort, sooner or later your mind will also figure it out. "Okay, I guess we're sitting here for a while. I might as well relax and pay attention."

Finding the Meditation That Works for You

Strictly speaking, zazen is the standard meditation for Zen, but Zen is your individual path, so another form of meditation might work better for you. Many excellent books about meditation are available that explain hundreds of meditation techniques.

We hope you won't go meditation-shopping just because zazen is difficult. All meditation is difficult in the same way. The difference lies in posture and position, and also whether the practice is more a meditation or an exercise. These exercises can be either a visualization exercise (where you picture a certain thing or series of experiences); a relaxation exercise (such as scanning your body for tension and consciously relaxing each part); or a concentration exercise (where you focus on a single point or object or a sound such as a chanted *mantra*).

All these techniques can help you train your mind to be more focused, clear, calm, quiet, and peaceful. Only when you are able to transcend technique, however, are you really practicing Zen meditation.

Zen-Speak

A **mantra** is a word or words you chant during meditation as a point of focus and to evoke certain energies in your body.

Techniques and Tricks

We've mentioned techniques, so let's look at a few in brief. In certain traditions, the techniques are the primary focus of concentration or meditation. *Mandala* meditation is a technique of Tibetan Buddhist meditation. Many different Buddhist, Hindu, and Western religious traditions employ the technique of mantra

Zen-Speak

A **mandala** is a circular, geometric design that draws the eye to its center, designed as a focus for meditation. In yoga, **kundalini** is a psychospiritual energy force in the body that can be released and used through certain techniques.

chanting for meditation and/or prayer. In yoga, the focus of meditation is on breathing techniques, or total relaxation, or rousing *kundalini* energy. In the Judeo-Christian tradition, meditation is often centered on prayer to God. More recent (or revived) traditions focus on moving meditation, dance meditation, different methods of mindfulness meditation, and creative visualization.

Of course, there are many crossovers in techniques between traditions, as well—mantra chanting in Christianity, breathing exercises in Buddhism, and so on. But for Zen, anything that is a technique is mainly for helping focus your mind, to get it into a mindful state. Techniques are like Zen first aid, and they can work very well for this purpose. Techniques are also used in Zen to help jolt the mind into a new awareness, such as with koan meditation. (We'll talk more about koans in Chapter 11, but briefly, a koan is an inscrutable story, riddle, or enigmatic saying the Zen practitioner contemplates until he or she arrives at an answer.)

Zen-Speak

Kinhin is Zen walking meditation. It is the walking counterpart to zazen.

Nirvana Notes

Practicing kinhin outside, especially out in the country or in a large park far from the traffic, noise, and pollution of the city, is a lovely way to work on mindfulness.

Kinhin

Kinhin isn't a technique, exactly. It is just zazen in motion. In other words, it is Zen walking meditation, as opposed to Zen sitting meditation.

In a Zen monastery, zendo, or at a Zen retreat, sessions of zazen typically alternate with sessions of kinhin, ranging from slow, steady walking to brisk jogging. The purpose of kinhin is not just to stretch your muscles so they don't atrophy while sitting on the floor—although walking does feel pretty good after a long session of sitting.

Kinhin isn't practiced to get anywhere, either. It is simply walking for the sake of walking, in full awareness. Some people say Zen priests encouraged kinhin so their monks wouldn't get too attached to or obsessed with zazen.

In a zendo, kinhin involves certain protocols. While walking, the hands are placed, typically right fist in left palm in front of the chest, elbows out at right angles, posture erect. Continue to watch your breathing or count your breath. In *The Three Pillars of Zen*, Philip Kapleau advises:

> Begin walking with the left foot and walk in such a way that the foot sinks into the floor, first the heel and then the toes. Walk calmly and steadily, with poise and dignity. The walking must not be done absent-mindedly, and the mind must

be taut as you concentrate on the counting. It is advisable to practice walking this way for at least five minutes after each sitting period of twenty to thirty minutes.

Different traditions have different methods for kinhin. Typically, in Rinzai Zen the walking is fast, but in Soto Zen it is slow. Depending on where you practice kinhin, the guidelines may vary widely. If you practice at home, simply walk along some easy, familiar, preferably circular route so you don't have to think about where to go. Walk mindfully.

Level Two: Just Sitting

Once you've got your mind under control, you'll find you can leave your techniques behind and progress to the next level: just sitting. Sit in full awareness, noticing thoughts and feelings, not engaging them, not judging them, simply being. This stage of meditation will imbue you with a deep, inner sense of joy, peace, and compassion. You'll wish everyone could experience such tranquility and inner serenity. You'll feel great.

But reaching this level doesn't mean you'll always be able to reach it. When you've been practicing meditation regularly for a long time (months or years), you will find it easier to practice pure zazen. But sometimes you will have less-successful meditation days and will need to use some of your techniques (counting your breath, visualization, or relaxation) to help center you.

Some Zen teachers advise students to count breaths and/or follow breathing for many weeks or months before they attempt "just sitting." Some might give koans only when "just sitting" is mastered; some when following the breath is mastered. But if you can achieve "just sitting," you'll know you are moving in the right direction. You are learning how to "be" under controlled conditions. This means you are ready for the next level.

One Hand Clapping

You should not be like an actor, who puts on a costume for the performance and takes it off immediately at the end. Many of us are like that. Although we undertake the practice very seriously during the meditation session, after it is over, we revert to the same negative person again. We do whatever we like—fighting, quarreling, and so forth …. Things are easy during the actual meditation session because there is no one to interfere with you …. When you meditate, you are trying to transform your mind, but the effect really shows only during the postmeditation period.

—From *Awakening the Mind, Lightening the Heart* by His Holiness the Dalai Lama

---

Level Three: Perpetual Meditation

Even though the most experienced of Zen masters continues to practice zazen to keep his or her body and mind disciplined and aware, the ultimate purpose is to carry that zazen into daily life. Remaining in a state of perpetual meditation—total awareness, mindfulness, a full immersion in the present moment—is the ultimate in Zen living. This condition might seem impossible when you are still struggling with your 5-minute mindfulness practice and can't even get to 10 in your breath counting without almost bouncing off the walls, but didn't some adult in your life always say, "Anything worth having is worth working for?"

This is worth working for, and we hope you'll stick with us. Very soon, you'll be glad you did.

The Least You Need to Know

- Techniques to help calm and focus your mind toward mindfulness include following your breath, counting your breath, visualizing, relaxing, or focusing on a visual point (such as a mandala) or sound (such as a mantra).

- Many religious, philosophical, and spiritual traditions throughout the world use different meditation techniques, and all of them may be useful for quieting mental clamor.

- Kinhin is the walking counterpart to zazen.

- Eventually, you will be able to sit in awareness without techniques and then carry that awareness throughout the day.

A Koan Is a Koan Is a Koan ...

In This Chapter

◆ The point of koans

◆ But don't koans seem so ridiculous?

◆ Transcending logic and duality

◆ Your personal koan practice

◆ Some thoughts on a few famous koans

Koans are probably the most familiar technique of Zen, beyond basic meditation, known to Westerners. Although many Zen practitioners (especially, although not exclusively, the Soto Zen sect) don't employ koans, many others do (particularly, although not exclusively, the Rinzai sect).

Koans are those enigmatic puzzles, strange utterances, seemingly paradoxical or nonsensical stories, questions, or anecdotes meant for pondering until they are internalized and understood on a level beyond logic and reasoning. They help anchor the wandering mind on one point, as does a mantra meditation or gazing at a mandala in other traditions. Koans are also meant to pop the mind into a state of more enlightened understanding.

But do they work?

Words to Live By

Koans aren't for everyone, and some people don't find them helpful, preferring instead to cultivate pure awareness without the mental machinations and somersaults required of koans. For others, however, koans are of great benefit for keeping the mind in place, similar to counting the breath but a little more interesting. For still others, the understanding koans can impart is as essential for Zen living as anything.

Nirvana Notes

Western Zennists may find it helpful to rephrase certain koans and stories in Western terms to remove the artificial "foreignness" of the traditional koans. This can help you detach from the koan itself and move to its content.

Koans are, of course, simply words put together by somebody. They aren't beamed down from some divine source. They aren't even really parables or wisdom or advice in the traditional sense. You can't get enlightenment from words. You already have truth within you, remember? It doesn't come from the outside, from printed words on a page, or even from words spoken by someone. The words are just a tool to help you reach what you have within you. The koan itself shouldn't get in the way. It is merely a gateway to the self and to the apprehension of truth.

Koans can indeed become words to live by if you see them not as advice, not as a divine message, but as a simple reminder that life isn't necessarily logical, certainly not fixed, and often not what it seems on the surface. Things don't always make sense or yield to the sword of logic. Or if they do theoretically, much in life is beyond our current ability to comprehend it (remember chaos theory?).

Illogical Logic

If life is absurd, that doesn't mean you should just give up and accept the absurdity without putting any effort into your life. Zen isn't cynicism, and absurdity isn't "bad." You have to internalize this illogical logic, and one way to do this is by internalizing a koan. Ironically, the result is that eventually you can accept the absurdity of life and you won't have to put any effort into this understanding. But it takes effort to get to that point.

When something happens that we don't expect, things don't work out the way we planned, someone doesn't do what we hoped or thought they would do, or the "good guy" gets it and the "bad guy" gets away, we might feel overcome with the illogical nature of things. We might even feel angry, dumbfounded, or despairing. Yet just because we don't understand something doesn't mean it's not going to happen! The world and the universe and the very nature of being aren't simple and nicely mapped out for us to understand.

This kind of thinking might sound familiar. Are we saying "everything has a purpose" or "trust in the divine plan" or something along those lines? Actually, no, we aren't saying that at all. Although Zen doesn't contradict these ideas and is compatible with them, Zen in and of itself doesn't ask you to believe that someone or something else has it all figured out. This is simply shifting the logic elsewhere: "You might not think life makes sense, but at least somebody else does! Somebody knows what's going on, so just trust them."

Nope, that is not how it is in Zen. In Zen, "not making sense" doesn't really mean anything other than the phrase's capacity to help you see beyond what you think you see and what you believe you know.

In Zen living, perceiving absurdity is like peeking through a keyhole to catch a glimpse of reality, as if the room you have been in all along is just the set on a stage and when you look through the keyhole, you see the actual room around the "fake" room. Life is absurd. Yes it is, sometimes. All that means is that the things we thought we knew, the things we counted on, hoped for, attached to don't really mean anything. They aren't the true nature of reality. They will pass.

Only being and doing are real. Existentialism, that philosophy that the individual is isolated in an indifferent universe, grapples with the concept of being and the great chasm of nothingness, while Zen frolics with the concept of being and doing, being and doing. There is no great chasm in Zen. Zen is more "somethingness" than "nothingness," but that "somethingness" has only to do with being and doing and nothing else. Be and do, right here, right now. The rest of it is clouds passing by, huge and towering, vast and opaque, until you get inside them and recognize that they are nothing you can hold on to; they are all mist without substance, ephemeral, ungraspable, soon to pass away.

Of course, this is easy to say and hard to do—to accept or embrace the notion that only being and doing are real and that the absurdity of the world is only a clue to real seeing. To really understand this, you must first take in the understanding that logic doesn't always work in life and that the greatest truths are perceived on a level beyond logic.

This is exactly where koans fit in. Koans are tools for unraveling that reliance on logic. They help you debunk the myth that logic is everything. By foiling logic, they clear the path so you can keep moving into post-logical territory, into that clearer sight and into the understanding that being and doing are the simple truth. But shouldn't you strive to stay objective when you are surrounded by a world of conflict, choice, unpredictability, and chaos? After all, isn't logic all you have in the face of such an insecure existence?

Not at all. In Zen, logic is irrelevant. It's something to "get over." *Star Trek*'s Mr. Spock probably wouldn't approve, but then again, Vulcans do spend a lot of time in meditation.

Duel With Duality

Koans also tackle the notion of duality. Being humans, we tend to think dualistically. In other words, there is an "I" and a "you," an "us" and a "them," a "subjective" and an "objective," a "self" and an "other." But is that really true? Or is duality an illusion, something temporary, like those ocean waves that all look so distinct but disappear and reappear somewhere else in the space of a breath? What happened to that one, choppy, foam-topped wave you were watching just a moment ago? Where did it go? Was it ever really a thing, or was it just a temporary manifestation of the ocean?

If a nonsensical koan is true, if logic doesn't make sense, if there is no "self" and "other," if a wave is just ocean, what is left? Ah, that's when it gets interesting!

Zen-Speak

Dokusan is a private meeting between a student and a Zen teacher, during which the student can ask questions, receive encouragement, or present the answer to a koan.

You can practice with koans on your own, and many Westerners prefer to contemplate koans privately without "presenting" answers to a teacher. Traditionally (and many Zen practitioners and teachers still do it this way), koans are practiced under the guidance of a teacher, who assigns koans he or she thinks are appropriate for the student. And then, in what is called *dokusan*, the student meets with the teacher to present the answer for the teacher's approval or rejection.

Long ago a monk, in private, would be assigned a koan he had never heard before. In those times, the koan system was secretive and mysterious. But today so many books have been published containing poems and responses to koans by various Zen masters, and certain koans have become so popular, that it is virtually impossible to replicate that kind of experience.

Today's open-book, Western Zen changes the experience entirely. Do you try to fool your teacher into thinking your answer is enlightened, even though it just happens to be the exact answer uttered by the famous Zen monk Joshu, which you looked up on the Internet and memorized?

The meditation on a koan to which you know at least one answer already accepted by a teacher presents a unique challenge. To the monk in a Zen monastery who needs to "pass" to move to a higher level of responsibility, knowing the answer could be an irresistible opportunity to "cheat" by trying to convince a teacher he or she has discovered the true answer. In *The Three Pillars of Zen*, Philip Kapleau attributes this trend to a degradation in the Rinzai tradition.

But we think that to meditate on a koan even if you know a "right" answer intellectually is even more of a challenge than never having heard the koan. Lay people have a freer, more open field in which to do this. We aren't getting "graded," and our koans don't determine our career path, so we don't have to cheat (unless our egos convince us to). We have the luxury of working past the intellectual answer to find our own answer.

Nirvana Notes _____

Koans don't come from anywhere special. Who's to say they aren't everywhere? Listen for koans in your daily life: a bus driver muttering, "Exact change only"; a child chanting, "My house has no roof and can fly!"; a friend commenting, "There is nobody in this crowd." You might find some truly engaging puzzles worth contemplating. Others might not yield much. Remaining open to the appearance of koans in your life can be enlightening in itself!

But Koans Are Silly ... Aren't They?

"If internalizing a koan means spending months and years obsessing over the sound of one hand clapping, forget it! That's silly!" you might be thinking. Some koans do seem silly at first, until you remember that the point isn't the koan itself. The point is to grow your awareness. And the point is also, to some extent, that very silliness to which you find yourself objecting.

Let's look at how you might approach a koan that sounds silly:

> A monk once asked Zen master Tozan, "How can one escape the cold and the heat?" Tozan replied, "Why not go where there is no cold and no heat?" "Is there such a place?" asked the monk. Tozan replied, "When cold, be cold. When hot, be hot."

Monkey Mind! _____

When contemplating a koan, if you feel like you are really stuck, let it go for a while. Store the koan in the back of your mind and do something active. Sometimes physical activity without direct contemplation can yield an enlightened answer to any problem, whether it be a career dilemma, relationship impasse, or koan (maybe all three have the same answer!).

Here's what you might ponder as you meditate on this koan:

Huh? Being cold hardly sounds like a way to escape the cold. A nice space heater and an afghan would probably work better. And being hot to escape being hot? Give me central air and a glass of lemonade, thanks.

Besides, how can a place where there is no cold be a place where you can be cold? That must be the illogical part. And what is the point of emphasizing cold and hot?

I guess I'm not normally the serious victim of the elements like a Zen monk might have been long ago. I don't spend my days huddled within the stone walls of a monastery without climate control. But for a Zen monk, maybe this question had more urgency to it.

Still, I feel discomfort in my life. Let me see. To escape cold, be cold. To escape hot, be hot. Life is full of discomfort and dissatisfaction. When did I feel it last?

One Hand Clapping

An old Zen story tells of a monk who saw a turtle in the monastery garden. The monk watched the turtle for a time, then approached his teacher and asked, "Why is it that most beings cover their bones with flesh and skin, but a turtle covers its flesh and skin with a bone?" Without speaking a word, the teacher took off one of his sandals and put it on the turtle's back.

This koan is meant to foil distinctions and duality. The monk saw beings as made of skin, flesh, and bones, here and there organized in different ways. By putting the sandal on the turtle, the Zen master attempted to demonstrate the absurdity of such a delusion.

Yesterday my friend criticized an idea I thought was great. That really hurt my feelings. This morning when I put on my jeans, I couldn't zip them, and I discovered I had gained 5 pounds. What an ego blow. And this afternoon I tripped over a bath toy and bruised my knee. Then there was that muscle cramp I got last week. That really hurt.

Of course, none of these are exactly life-threatening discomforts, but they weren't any fun, either. They can still count as suffering.

So when cold, be cold. When hot, be hot. When in pain, feel the pain? When having a cramp, or hurt feelings, or a bruised ego, feel the cramp, feel the hurt, feel the bruise—is that it? Hmm. Won't that make the feelings worse?

What was that Zen explanation for suffering? Suffering comes from attachment. A bruised knee hurts because I am attaching to the pain. I'm angry for not seeing that toy. I feel clumsy. The pain makes me regret the incident. I wish it had never happened! I wish I had never bought that toy for Junior, who never plays with it anyway! I'll probably have a big bruise that will remind me of my inner klutz whenever I see it. Then it will turn an ugly yellow. It's throbbing! Ow!

Yeah, that sounds like attaching to the feeling, all right. I wonder what would have happened if I would have sat down and concentrated on the pain without forming any opinions about it. Just felt it, really felt it, moved into it and through it? Sounds intense. I guess all that attaching helped distract me from the intensity of the actual experience.

But if I had let myself feel it without attachment, it would have simply become an experience rather than a matter of suffering, ouch, ow, oh poor me, poor me. I would have really lived it. And I would have escaped the suffering.

Oh! I get it. To feel hot, you have to embrace the heat, really feel it, without attaching the old spiel, "It's the humidity that kills me! I hate living here in the summer. Oh, the heat is horrible! How can I get anything done? Am I sweating through this shirt? This whole house is like a sauna,"—yadda yadda yadda. Instead, be the heat. Be hot, period. Then you don't suffer.

That makes sense! Wow, I'm pretty good at this koan stuff. It's a snap!

Before you get too proud of yourself, let's remember one important thing:

Understanding a koan intellectually is not understanding a koan.

Sure, that was a great little session of personalizing a koan. But it is one thing to say, "Oh! I figured it out! Don't complain, just experience!" and quite another to understand it on such a level that you make it part of yourself.

We're guessing that our imaginary Zennist thinking these thoughts would probably attach just as vehemently to the pain the next time he or she falls on another discarded toy, gets a muscle cramp, or feels insulted by a friend.

Nirvana Notes

Whenever you get caught up in frustration, irritation, pain, sadness, or any other brand of suffering, a simple reminder— a sort of Zen-in-a-nutshell—can help a lot (at least, it helps us!): Suffering is ignoring this moment. Freedom is in this moment.

Our imaginary Zennist understood one possible interpretation of the koan, and it is a good interpretation. We like it. We even agree with it. (Maybe because we wrote it!) But if our Zennist paraded that answer in front of a Zen master, he or she would probably get waved away. Getting it isn't getting it. You don't internalize a koan in 3 minutes.

Now, if our Zennist friend decided to keep going, that might be a different matter.

Be the heat. Be hot. Then you don't suffer. Let this sink in. Let it ring within me. Be hot to escape the heat. Be cold to escape the cold.

Maybe our Zennist kept this koan in mind all day, all night, mentally pulling it out and looking it over every so often, during a free moment.

Be hot. Be cold. Feel the pain.

Maybe the Zennist lets the koan linger for weeks, or months, or longer.

And then one day, the big *Oh!* happens. Our Zennist becomes the koan. Suddenly, the koan has personal meaning beyond the intellect. It has intuitive meaning. One day, perhaps on a particularly sweltering August afternoon or at the peak of a frigid February night, our friend becomes the heat, or the cold, and it all makes sense. The suffering stops in a moment of kensho.

Were our Zennist to visit a Zen master now, the result might be quite different: a serene nod, perhaps a smile—and the assignment of another koan!

One Hand Clapping

On his deathbed, the Buddha said, "Be a light unto yourself." Commenting on this message, Zen priest Steve Hagen, in his book *Buddhism Plain and Simple*, wrote:

> To awaken is not to hold the idea of awakening. You can't practice waking up. And you can't fake it or imitate it. You have to actually want to wake up. You're the one you can count on. You're not other-dependent. Everything you need is here now. Just rely on this—immediate, direct experience. You're the final authority. Whether you awaken or not is completely up to you.

Now that we've talked about what it means to really apprehend a koan, let's look at some famous koans and how you might start thinking about them.

The Sound of One Hand Clapping

There is an old Zen story about the famous "You can hear the sound of two hands clapping together. What is the sound of one hand clapping?" koan. In the story, as it is related in the koan collection *Zen Flesh, Zen Bones*, transcribed by Paul Reps and Nyogen Senzaki, a 12-year-old boy had the desire to study Zen. He worked in a Zen temple but wanted to meet privately with the teacher, just like the older Zen disciples did. One day he approached the teacher, but the teacher told him to wait. "You are too young yet," the teacher said.

But the little boy persisted, and at last the teacher relented. He met with the boy and gave him the koan. "You can hear the sound of two hands clapping together. What is the sound of one hand clapping?"

The little boy bowed and retired to his room to meditate on the koan. Outside his window, he heard the geishas playing music. "Aha!" thought the little boy. "That must be it!"

The next evening, the boy met with his teacher and played him the music he had heard. "No!" said the teacher. "That's not the sound of one hand clapping. That is music."

Crestfallen, the boy went back to meditate some more. During his meditation, he heard water dripping. "That must be it!" thought the little boy. But the next evening, the teacher sent him away again. "That is the sound of dripping water, not one hand," said the teacher.

The boy tried many sounds in front of his teacher: the wind blowing, an owl hooting, locusts buzzing, and again and again and again.

The boy meditated on the koan for one year. Then one day (at the ripe old age of 13), the boy got it. After using up the possibility of every sound he knew, he suddenly understood what was left: soundless sound. And soundless sound is the sound of one hand clapping.

Had someone told the boy the answer on the first day, he wouldn't have understood, at least not on a deep level. In the same way, knowing the answer this boy finally came to won't keep this koan from working for you. You can meditate on it, contemplate it, and turn it over in your mind for the rest of your life. When you finally get it—really get it—you'll know it.

Monkey Mind!

Keeping a koan in mind over a long period of weeks, months, years, is different from obsessing about the koan. Obsessing means you are too attached to the koan. You might only be able to understand it by stepping back a little and loosening your hold on it.

Does a Dog Have Buddha Nature?

An oft-quoted koan, and probably the most famous Zen koan in the East, is, "Does a dog have Buddha nature?" This koan is often assigned to new Zen students.

The story attached to this koan goes something like this: A monk approached the famous Zen master Joshu in an attempt to understand the concept of Buddha nature. As he started to speak, he noticed a dog wandering by and asked Joshu, "Does a dog have Buddha nature?"

Almost before the monk could finish asking the question (so the story goes), Joshu shouted, "*Mu!*"

In Japanese, *Mu* has two meanings. One is the opposite of *U*, which means "is." *Mu* means "is not." The other, according to Gyomay M. Kubose in the book *Zen Koans*, is the Absolute Mu: "The Absolute Mu of Zen Buddhism transcends 'is' and 'is not.'"

Joshu's answer, therefore, isn't "No, dogs don't have Buddha nature," or even "No, don't ask such silly questions." Neither is the answer "Of course a dog has Buddha nature. We all do!" The answer doesn't avoid the question, either, as it might seem to.

The shouted "*Mu!*" was meant to break the monk's obvious obsession with the concept of this being and that being and all beings having Buddha nature. In response to this koan, Kubose writes:

> The essence of Buddha's teaching is non-attachment. All human troubles and sufferings, without exception, are due to attachment. Even attachment to the idea of non-attachment is attachment! Joshu wanted the monk to transcend the relative world, transcend the teachings, transcend U and Mu, transcend Buddhism, and gain the free and independent world of enlightenment …. Thus, Mu is crucial: it offers no surface upon which the intellect can fasten. The word Mu must be experienced as the world "MU!"

Joshu's answer was the "right" answer. Yet, if someone asked you the question and you responded "*Mu!*" because you had read it in this book, you wouldn't have the answer. Or you wouldn't *necessarily* have the answer.

You would have to turn the koan over and over in your mind, live with it, and meditate on it until you become it and are finally able to respond intuitively—and from an internal place rather than from the place in your brain that receives information and spits it back out. Maybe then you would shout, "*Mu!*" or something else. But only then would you understand.

One Hand Clapping

A famous Zen koan tells of a monk named Wakuan who looked at a picture of the heavily bearded Bodhidharma and said, "Why doesn't that fellow have a beard?" Of course, Bodhidharma did have a beard. This koan urges us to foil our preconceptions based on appearances. In *Zen Koans*, Gyomay M. Kubose writes:

> When we say "Bodhidharma" we immediately conceptualize him. If we say "Buddha," we conceptualize the Buddha. If we say "Christ," we conceptualize Christ. We make ourselves victims of concepts. By refuting appearances, Wakuan invites us to go beyond the duality of beard and no-beard and see the real Bodhidharma.

Why Did Bodhidharma Come from the West?

"Why did Bodhidharma come from the West?" is also a famous koan often quoted in popular culture, including in Jack Kerouac's novel *Dharma Bums*. Remember, Bodhidharma was the one who brought Buddhism from India to China—in the Far East, India is considered the West. You won't find the answer to this koan searching around to discover some evangelical intention on Bodhidharma's part. The Zen master Joshu's answer was, "An oak tree in the garden," but you won't find your answer by spouting something irrelevant to the question as Joshu's answer seems to be. You don't need to know any historical facts to answer this one, so don't go to the library to start researching it.

Maybe you will start thinking about the things in front of you, everyday life, or your own intentions for moving forward or doing anything. Perhaps you will consider whether or not Zen is related to place or why anyone ever embarks on any difficult journey.

No one can tell you the answer. Only you can discover within yourself if Joshu's answer was correct and what your answer would be.

Nope, we're not going to give you any more than that. As we've been saying all along, you need to work through these koans on your own!

The Broken Vase

This koan is a question and an answer together, and the koan consists of understanding why the answer was the right one. The story goes that a monk wanted to open a new monastery and needed someone to run the place. He told his students that he would ask them a question, and whoever gave the best answer would run the new monastery. The monk Hyakujo placed a vase of water on the ground and asked, "Who can say what this is without calling its name?"

Thinking he had the absurdist nature of Zen all figured out, the chief monk at that monastery answered, "No one can call it a wooden shoe." Just then, the cook came in, kicked the vase, knocking it over, then left the room. Hyakujo turned to the chief monk. "You lose," he proclaimed. "The cook will be the master of our new monastery."

This koan asks you to question the notion of naming. Naming something puts a label on it, and this labeling only further highlights the false nature of difference and separateness. What is the vase? No, it's not a wooden shoe, but this is the wrong answer because this answer supposes that a vase and a shoe are two different things. The cook, instead, knocked over the vase and broke it. This action foils the very notion of a vase by breaking the object in question. Vase, no vase, shoe (wooden or not), foot, bowl, Hyakujo or the chief monk or the cook—all seem different, but they might as well all be tipped over because they aren't actually separate at all. They are one.

If this doesn't make sense (or even if it does—remember, that's just logic), keep thinking on this koan. Think until your mind pops out of the intellectual space and sees the broken vase for what it is.

What Is Buddha?

Many responses have been written to the koan "What is Buddha?" Some familiar answers are "Mind is Buddha," "This mind is not Buddha," and from the sublime to the ridiculous, "Dried dung."

The point of this koan is to demonstrate the inexpressible. Buddha cannot be described or defined. Your answer will come from your own true nature. Contemplating "What is Buddha?" is just like contemplating "Who am I?"

We think "Who am I" is a great koan to launch your own personal koan practice.

The Least You Need to Know

- A koan is a puzzling or illogical question, statement, or story to help the Zen student transcend logic, intellect, and notions of duality.

- Koans seem silly or absurd precisely because they are undermining preconceived notions. To take the absurd seriously is to foil logic.

- Knowing the intellectual answer to a koan, or someone else's answer, is not knowing the answer to a koan. Each individual must perceive the answer on an internal and intuitive level.

- Traditionally, a Zen teacher assigns an appropriate koan to a student who periodically meets in private with the teacher to offer answers. The qualified Zen teacher can tell whether the student has truly understood the koan or not.

- Some of the more famous koans are "What is the sound of one hand clapping?"; "Does a dog have Buddha nature?"; "Why did Bodhidharma come from the West?"; and "What is Buddha?"

Eating, Moving, Breathing: Maintaining a Zen Lifestyle

In This Chapter

- ◆ Ways to maintain your meditation practice
- ◆ The Zen of eating and exercise
- ◆ The Zen of sports
- ◆ Stop and take a moment

Meditating once or twice is easy; meditating every day is not. Remembering to live in the moment every now and then is easy; reminding ourselves to live in the moment every day is not. Most of us aren't in the habit of living Zen, but we can change habits.

In this chapter, we'll go through your day with you and help you find opportunities for Zen living. Meditation isn't the only time to live Zen. You can live Zen every minute—when you eat, when you exercise, when you read, when you work, when you create or cook or clean, or when you aren't doing anything at all. Only when you have established a Zen lifestyle in your daily life can you truly say you are living Zen.

Zen and the Art of Meditation Maintenance

Meditation, talking about it is easy. Getting excited about it is easy. Doing it is tedious. How do you get yourself to meditate every day? And do you even really need to meditate every day?

If you want your zazen to make a difference in your life, you really do need to make it a habit. We know, we know—just like any habit, this is easy to say but really tough to do. As you progress through the weeks trying to meditate, you will probably find that you do it here and there when you have a spare moment, when you happen to wake up a few minutes early or get to bed a few minutes early, or when you are particularly stressed in the middle of the day. But meditating on a regular basis, when you don't "need" it? That's like taking an aspirin when you don't have a headache, isn't it?

Ah, but health professionals say taking a daily aspirin can prevent a heart attack! Daily meditation may have a similar effect. According to Jon Kabat-Zinn in his book *Full Catastrophe Living*, "Greater resilience in the face of stressors and reduced reactivity are characteristic of people who practice meditation regularly." To get the full range of benefits, the habit—be it meditation or taking vitamins or herbs, exercising, or eating a healthful diet—has to become a part of your lifestyle.

Daily meditation won't magically transform your life into one of immediate and perpetual stress-free tranquility. But you will be able to tell the difference.

Meditation does more than change your response to stress. It changes your response to yourself. Or we could say it eliminates your response to yourself because you begin to see things the way they really are. You are simply you, and the world and your life are simply the world and your life. You start to appreciate the beauty and the wonder of the mundane.

Those daily meditation moments will gradually spread across your entire day until you feel as if you are meditating—as in responding in total awareness—all day long.

Practice Makes Practice

Don't expect big changes like that right away, though. You don't play Rachmaninoff after your first piano lesson. And just like the piano, meditation takes practice and more practice—daily practice.

We won't say "practice makes perfect," either. You are already perfect. Remember, you aren't striving for anything other than access to what you already have. You are who you are. Practice only makes practice, just like being is just being. Practice meditation for its own sake, to uncover your perfection. Meditation isn't training for some quest to find happiness "out there." It *is* happiness.

If you like nice, neat guidelines, we'll be happy to start you on your way. You can use this meditation plan to set up and begin practicing your new habit. Commit and stick to the plan.

Use the following chart as a meditation record. Fill out the particulars and check the box when you have accomplished each meditation session. This chart provides for two 5-minute meditation sessions each day. With some rearranging, just about anybody can spare 10 minutes. You know that's true.

We suggest that Session 1 be first thing in the morning and Session 2 be before bed, but work these sessions into your schedule whenever you can in whatever way works for you. Not everyone can meditate first thing in the morning. Maybe you will be more consistent if you meditate at 10 A.M., on a break at work, or on your lunch hour.

To time your sessions, use a watch with an alarm, a kitchen timer, your microwave or oven timer, or whatever will alert you to the end of your meditation without your having to look at the clock every 30 seconds while meditating. If you can see a clock, you will keep looking. By the way, if your timer makes a ticking sound, and you find it distracting, you might want to use a silent timer.

Day	Session 1	Session 2	
1 _____	Time: _____	Time: _____	❏
2 _____	Time: _____	Time: _____	❏
3 _____	Time: _____	Time: _____	❏
4 _____	Time: _____	Time: _____	❏
5 _____	Time: _____	Time: _____	❏
6 _____	Time: _____	Time: _____	❏
7 _____	Time: _____	Time: _____	❏

After your first week, add 1 minute to each meditation session per week until you have worked up to a satisfactory 30 to 60 minutes of daily meditation. For some, 30 minutes is plenty. For others, 60 is a delight. You'll be up to 30 minutes in about 3 months. You can make copies of this chart and use it every week if you wish.

You will probably be tempted to meditate for longer sooner than this though. We advise against this, no matter how impatient you might feel to progress quickly. You might be able to do it for a while, but then you will likely get burned out and quit. This nice, slow, gradual pace doesn't take a big time commitment and is much easier for the beginner to handle. Stick with us. We won't lead you astray!

Zazen, Kinhin, Zazen, Kinhin

When you are meditating for longer periods, you will probably experience some discomfort from sitting. Your joints might get stiff or creaky or even painful. You might get a cramp, or your legs might fall asleep. Your back might hurt, your neck get tired, and so on. Meditators describe a range of complaints.

Before your body is accustomed to this new habit of meditating, physical discomfort during meditation is one way your body tries to convince you to stop meditating and get up. Unless you have a specific medical condition, in which case you should follow your doctor's advice, "just sitting" should be perfectly harmless, even if it is, at first, uncomfortable.

When you feel discomfort, try to really feel it rather than attach to it and let it distract and carry you away. Another good way to handle the discomfort of sitting is by alternating periods of zazen and kinhin.

Monkey Mind!

Trying to meditate for too long at first is just like trying to exercise beyond your ability when you first start a workout program. You will get frustrated, even injured, and you won't want to continue. To keep from foiling your own efforts, work into all-new activities gradually.

Nirvana Notes

If you can work up to 20 minutes of zazen and 10 minutes of serious meditative kinhin per day, you will start to see real changes in your life.

Kinhin, you might remember, is Zen walking meditation. In Zen monasteries, monks typically alternate zazen and kinhin. You might practice zazen for 8 minutes and kinhin for 2 or zazen for 5, kinhin for 2, and zazen for 3. Or perhaps try zazen for 5 minutes and kinhin for 5. Just make sure you continue in your meditative awareness as you transition from one to the other. Don't use the change of activity as an excuse to just get up and move around and think about all the stuff you have to do.

When you practice kinhin, walk slowly or briskly, in full awareness, in circles around your meditation space. Or if you can do so without becoming too distracted or attached, walk around your yard or down your road (this also works well if your meditation space is outdoors). If you walk along your road, be sure you are far enough away from the edge of the road to avoid oncoming traffic. This works best if you live in the country. In the city or in a busy neighborhood, maintaining a meditative state while walking is extremely difficult. It's best to stay in your meditation space.

This is also the reason why we don't just suggest doing kinhin and no zazen at all. Zazen provides the most stable, least distracting atmosphere for meditation. Kinhin is wonderful, but it is harder to keep from getting distracted and to notice when you are distracted. If your mind wanders while you watch the passing trees and flowers, you will be so entertained that you won't notice nearly as quickly that you are also thinking about what to add to your shopping list and when you can get your car in for an oil change. Total awareness of your environment is great, but when you are a beginner, this is much easier in a simpler environment with less stimulation.

In zazen, your mental wandering is much more obvious because nothing distracts you from noticing that you aren't concentrating on your breath. In a way, zazen is also harder because mindfulness is more challenging if your brain isn't being entertained by moving scenery, and this is also important to understand. Together, zazen and kinhin are perfectly complementary.

You can also add extra kinhin throughout your day—a meditative walk at lunch, a stroll through the park after work, or an evening meander around the neighborhood. Whenever walking in kinhin, keep your mind totally focused on your environment and not on the thoughts that try to distract you.

The Brown Rice Myth

What about the rest of your life? Besides being aware, are there Zen "rules" you have to follow? Do you have to eat brown rice and vegetables every day, dress in robes, quit wearing makeup or expensive neckties, and start doing tai chi? Do you have to—*gulp*—shave your head?

Of course not! Awareness. That's it. That's all there is to it. Remember our summary of Zen? "Now."

Nirvana Notes _____

When undertaking daily life—meditating, eating, drinking, exercising, or resting—remember the Buddha's discovery that the Middle Way, or moderation, is the most conducive to self-realization. Neither too much nor too little, neither overindulgence nor denial will keep things clearly in focus because your mind and body will be distracted by a state of extremes. Keeping things in balance makes mindfulness easier, and mindfulness makes it easier to keep things in balance.

By learning how to be, how to wake up, how to live in the now, you learn how to savor every drop of life. You probably won't feel compelled to shave your head, but you might feel compelled to simplify your life. You might find you don't want to waste a moment stuffing potato chips down your gullet, staring at a really, really bad television show, or all those other things people do to distract themselves from themselves, from the present moment. You will want to live in that present moment. As long as you are really noticing, experiencing, living your present moment, you will find you want to make it worth living. Through the practice of zazen, you'll start to understand exactly *how* to live that present moment. And that's exciting.

Do You Have to Be a Vegetarian?

A lot of people, especially Westerners, struggle with the Buddhist precept of nonviolence. Does that mean never eating meat? Let's look at that precept again (as stated in Chapter 8):

> The destruction of life causes suffering, so I vow to cultivate compassion and learn how to protect the lives of people, animals, and plants, refusing to kill, to let others kill, or to condone any act of killing in action, thought, and lifestyle.

Monkey Mind!

Many of us attach guilt to food. Feeling guilty about eating too much or not enough or of eating the "wrong" things such as sweets, high-fat foods, red meat, or dairy products is perhaps just as damaging as the foods themselves. Whatever you eat, eat it with full awareness and joy at each bite, and it will nourish you.

This wording seems to support vegetarianism, yet Zen Buddhists in some countries are not vegetarians, and Jack Kerouac (in his novel *Dharma Bums*) writes (we are paraphrasing here) that being a vegetarian always seemed to him like splitting hairs because all sentient beings eat what they can.

In other words, do what makes sense and feels right to you. If you feel it is truly important to practice nonviolence in all ways and you don't feel right about condoning the killing of animals for food by buying and eating meat, then be a vegetarian. If you want to keep eating meat because you like it and it makes you feel healthy or if you simply don't want to give it up, then don't.

Every Last Bite

Even if you eat meat, however, eating in a Zen way means really experiencing your food. We all have a lot of reasons for eating what we eat, eating the way we eat, or eating when we eat. But how often do you gulp down your food on the run, eat at your desk while working, or stare at the television or newspaper as you eat? Few of our reasons have to do with sensible choices about nutrition or even about really enjoying our food in the moment of eating it.

We eat to socialize; to comfort ourselves when we are lonely, scared, or depressed; or to keep stress or anger from getting out of control. All these reasons for eating are self-destructive, yet even though we know this, we still do it.

As we've talked about earlier, part of having a Zen attitude is to have and then release our feelings. Eating to cover up feelings is antithetical to this process. If you can stuff yourself, thereby dulling your feelings of loneliness or fear, you are negatively impacting both your physical and mental health. You are interfering with your own wholeness and personal growth.

We don't all have to eat brown rice or give up meat or go macrobiotic or Ayurvedic or whatever else, but to really practice Zen living, we do need to take a look at the role of food in living a balanced life. This means that we need to recognize when we are using food in a way that is mindless, defensive, or protective—or for any reason other than simply to eat food.

That takes some discipline, and it isn't easy. We've found the only way to make it work is to keep coming back to the present moment, to the Zen of eating: When you eat, eat. Live in the moment of your eating. Really taste. Really experience the flavor, the texture, the whole process. To help you see what we mean, try the following exercise.

Zen Exercise: Zen Eating

To eat in the Zen way, you should fully and completely taste every bite and every crumb. Even food you don't really like will become an experience—not a "good" or "bad" experience but simply an experience. If you are present in your eating, you won't binge or eat things that don't satisfy you. You won't eat without noticing you are eating, and you won't eat obsessively. You might find more enjoyment from healthful foods and discover a more awakened awareness that unhealthful foods aren't as good as you thought they were. Of course, if you really plan to savor every single bite of that chocolate cake or those french fries, go for it. You won't need much because the experience will be so vivid, so *right now.*

To do this exercise, find a piece of fruit: a pear, an apple, even a single grape. Sit in a quiet place where you won't be disturbed. Relax, breathe, then slowly, very slowly, eat the fruit. Notice the look of the fruit, the taste, the texture, the juice, and the sweetness. Notice everything you can about what you are eating. Let your whole awareness encompass the eating experience. Take your time. Savor. Live the experience. The more you eat in this way, the more you will understand the reality of the present moment.

The Zen of eating can completely transform your relationship with food. Let yourself have a relationship with it, not a secret affair. Enjoy it! Relish it! Food gives you energy and life. You don't need to overindulge. Allow yourself the pleasure of tasting. Food is wonderful, and when you eat in the Zen way, even a fresh salad and a ripe pear can be a banquet.

One Hand Clapping

An old Zen story tells of two Zen masters traveling with their disciples, camping on opposite banks of a river. Two disciples, one from each master, saw each other across the river. "I bet our Zen master is greater than yours," called the first disciple. "He has amazing powers. He can hold a brush and write in the air on one side of this river, and when one of us holds a paper on the other side of the river, the writing will appear." The other disciple responded, "Our master is even greater. When he eats, he does nothing but eat. When he drinks, he does nothing but drink. When he sleeps, he does nothing but sleep." Stunned by this far greater feat, the first disciple came to follow the other Zen master.

The Zen Workout

As you know by now, Zen isn't all about sitting still in silent meditation. It is about living in the now, and the best way to do that is to feel good and have a healthy body that won't distract you with lots of physical complaints. How do you get that healthy body? Through exercise, of course.

We all know that getting or maintaining a healthy, fit body means getting up and moving. We need to exercise. Modern life doesn't require a lot of physical movement (unless you have a very physical job—we sure don't, sitting at our computers!), so we have to invent our own ways of putting that movement back into our lives. But that's all exercise is: putting movement into our lives.

Nirvana Notes

When you are exercising, it is difficult to focus on what you are doing if the movement is too easy. A wandering mind can be a sign that you are ready to take your activity to a faster pace, a heavier weight, or a more complicated routine. If you are trying to keep track of challenging steps, balance, or breathe, your mind has little chance to wander.

Exercise is another one of those things like eating more healthfully that many of us know we should do but have a hard time actually doing.

Gary admits to having often been vaguely annoyed with people who are obsessed with their workout, leaving important meetings to go on a lunchtime run, as if that were more important than anyone or anything. And what about people who expect to be scheduled around so they can get to the gym? They might elicit responses such as "Oh, I really need to work out more, too," but some of us are probably thinking, "Please. Chill out. Eat a doughnut."

Some people do get obsessed with (attached to) exercise, using it to control others or avoid feelings (the way we can avoid feelings with food). But exercising doesn't mean you have to be obsessed. It also doesn't mean you earn some kind of societal privilege. Those of us who get into the exercise habit may see things from the other side. We may find ourselves getting annoyed at those who don't seem to have the discipline or the will to exercise. Can't they just get up and move? A few push-ups wouldn't hurt that guy. That girl obviously isn't doing her sit-ups. If only those people would exercise, they'd look a lot better!

Because our culture is so obsessed with appearance and youth, exercise, like food, has become a complex social subject, full of dread and status and obsession, either with not exercising enough or exercising too much. But exercise needn't be burdened with all that societal garbage. The Zen approach to exercise is simple. Are you listening? Okay, here it is:

Exercise.

But wait, are there no justifications? No rewards?

Sorry. The Zen of exercise means that when you exercise, you exercise with your entire attention. And that's all.

One Hand Clapping

One story goes that when Bodhidharma first visited monasteries around China, he was appalled at the low level of physical fitness of the monks, so he taught them moves some say were the beginning of chi kung, a precursor to tai chi. Chi kung is an ancient Chinese art of health management. It means "energy skill" and is tai chi without the martial arts aspect, a holistic approach to health using movements and breath to manipulate the body's energy. Tai chi developed later as a martial art, but its slow, deliberate movements are widely practiced today for health, not self-defense.

Of course, you know there are benefits, justifications, and improvements from exercise. You've heard all the reasons why you'll be glad you got in the habit of exercising: a better, more positive outlook; more energy; better muscle tone; more stamina; better ability to manage stress. But if you think about all these things while you are exercising, you won't be exercising in the Zen way. To exercise in the Zen way, you exercise—and that's it.

Doing push-ups? Concentrate on your form, how your muscles feel, your breathing, your sweat, your effort, even the discomfort, if you have any. Feel it. Experience the sit-ups or Pilates moves or reps on the weight machine.

Running? Kick-boxing? Elliptical trainer? Cycling? Tai chi? Interval training? Tennis? Racquetball? Basketball? Beach volleyball? Mud wrestling? Taking a simple walk around the block? Whatever your activity of choice may be, to exercise in the Zen way, you need to exercise with your full and complete attention, not to get somewhere or be something, but with a full immersion and oneness with your activity. Only then can you notice how your body responds and adjusts, fine-tuning your movement to your body's needs and abilities. You'll find you move with more coordination, control, and confidence. You'll get more from your workout. You'll see results faster. You'll find your whole self becomes better integrated, calmer, and more creative.

But don't think about that part! That isn't the point. The point is to be the ball, be the yoga pose, be the exertion, be the running. Be the movement, be in your doing.

Nirvana Notes

It's easy to say you will detach yourself from your feelings of exercise dread, but in the meantime, how do you get started when you can't stand the thought? Give yourself a choice: Exercise, or sit in zazen for 30 minutes (in addition to your regular practice). Start sitting in full awareness. If you sit for 30 minutes, what a great job of zazen! If you can't sit still, get up and exercise—you've motivated yourself! Either way, experience whatever you do with full awareness.

As soon as your mind starts to wander, you aren't practicing a Zen approach. When you grasp for or attach to these "results," your effort becomes fragmented. Notice and detach from your feelings, and you might find yourself dreading exercise, patting yourself on the back, looking down on others who don't exercise, expecting yourself to feel or look better, fearing the effort, or feeling pride at how good you are or frustration because you can't "get it." You probably will generate feelings out of an attempt to define, understand, put off, or become obsessed with exercise, but the Zen trick is to notice those feelings without attaching to them. See them, then let them move on. You have more important things to do—like run that last mile or experience those final three sit-ups!

Zen: Performance Booster?

The traditional practice of zazen may not look very athletic or artful—you're just sitting on the floor, meditating. But Zen, sports, and the arts are not only good matches but also historical ones as well. For centuries, people have paired them—or it might be more accurate to say people have *unified* them.

Zen is as natural on the football field, the volleyball court, the craft studio, or the art gallery as it is in the martial arts dojo or the tea ceremony because Zen is the art of doing.

Can Zen improve your golf game or your drawing skill? The answer is yes, but the question, from a Zen perspective, is meaningless. Why would you want to be "better" or "faster" or "stronger" than you are? You are already perfect. Just be. Just do.

One Hand Clapping

Once there was a wrestler named Great Waves who was so strong and skilled that he could beat even his teacher. But he became so overcome by anxiety in a wrestling match that his own students could throw him. Great Waves sought a Zen master's help. The Zen master advised him to sit in zazen and consider his name. "You are called Great Waves. Find those great waves within you, and see how they can sweep away anything." Great Waves meditated all night. In the morning, the Zen master found him in zazen with a faint smile on his face. "You have found your great waves. Now no one can beat you," he said. That day, Great Waves won easily, and afterward, no one in Japan could beat him. Through zazen, we can see into our own natures to make the most of our abilities.

The Zen of the Game

Sports hardly sound like an important activity. It's just a game, right? You toss around a ball, or you hit a ball with something, and you run around some. So what? It's just a way to pass the time, right?

In college, Eve had a friend who was mystified by her lack of interest in sports. "How can you not see the artistry of it?" he said. "It's the human spirit pushing itself to its limits. It's beautiful. They are tapping into the energy of life." Eve wasn't so sure, as she suspiciously eyed the football game on television. It looked like a bunch of guys in padding crashing into each other and chasing an illogically shaped ball.

But since then, she's begun to look at sports a little differently. Sports are an opportunity to practice mindfulness, and with the practice of mindfulness comes a skill, a finesse, and an immersion in what one is doing that can result in a performance he never thought possible.

Nowhere more than in sports do you hear people talking about getting "in the zone," that place of complete oneness with your activity, where you seem to tap into something higher. Suddenly the team moves as a unit, the ball does what you want it to do, or your body moves just as you intend.

Nirvana Notes

Even if you have never been athletic, you might find satisfaction in a Zen approach to sports. Many people shy away from sports because of the pressure of competition or even stage fright. With a Zen approach, sports are just another form of zazen. Consider starting with a sport that isn't necessarily competitive, such as tai chi, yoga, walking, running, weight lifting, or dancing, to ease your transition from nonathlete to athlete.

"Being the ball" (or the bat or the arrow or whatever) might improve your sports performance, but that isn't the point of a Zen approach to sports. There is no point, other than the process. Winning isn't the point of the Zen of the game. Like the Zen of anything else, the "point" is the right now—the doing—that matters.

In sports, as in life, if your energy is fragmented, it shows. If you are thinking about the end result, winning, or what you just did wrong—that fumble, that stumble, that fall—you aren't present in your action. But when you become fully present in your action, watch out. You'll find that you're better at this game than you thought you were!

But your skill doesn't matter any more than winning matters. If it matters to you, you are thinking ahead again and you have lost your mindfulness. Instead, becoming the game—being the ball, bat, basket, goal, target, arrow, bow, bar, hurdle, finish line—is a powerful exercise in simply being. Everything, every tool or every movement of the sport or activity you are doing, is you.

When that fragmented energy—yours, your body's, your mind's, your equipment's, your thoughts and feelings about your activity—comes together, the result is something spectacular, beautiful, and, when you think about it, completely unsurprising. You are existing, as your true self, fulfilling your potential.

One Hand Clapping

"Your arrows do not carry," observed the [archery] Master, "because they do not reach far enough spiritually. You must act as if the goal were infinitely far off. For master archers, it is a fact of common experience that a good archer can shoot further with a medium-strong bow than an uninspired archer can with the strongest. It does not depend on the bow, but on the presence of mind, on the vitality and awareness with which you shoot …."

—From *Zen in the Art of Archery* by Eugene Herrigel

Stop! (In the Name of Zen)

One last suggestion for putting more Zen into your day: Every once in a while, stop. We get so used to go-go-going, never stopping in the middle of a chore or a job or the morning commute to say, "Look at this view, look at these people, look at this city street, look at this tree."

Every so often, just stop what you are doing, breathe, and notice the world as it stands right now all around you. Open your senses to your environment. Experience your present moment in complete stillness, if only for a few seconds—a microzazen moment to remind you how it feels to pay attention.

Breathing is an important part of this moment. Breathe in. Breathe out. Feel your breath going in and out of you as you notice the world around you. Here you are. Right now.

Now you're living Zen!

The Least You Need to Know

- Maintain your meditation by committing to very short periods twice each day, then gradually working up to longer periods.

- Alternate sitting meditation with walking meditation to train yourself to meditate under different circumstances.

- You don't have to be a vegetarian, eat brown rice, or be anyone you aren't already to live Zen in your daily life.

- You know you should exercise. Zen can help you cut through all the dread, pride, and other feelings you attach to exercise so you can "just do it."

- Every day, indulge in microzazen moments and stop what you are doing, breathe, and pay attention to the present moment.

Part 4

Personal Zen

Part 4 is all about you. Who are you, anyway? Have you ever met the "real" you? Has anyone else? Zen can help you gain self-knowledge and can keep you from allowing your life to slip away unlived. People feel. People think. But how do we feel and think without letting the feeling and thinking take over? How do we keep it all in perspective? With a Zen attitude!

Zen can also help you improve your love relationships and, even more important, it can help you appreciate who you are and who other people are, both in and out of relationships. Zen can also help with family relationships. We'll cover a Zen approach to parenting, Zen for kids, and Zen for adult children forging a new kind of relationship with their aging parents. Finally, we'll look at your own personal dukkha: the desires, fears, and worries that cause you to suffer and how Zen can help you master them all.

Chapter 13

The One Who Stares Back at You

In This Chapter

◆ Your reflection in the mirror

◆ How to be perfect

◆ What to do with all those feelings

◆ What to do with those racing thoughts

Once you've integrated Zen living into your life, you might find you have come right back around to the question that got you started: "Who am I?" So now let's look at that question, knowing all we now know about Zen.

There you are, in the mirror. Yes, that's you. Your friends and family recognize your image. You recognize it. But who are you, really? Humans have been struggling with this question for thousands of years. Who is that person reflected in the mirror (or the lake, before the invention of mirrors)? Why am I here? What characteristics define me? What can I make of myself?

Perhaps the extreme popularity of self-help books has something to do with this eternal question. People are dissatisfied with their lives (that's dukkha, remember, from Chapter 2?). They think they can be something better. Self-help and self-esteem books promise the realization of these changes. They promise that you can be whatever and whomever you want to be.

Is this true? Or are we getting duped? Are we stuck with what we've got? Or are we asking the wrong question entirely?

The Real You vs. the Potential You

One difference between the philosophies offered by many general self-help or self-esteem books and Zen is that in self-help books we are told we can become something new. You don't like the old you? No problem! You can create a new you! Many of these books and systems help you formulate some kind of major goal—get the perfect job, find your soul mate, even change your personality—then develop practical strategies toward achieving it.

But these systems encourage people to focus their entire beings on becoming something they are not. Is that realistic? Is it possible? How many times have you tried to change and been successful for a day or two (or an hour or two), only to slip back into your old patterns, which, even if they are destructive or unhealthy, feel suddenly as comfortable as an old shoe after your foray into the world as someone else?

Living Zen means giving up something you might find pretty difficult to give up: the idea, the promise, that the present will get you what you want in the future if only you do the right things, say the right things, or feel the right things. You also need to give up the idea that your future perfection, even your future transformed identity, is in your hands and that with the right tools, you can have it all.

CAUTION Monkey Mind! _____

We don't want to underemphasize the power of society's emphasis on appearance. It is extremely difficult not to judge one's own appearance, especially when it differs from societal perceptions (or perceptions in our immediate social group) of perfection. The key is to let yourself have these feelings and yet recognize what they are. Acknowledging negative feelings about appearance helps deflate those feelings.

We have two things for you to think about:

◆ How do you know what you will want in the future or who you want to be? How do you know your emotionally charged or intellectualized solution will work, make you happy, or be any better than what you have right now? Is it because it worked for someone else? Because money, or a soul mate, or talent, or prestige would make anyone happy? How do you know that's true—and true for you?

◆ Is it really in your control to do anything you want with your life?

We would like to suggest the following answers:

◆ You don't know.

◆ It isn't.

If you think those answers are depressing, pessimistic, hopeless, or real downers, you have yet to grasp the essence of Zen. Zen goes beyond optimism or pessimism, both of which presume to make judgments about the future. You don't know who you will be tomorrow or what you will want, and you can't control what will happen to you in your life.

But that's just fine. It doesn't matter. Why?

Because you are already who you are, and you are already everything you need to be!

In this moment, you are complete. You can still have goals. You can still work toward changes in your life. But if you scramble desperately toward some ultimate idea of you that is somehow better, superior, or improved, you won't get there. Worse, you'll miss your *right now*. You need to see how complete you are right now before you can make tentative plans for a direction in your life.

We say "tentative plans" because as we live each moment, the world spins on and all kinds of things happen to determine what will happen next. You can't control what might happen to you or how you will feel about it. All you can do is point that old boat of yours in a general direction and go with the flow.

And your goal? Your goal is to be, right now. The point of your journey? To be, right now. (We figure it can't hurt to remind you!)

Nirvana Notes _____

One way to help de-emphasize your dependence on external notions of perfection is to break habits that tune in to those cues. Stop reading those magazines that make you so miserable. Quit watching that television show with all those beautiful people. Is it really that interesting? When you catch yourself attached to the mirror, redirect yourself out the front door for a mindfulness walk instead.

So Who Are You?

"If I'm so complete, why do I feel so unsure of who I am?" Many of us feel unsure of ourselves or wonder who we really are. Our culture encourages our dissatisfaction. Images of perfect-looking people, celebrities (at least for the moment), and success stories of those who have "made it" in one way or another surround us. How are we supposed to compete with the single mom who writes a billion-dollar novel complete with movie deal; the overweight young man who loses hundreds of pounds, lands a contract to do ads for healthy fast food, and becomes a household name; or the poverty-stricken kid who becomes the most famous rap star ever?

We all get the message that we, too, should keep striving, that if we work hard enough, we, too, can be rich or famous or have the perfect body—or all three! We are continually encouraged to strive for these very external symbols of accomplishment. Affluence, good looks, adoration by the masses—aren't those the ideal markers for success?

And although we might get the message from some sources (parents, teachers, social or religious organizations) that "it's what's inside that really counts," do we really believe it? We say we do, but do we really? Or do we spend time staring in the mirror, pulling back our faces to get rid of the wrinkles, hating the body parts we find imperfect, or longing for youth or strength or less fat or more shape or anything other than what we have?

We aren't going to tell you what you "should" be doing. You already know. But we would like you to become aware that the struggle you experience when you look in the mirror is an internal struggle. You are attached to ideas about what a "self" in our culture should be, and those attachments are causing you to suffer.

When we strive to be perfect, we deny ourselves because in knowing we aren't perfect right now, we know we aren't yet good enough. We are inadvertently putting ourselves down in our effort to "improve."

Who defines perfection? The latest article in a men's or women's magazine? Actors in the movies or on television? Supermodels? Those people you've never met whom you see on the street, in a nightclub, or at the coffeehouse? Does perfection mean youth, beauty, strength? Is perfection that older sibling your parents always compare you to, the next-door neighbor who always had something a little better than yours, or the best friend who always came out ahead?

When Gary worked in a substance abuse program, he encountered this attitude all the time. Many of the clients experienced such suffering because of the image of perfection they had in their heads—an image totally unrealistic for who they were, an image that was ultimately destructive. The difference between that image of perfection and the reality of their lives was a wide, wide chasm, and when they perceived the reality of the chasm, they could find no joy in today, no reasonable way to get across. Defeated, they would slip back into substance abuse.

Monkey Mind!

Many people experience a pervasive feeling of emptiness, and in an effort to fill a void, they engage in destructive behavior: overeating, excessive drinking, substance abuse, gambling, spending, or other impulsive, risky behavior. Zen urges us, instead, to embrace the emptiness as part of our being. We should step into the emptiness and experience it, rather than fear it, judge it, or try to fill it. Then we won't need those other things anymore.

One client was barely scraping by in a medical job as he worked to maintain his sobriety. He clung to the idea that he was going to be a doctor. Was this a possible future for him? Of course. Would it happen in a day or a week? Certainly not. Yet in clinging to this idea, the man remained in a kind of limbo, treading water and searching desperately for a faraway shoreline, without any appreciation for the sunlight, the gentle waves, the bright green water around him. He was looking for the "someday," but without the "now," he had no roadmap. Without the "now," we can't get to the "then."

This client, and so many others in Gary's experience, did not want to look at who he was or where he was, let alone begin to take those baby steps necessary to start moving. But in clinging to some future notion of a life to be, a potential you, today, slips away. We can learn so much about ourselves, and our lives can be rich beyond measure if we pay attention, look around and take it all in, then fold up our binoculars and put them away. The future will happen, gradually becoming present moment by present moment. Only in living now can we understand the flow of life, how we can begin to move with it, and where we might end up.

Perfection has nothing to do with anything outside yourself. Why would you think that someone else, with his or her own personal struggles and insecurities, has anything to do with you? Who wrote that magazine article? Who photographed that supermodel? Who

Nirvana Notes

Cultivating balance in your life can help you get in touch with your inner self. Each day, think a little, feel a little, move a little, rest a little, eat a little, drink a little, sleep a little, and meditate a little. Don't let any one activity dominate, and you will cultivate an inner sense of equilibrium and contentment.

hired those actors? Who told you you should be somebody else? Whoever it was struggles with the same questions of identity and perfection that you do.

People will try to tell you how you should be. They can't help it. Yet no one can define your perfection but you, and the only way you can define perfection is by looking inward, quietly, calmly. There it is, looking back at you. Let the world's external chaos die down a bit, and you'll see it: the perfect you, right there all the time.

One Hand Clapping

The concept of time is one of the great ways in which we are fooled. We believe that the past and the future are, as it were, more solid and of longer duration than the present .... We live in a sort of hourglass with a big bulb at one end (the past) and a big bulb at the other end (the future); we are at the little neck in between, and we have no time. Whereas when our vision becomes changed, we see that ... we have, in fact, an enormous present in which we live and that the purely abstract borders of this present are the past and the future.

—From *Zen and the Beat Way* by Alan Watts

Once More with Feeling

Letting your life begin right now is easy to say, just as all the suggestions in this book are easy to write. But as you might find, a few things get in the way. One of those things is your feelings. You can plan and plan until you turn blue in the face, but one highly charged feeling can turn a million plans on their heads. You can have a zazen schedule—or anything else—perfectly orchestrated, but then something happens to spoil your mood and your intentions dissolve.

Nirvana Notes

How would your life be affected if you turned all your mirrors to the wall or draped towels over them for one week, and you resorted to using your car's narrow little rear-view mirror to check for spinach between your teeth? Try it if you're feeling brave. You'll find it isn't easy, but it could transform your idea of yourself.

Humans have feelings—some pleasant, some not so pleasant. We react to our world largely by feeling. Someone criticizes you or something you say or do, and your day is a loss. Someone compliments you, and you can do no wrong. Our feelings are largely tied to our self-image. If we get an external nod, we feel great. If we get an external thumbs-down, life seems hopeless.

Other feelings aren't so obvious or so directly tied to an event. Feelings from long ago can get buried and can rise to the surface unexpectedly during meditation or at the onset of a new relationship, during an argument with a loved one, or when stress gets the better of us. Just looking in the mirror can bring on a whole avalanche of feelings: "This is not how I want to look! What happened to me? What's wrong with me? When will I finally become the person I wish I could be?"—and on, and on, and on.

How to Feel

A Zen approach to living with this roller coaster of feelings means acknowledgment. Give your feelings a chance to happen. Hear them out, then let them move on. Even if they aren't yet resolved, you can decide to meet up with them later. Living Zen means learning to recognize your feelings and letting them have a voice, but not letting them control you.

You are in control, even if it doesn't feel like it as you let a feeling play itself out. Feelings are just something you have, not something that rule you.

Think of feelings as your children. You made them. Sometimes they are pure joy. Sometimes they give you grief. But you are the parent and the one who sets the rules. Sometimes, in the proper environment, you let them go wild. Sometimes you have to rein them in. You don't ignore them, of course. You let them be. But they have to follow your rules.

> **CAUTION**
>
> **Monkey Mind!**
>
> If you don't learn to live in the present, what good are all those plans you have for the future? When your plans come to fruition, you won't be able to enjoy them because you never learned how. You'll be too busy planning for the future!

Whenever your feelings start to get the best of you, try to remember this metaphor: If you let your children rule the house, you're going to have a pretty chaotic house. But if you ignore them or refuse to let them express themselves in any way, your family won't be healthy and you won't be doing your job as a parent.

Embrace and Disarm

Ignoring or refusing to acknowledge your feelings gives them power. Obsessing over your feelings also gives them power. Embracing your feelings, really letting yourself experience them, gives you just what you need: the chance to be your human self. Feeling your feelings lets them be, so they can go move on and make way for the next present moment.

Have you ever noticed how some people seem to be angry all the time while others are cheerful all the time? Both are likely a cover-up against the wide range of human emotions we all experience. If you are always angry and let your rage control you, you can feel safe. You don't have to take responsibility because you are a victim of your rage. Something bad happens? You've got it covered. Something good? You can be safely suspicious.

Nirvana Notes

Sometimes the best way to let yourself feel your feelings or think your thoughts is to give yourself the gift of silence. Turn off the television and go into a quiet room by yourself. Sit and simply enjoy the silence. Listen to the silence. Your feelings and thoughts will have a space to live in for a while.

The same goes for the cheerful sort. Putting a good face on everything makes it safe. If everything is always sunny, you can pretend the bad feelings aren't there. But they are still there, and they will stay there if you don't let yourself feel them.

When Eve and her husband separated a few years ago, Eve thought everything was great. What an improvement. How great her life was! Deep down, she sometimes wondered why she wasn't upset about it all. But deeper down, she knew she wasn't going to let herself feel those scary emotions. It was much safer to be happy about everything.

But then something strange started to happen. Eve would suddenly start to cry for no apparent reason. Or she would lose her temper, completely without cause. Her emotions were rebelling at being kept way down in that dark little closet where she had stashed them. Finally, little by little, she realized she had better let them out. As each saw the sun, it wasn't pleasant, but there they were—grief, sorrow, pain.

Then, gradually, as each got its time to be, these emotions packed up and moved out.

Monkey Mind!

Remember those inflatable punching clowns made for children? Weighted on the bottom, they pop right back up when punched. Imagine if they were weighted in their heads. One bop and they would topple over. Likewise, we can become unbalanced if we put too much emphasis on our thinking.

Think About It

Feelings aren't the only things that characterize the complex workings of the human brain. We like to think, as well. We like to think a lot. Thinking makes sense. It is a logical approach. It can also be a great way to avoid feeling.

Thinking gives us a sense of control: If we think about every possible outcome, we can avoid a negative outcome. If we think about all the ways to handle a situation, we'll handle it better. If we think, think, think, we'll have control. Right?

Thinking has its place. We need it to solve problems, communicate, and generally get along in society. But like anything else, we tend to overdo it. We think so much, we think ourselves in circles. When our brains need a rest, we keep thinking. Thinking keeps us up at night, distracts us from concentrating, and even convinces us that things are true when they aren't. We assign motives, project outcomes, and create scenarios. We drive ourselves crazy!

How do we get our thinking under control? We do it in the same way we get a handle on our feelings.

Nirvana Notes _____

When you come to a busy four-way stop, do you try to speed up and take your turn first, do you go strictly by the rules (whoever is on the right goes first), or do you hold back and let everyone else go first? Think about how your stop-sign style is reflected in your emotional reactions. Recognizing your emotional patterns is a good way to start putting them into perspective.

How to Think

Just as it is human to feel, it is human to think, and a Zen approach to thought is to acknowledge rather than deny it. Some people believe, for example, that meditation is about suppressing thought. That is not it at all! Meditation, and mindfulness in general, is about acknowledging, but not attaching to, our thoughts.

If we acknowledge our thoughts and the processes our brains go through to evaluate situations, we can put our thoughts into perspective. Some people keep lists of their thoughts so they can keep track of them and come back to them later. Some simply name their thoughts: "Oh, there is a thought about what I believe someone might be thinking." "Now here's one about how to solve that same old problem again."

If you give your thoughts too much control, they can block your creativity, your emotions, even your ability to communicate clearly. Let yourself have your thoughts, then let them pass on—it's the Zen way to think.

Monkey on Your Brain

In this book, we call our "warning" sidebars "Monkey Mind!" Monkey mind is that familiar mental state in which your thoughts are racing, impeding your concentration and action.

Gary has a friend who was in a hotel in Central America some years back and had an experience so representative of monkey mind we could hardly have invented a better example.

Gary's friend recalls someone bringing an actual monkey into a restaurant. Everyone was laughing until the monkey jumped on the head of the woman who brought him in. Then everyone but the woman was laughing. She became very afraid the monkey might bite her. What if it was infected with some horrible virus?

Gary's friend watched the woman begin to panic. He felt helpless. If he tried to pull off the monkey, the monkey might panic and bite her or him. The more distraught the woman became, the tighter the monkey clung to her head.

At last, Gary's friend decided to approach the situation differently. He urged the woman to relax. The monkey hadn't bitten anyone yet. Why panic about the assumption that it would? Then he grabbed a banana and started jumping around, clowning to distract the monkey. And it worked!

The monkey jumped off the woman's head and darted toward the banana. Gary's friend threw the banana to the monkey, and everyone was happy.

What a perfect illustration of the Zen approach to thinking. The anxiety and panic the monkey (your thoughts) can induce will only give them more power over you. But to engage your thoughts with a lightness and playfulness, with an attitude that they don't have power over you, will help them move along.

Human thoughts are like monkeys—funny, curious things, unpredictable, sometimes a little wild, but easily diverted. Taking them lightly and teasing them away reminds you what they are: just thoughts, not truth. Your thoughts aren't you. They are just monkeys.

Zen Exercise: Barrel of Monkeys

The next time you feel overwhelmed or your mind is racing, try this exercise. Take just 5 minutes to yourself. Sit and relax in a place where you won't be disturbed. Close your eyes, breathe deeply, and visualize a big wooden barrel with a top—you know, the old-fashioned rainwater-catching kind that people used to ride over waterfalls before they invented extreme sports.

Now, begin to count your breathing: one inhale, one exhale. Two inhale, two exhale. When you reach 10, start again at one.

But wait! Who says you are going to reach 10? You are feeling pretty stressed right now, and we are fairly sure that as you try to focus on your count, thoughts and feelings will get in the way. And that's good! Let them come, but every time a thought distracts you from your count, immediately focus on it and visualize it as a monkey wearing a little jacket and hat. Look at the monkey's hat, and visualize a label for the monkey printed on his hat. Then imagine taking the monkey by the scruff of the neck and popping it in the barrel, then clapping on the lid.

As you count, keep track of your monkeys. One monkey might be labeled "Worried about son's recent rebellious behavior." You dress it, then, duly labeled, into the barrel it goes. Three inhale, three exhale. Another monkey … maybe this one will be labeled, "Wondering what to cook for dinner." Into the barrel it goes! Four inhale, four exhale. Five inhale … and another monkey! This one might be, "Worried about impossible deadlines." Another one goes into the barrel!

When 5 minutes are up, visualize taking that barrel and throwing it over Niagara Falls yourself. You saw the thoughts, you named them, then you moved them right along. Good for you!

The Thinking, Feeling Zennist

Whether you take pride in your mental abilities (there is nothing wrong with cultivating your strengths) or suffer from your tendency to overthink (or both), just remember that you are not your intellect and you are not your feelings. You have thoughts and feelings just as you have a cat or a car or a computer or a utility bill.

You might think of yourself as an intellectual or an emotional person (or a computer person, or a cat person), but these labels are antithetical to a Zen approach to life. You can be intellectual and you can be emotional while living Zen. But these thoughts and feelings come and go. They are not you.

One Hand Clapping

Mind contemplating mind is like an object and its shadow—the object cannot shake the shadow off. The two are one. Wherever the mind goes, it still lies in the harness of the mind …. Once the mind is directly and continually aware of itself, it is no longer like a monkey. There are not two minds, one which swings from branch to branch and another which follows after to bind it with a piece of rope.

—From *The Miracle of Mindfulness* by Thich Nhat Hanh

You are the someone who wakes up and pays attention. You are that perfect being alive in the present moment, not missing a beat. You are someone discovering yourself and the life with each present moment, even after you've lived your Zen for years.

Living Zen, you can see your thoughts and feelings as flotsam and jetsam in the river that is your life. You might pick out some treasures or let the rubbish flow past. Some of it might bump up against your boat, and you might look at it for a while in amusement ("Look at that funny-looking thought!"), with pleasure ("Mmm, I really like this feeling"), or with a little disgust ("Yuck, what's that mucky, seaweed-covered piece of junk?").

But you have the power to nudge it all past with your oar so you can get on down the river.

The Least You Need to Know

♦ Cultural perceptions of perfection are compelling, but you already have perfection inside you.

♦ Rather than striving for some perfect future life, Zen encourages you to live your life right now.

♦ Humans feel. Acknowledge your feelings so they can pass.

♦ Humans think. Have your thoughts, but don't mistake them for who you are.

Chapter 14

Zen and Your Relationships

In This Chapter

◆ The reasons why we love and argue

◆ Zen advice on your love life

◆ The dangers of expectations and assumptions

◆ Zen dating tips

◆ You don't *need* a partner

You can work on your inner self all you want, but eventually you are going to interact with people. (Even if you are one of those Zen hermits living in a cave in the remote wilderness, you will probably have to go into town occasionally to get supplies.) And even if you try not to interact with people, you are always interacting with something: your environment, your own thoughts and emotions, or your own body.

Life means being in relationship to ... well ... life. But this chapter is about your relationships to others, and more specifically, your love relationships (or your lack thereof!). So what does Zen have to say about living with and loving our fellow sentient beings? Plenty—and not much at all (another Zen contradiction). A Zen approach to relationships won't prevent all future conflict, and it won't give you a magical way to find and immediately secure that one perfect person for you (if there is such a thing). But Zen can help make your relationships better.

Zen and the Art of Love

What is love, exactly? Is it physical attraction? Habit? Comfort? We once heard love defined as (we are paraphrasing) an almost inexplicable affection. Various branches of science have attributed love to hormones, to the subconscious perception of another person's scent, to the psychological need to find someone similar to a parent or a sibling, or to the basic biological urge to procreate.

We won't try to define love for you (although we do like that "inexplicable affection" definition); only you can do that. But we can tell you how to approach the concept from a Zen point of view:

When you are with the person you love, be with the person you love. Just be there. Don't assume, expect, project into the future, or dwell on the past. Just be with that person in total awareness.

That's not so hard, right? Or is it?

This isn't exactly a revolutionary idea, but you might stumble over that "don't expect" part. Don't expect anything? Well, shouldn't you be able to expect certain things from a mate? What about responsibility? Support? Public displays of affection? Or at least a little help with the household chores?

Nope.

Nirvana Notes

A Zen approach to relationships doesn't mean your relationships will be without suffering. It means your acknowledging and feeling the suffering and letting yourself remain open to it so you can understand where it comes from. Be there for the suffering rather than inventing complex devices to avoid it. Only then can you move through it to build something strong or dissolve something unworkable.

Now, before you decide you aren't liking the way this chapter is shaping up and are thinking you might just skip it, bear with us for a minute. We aren't saying you should be long-suffering and your partner should get to do whatever he or she wants. Of course not. In a strong relationship, both people have the same attitude: "I am whole, you are whole, and we choose to go in the same direction together."

This is important. If you are a whole person who can exist as yourself, without needing someone else to "complete you" (sorry, Jerry Maguire) and you can enter into a love relationship with someone else who is also a whole person, you may develop an "almost inexplicable affection" for each other. Then your relationship will be strong. It will be a bridge between two cities under which the river of life can flow freely.

On the other hand, you might be waiting for someone to fix you, help you, make it all better, solve all your problems, save you, and kiss your boo-boos. Or you might be looking for someone you can fix, help, solve, save, and patch up. If you are lucky, you might find someone who fits your profile and is willing to play that game, but we wouldn't drive a car over that bridge. (Can you say "co-dependent"?)

Let Zen Be Your Baggage Handler

Our Zen paradigm for relationships is a lot more difficult than it sounds, of course. We all bring a lot of our own baggage to relationships: fears, hurts from the past, expectations that the relationship will be like or unlike other relationships we've seen or experienced (such as that between our parents or the relationships we've had before). Maybe we have friends in relationships that appear to be perfect and we feel competitive. ("Why can't you be more like Lorenzo? He *always* brings his wife flowers!")

All these feelings are normal human feelings. But they are also just that—only feelings. If you recognize the load you bring to a relationship for what it is and then consciously put it down instead of dragging it around with you everywhere you go, you are taking the first step toward a Zen approach to love.

The next step is to look your potential partner in the eye: "Here you are. Here I am. Let's be together."

Couples get into all kinds of destructive patterns that aren't easily broken. Sometimes one person always asserts an opinion and the other always gives in. Sometimes both are so set on getting their own way to avoid feeling put upon that they argue constantly. Sometimes both are so afraid of offending the other that nothing ever gets done because each is being so polite.

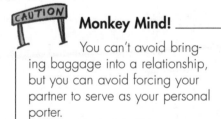

Monkey Mind!

You can't avoid bringing baggage into a relationship, but you can avoid forcing your partner to serve as your personal porter.

How much simpler would it be to just speak what you feel and let all the assumptions and double-speak go?

Now don't get us wrong. The Zen approach to relationships is a process of learning and adjusting perceptions, so chances are, you will still have assumptions as you go. That's a hard habit to break, not to mention a natural human tendency, too. But the trick is to recognize the assumption as an assumption ("Oh yes, there it is again!") then let it go without engaging it or speaking it to your partner. Save your words for the genuine stuff. The more you practice, the more you'll learn to recognize when you're holding on to assumptions.

For example, if your partner says, "You look great today," or "I had a really nice time last night," or "What do you want to do today?" you don't need to say, "What do you mean? Do I usually look bad?" or "What, normally our evenings are a great big bore?" or "Is that your passive-aggressive way of telling me you never get to pick what we are going to do?"

Don't express these ideas even if that's what you're thinking. These thoughts are based on assumptions, not the present moment. You assume you know what your partner was thinking or what prompted the comment, when you can't know either. You might even be right in your assumption, but you'll fuel it if you engage it, and the assumptions will start flying back and forth like tennis balls. Pretty soon neither person will know what the other really means anymore.

Why not just assume what a person says is what he means? It is the safest and probably the most accurate route. People tend to attribute much more to the words of others than is often intended.

So think your human thoughts, no matter how silly, paranoid, or irritable. See them for what they are. Notice your assumptions, your expectations, your mental gymnastics; smile; then let them go.

One Hand Clapping

Our life is like a wheel out of kilter. It's not satisfying. "There's something out there I've got to get. And there's something else out there I've got to keep away from me." This is bondage—this wanting, leaning, craving for something outside ourselves. It comes from that illusory vision of seeing our selves as separate and real. The only choice we have in life is whether or not to be awake .... There isn't anything "out there" that ultimately satisfies. There isn't anything "out there" that we must acquire or repel. In fact, there isn't anything "out there" at all. Nothing enters or leaves the mind.

—From *Buddhism Plain and Simple* by Steve Hagen

Relationship Reality Check

Be present in the moment with the one you love, without assuming or expecting anything.

This simple concept can carry you a long way. You and your partner can build your relationship on communication grounded in the present moment, and you will get much more out of your time together if you are both there, really paying attention to each other and to what you are doing. It might be the only thing you need to know to communicate effectively with the love of your life.

We're not saying you and your partner won't ever have problems, slip up, make mistakes, and have to talk it out, work it out, forgive each other, or maybe even end the relationship. Human life is full of big and small problems, dilemmas, and things that need to be worked out.

But being present for your partner is the greatest gift you can give, and your relationship will develop integrity and a reality. Relationships that are based on false ideas people have of who the other should be or unclear or unrealistic expectations based on an idea or assumption about how relationships should be, will find disappointment when expectations aren't met and confusion and misery if the relationship ends.

> **Nirvana Notes** _____
>
> In Buddhism, the notion of right action involves acting to promote harmony and unity rather than discord and disagreement. That doesn't mean going along with things just to avoid an argument, however. It simply means refraining from allowing your attachments and expectations to cause or further an argument.

Just be there. The rest will work out one way or the other, and realize you can't do anything about your partner's actions or feelings anyway. Sure, you can still remember the past (that spectacular first kiss, that romantic proposal) or envision the future ("Is this the person I'll grow old with?") but keeping one step back from attaching desperately to these memories or projections is the key to letting your partner and yourself be just who you are, separately and together, right here, right now.

Remember that your partner doesn't owe you anything and you don't owe your partner anything. Yet in good relationships, partners choose to give to each other, support and help each other, nurture each other, and love each other. They give without compulsion, without the idea that they are repaying some debt or fulfilling some obligation. They love, not because they are expected to love, but simply because they love. Isn't that nicer?

To move beyond your own ego, past all that stuff you think you "need" from your partner, to a place where you can each become fully developed people traveling through life together—that is the stuff of strong relationships.

If you are present for your partner without expectation, grasping, attachment, or need, you are doing everything you can do. That old cliché about "if you love something, set it free" applies here. Love, and let the rest go. The love will stay or it won't, but you can't force it to stay. Let go, release your grip, and see what happens. Be there. Live it, whatever it is.

Now, if your relationship sounds a pretty far cry from all this enlightened engagement, don't think we're saying you should throw in the towel. "Sorry, Charlene, but you just aren't Zen enough so we have to break up." But it also doesn't mean you must stay in a relationship that doesn't work until you get it right. Again, Zen living is a process of adjustment, a continual starting over and recentering in the now. You can start being present with your partner right this moment. The past is gone. The future, as they say, never comes. Right now is all that matters. Be here now, and start living in your relationship, not hovering over it like an albatross.

Monkey Mind!

Many relationship problems can be worked out between the involved parties, but if you are having serious relationship trouble, such as domestic violence or alcohol or drug abuse, please seek guidance from a social worker, counselor, or licensed mental health professional right away. Help is out there.

Or if this isn't the relationship that fulfills you in this present moment, perhaps you will decide to end it. It's never too late for you to begin again, and you can't control anybody else, anyway. Just be there, awake, alive, present, in your own consciousness and being. You'll have a much easier time discovering what you need to do.

Zen Exercise: Expectation

This exercise is a good one to do with your partner to help you both step back and see your relationship in a more realistic light. Take a few minutes to think about the things that (despite our Zen advice) you expect and assume about your partner. Do you expect him to open doors for you? Do you expect her to do the cooking? Do you assume he will always side with you against his mother? Do you assume she will always order something different from you in a restaurant so you can share? Do you expect respect? A good-night kiss? Do you assume fidelity, support, a listening ear? Big, small, or in between, think about all your expectations and assumptions.

Now, on a piece of paper, each of you draw a line down the center and write "Expectations" at the top of one column and "Assumptions" at the top of the other column. Then, write your list of the things that (even if you feel you shouldn't) you really do tend to expect from your partner and the things that (even if you feel you shouldn't) you really do assume about your partner. Naturally, these lists could be never-ending, so try to keep it to the things unique to your relationship or that are particularly important to you.

After you have finished, in the true spirit of open communication, exchange lists and take a good, hard look at what your partner expects and assumes about *you*. This can open the way for an honest discussion about relationships, but keep your discussion free from expectation and assumption as well. Instead of saying, "What do you *mean* you think I should always do the cooking?" say, "I always assumed you would one day volunteer to cook a meal, but maybe we should both stop assuming that and set up something that makes us both happy." Also avoid saying, "It's okay, honey, you *can* assume I will always kiss you good-night." Instead, say, "I love to kiss you good-night." That keeps it real and doesn't further expectations that could potentially be foiled someday and cause suffering.

You can repeat this exercise every so often just to keep a reality check on your relationship and help raise your relationship awareness about what the other is thinking, feeling, expecting, and assuming.

A Zen Guide to Dating

But what if you haven't found the love of your life yet? What if nothing seems to live up to the cultural perceptions of love you observe in movies and on television? Where is your Meg Ryan or your Tom Hanks? Your Brad Pitt or your Jennifer Aniston? Why can't anyone you meet act even remotely like those movie characters who are so sweet, giving, vulnerable, romantic, and achingly adorable?

Zen can't help you find your "soul mate." Zen can help you find yourself. Whether or not such a thing as a soul mate exists (we tend to think each person has many potential compatible partners, friends and lovers alike), Zen can simplify the process of that search in the same way it simplifies the process of living life:

There is no search.

Being present in the moment means you aren't searching at all. If you're searching for some perfect relationship, you're living in the future, always waiting for your life to start happening. If you are awake to your life right now, you will not only be more likely to recognize people who come into your life who might make potential partners, but you also won't feel that desperate need for them. You will find a joy and contentment, even in your own feelings of loneliness.

Being present in the moment gives you a real, grounded sense about yourself that will make

> **Monkey Mind!**
>
> Our culture does us a disservice by idealizing and simplifying relationships in the media. Relationships are big, complex, and difficult, not the cute, picturesquely resolved scenarios portrayed in movies by perfect kisses and horses galloping into sunsets. Relationships can be ultimately rewarding, but they aren't the solution to loneliness. The solution is within you, not within someone else.

you attractive to people. And when you meet people, if you are really there in the moment, they will notice. Really being there with someone is a great gift.

If you and that person are compatible, you are doing everything possible to further the possibility of a relationship—which is to say you are doing nothing at all. (And you can't force compatibility—trying to be someone you aren't simply doesn't work, at least not in the long run.)

Nirvana Notes

A Zen approach to dating doesn't mean sitting and waiting for love to come to you. You can take action, get out, ask people out, accept when asked, enjoy yourself, or be a social butterfly. The key is to interact with others sincerely and without expectation, really being there in the moment with others.

Zen doesn't have any tricks to getting you dates, getting people to say yes when you ask them out, or getting people to ask you out in the first place. All Zen does for you—and this is a lot—is help you make the most of the beautiful person you are, and help you be present for the moment if a good match for you comes along.

But in the spirit of all those dating and advice books out there, we'll give you a handy little list, just so you can keep all this stuff in mind when you are wondering (as you will, being human) where Mr. or Ms. Right might be.

Here are our 10 Zen rules for dating. Cut out this list, stick it in your wallet, and live it:

♦ Spend time each day in meditation so you can stay in touch with who you are inside.

♦ Remember that you can control only your own actions and your own words, not anyone else's.

♦ Recognize, acknowledge, and release each of your assumptions and expectations.

♦ Speak and act in accordance with your character. A successful relationship is based on truth.

♦ Don't say or do things based on what you think someone is thinking. You have no way of knowing what anyone else is thinking.

♦ Remember that nobody else can fix your life or make you whole. You are already whole.

♦ Recognize your impulse to cling to or attach to someone else. What are you trying to accomplish? You can't own anyone else. Let go. They just might stick around.

♦ You can make plans with a potential partner, but don't attach to those plans. You never know what life will throw at you, and it doesn't do anybody any good to suffer and rage at foiled expectations.

♦ Always listen with an open mind and respond with a generous heart. Wait to speak, and avoid interrupting.

♦ Be genuine, truthful, kind, compassionate, and respectful of your fellow sentient beings, whether you want to date them or not.

How Zen Is Commitment?

Living in the moment might not seem conducive to commitment. Can you practice Zen and make a long-term commitment to someone? How do you commit to the future if you are so busy living in the present?

Make plans but hold them lightly.

If you find someone you love and the relationship makes you feel strong and happy (rather than diminished or compromised) and your partner feels the same, and if the two of you decide to make a commitment, then more power to you. Steer your boats together in the direction of commitment. But remember, commitment means two boats traveling the same river, not one boat with a captain and a passenger, or two captains duking (or *dukkha*-ing) it out for control of the helm.

Nirvana Notes

A Zen approach to a sexual relationship enhances the experience just as it enhances any experience. Be present in the moment, and you will experience the moment fully. Buddhism also advises against allowing sexual desires to control your mind and body. Desire leads to attachment, which leads to unhappiness. To see your desire as a desire separate from yourself can help put it in perspective.

But What If I End Up Single?

Single? You, who always thought you'd be married, or bonded to a life partner who is, of course, the perfect, supportive, kind, generous, loving, affectionate, sexy, drop-dead-gorgeous mate? What about your "happily ever after" plan?

Or maybe you never really thought of yourself as marriage material, but now that you aren't a teenager anymore, people are starting to ask those questions. You know the ones: "When are you going to settle down?" "Aren't you ever going to get married?" "Don't you need to find someone to grow old with?" "Aren't all your brothers and sisters married already?" "What's *wrong* with you?"

Nirvana Notes

The Buddha said, "Be a light unto yourself." This means that only within can you find truth, meaning, and fulfillment. Find your inner light and you will be whole. Your glow will also be irresistible to others.

Or maybe you find yourself unexpectedly single after a long relationship.

Our culture constantly teaches us that we must be in love, or at least in a relationship, to be fulfilled human beings. And where popular culture stops reminding us of this, our families start. But being single is far from being a failure. It isn't even a problem unless we make it a problem. Being single can be a wonderful opportunity.

In fact, Gary and Eve are both single. Gary lives in New York and is surrounded by single people, some happy that way, others "looking."

Over in the middle of the country, Eve also sees lots of people looking, looking, looking—and trying to help her look, too. Never mind that neither Gary nor Eve mind being single. It's actually kind of fun! Sure, being single can be hard sometimes, especially during times when everyone else seems to be happily partnered, or with kids in tow (and people with children have a hard time calling themselves "single" with a straight face). But being single means learning to meet your own needs, to look inward rather than to another person for support and strength. You have the freedom to express yourself in new ways, to change direction, to make plans that are all your own, without having to compromise, debate, discuss, or agree with anyone else.

When it comes to parenting, being single means making the house rules without having to discuss everything first, disciplining in a way that is totally in concert with your own beliefs, and the opportunity to really stretch out in the bed at night. (Unless a child has a nightmare—then there is plenty of room for two!)

Nirvana Notes

Everyone gets lonely. Loneliness has nothing to do with being single or divorced, even though people suffering from loneliness often believe that finding a partner will alleviate their suffering. People in unsuitable relationships are often the loneliest of all.

These days, plenty of people are coming to terms with the idea of living as single people. We are all single people, in a sense, and those of us who feel an urgent need to be partnered might examine why. Being single doesn't mean being lonely or even alone. Single people often have closer relationships with their friends than married people. Some of Gary's married friends tell him he has closer relationships with his friends than they have with their spouses! Being single also means getting to meet lots of different people, discover different kinds of connections, and explore the world of personalities and differences.

But if the best way to find a strong relationship is to be whole, to not need anyone to be whole, then why do it? If you are whole and don't need anyone else, why make a commitment, why get married, why spend all that time "looking"? If being single is so fun, why does anybody want anything else?

Being with a partner does have many advantages. When you feel like a whole person, a good relationship—one that isn't based on need but on mutual respect and support of each person's personal growth—can be a wonderful life enhancer. For some people, life is more enjoyable together than apart when they find someone compatible, going along on a similar path. A life partner provides companionship, affection, love—all nice things to have!

But being with someone just because you think you are supposed to be with someone or because you want them to fill some void in yourself is a shallow substitute for fulfillment.

Marriage, or life partnership, isn't for everyone, and no one should feel he or she "should" get married or commit to someone for life. And just as relationships aren't guaranteed, neither is the single life. Many people find kindred spirits on parallel paths later in life, after they have become completely comfortable with living single.

The key to being happily single is to accept it, embrace it, look for opportunities to make the most of it, and be willing to work with yourself and reach out to others to establish meaningful relationships. When you least expect it, you might fall madly in love. Or you might not. In either case, you can be fulfilled. After all, all you have is right now. Don't waste it worrying about "someday."

The Least You Need to Know

- Humans are social creatures, but because we tend to expect things from each other, we are also constantly at odds.

- Assumptions and expectations can compromise love relationships. Live in the moment with the person you love.

- A Zen approach to dating means keeping in touch with yourself and working to be a whole person while being completely present with others.

- So what if you never get married? Being single means a life full of opportunities for personal growth.

- Whatever your relationships, work to be your own person making the most of your now.

Zen and the Family

In This Chapter

♦ The importance of daily zazen for parents

♦ Ways to be there for your kids right now

♦ Help kids enjoy their families more with Zen

♦ Tackle mixed emotions about caring for aging parents using a Zen approach

Our families see our best and worst sides. Unless we choose to cut off all contact, we are stuck with our families. You can't divorce your parents (a few unusual court cases aside) and get new ones. You can't trade in your kids. Your siblings are your siblings, like it or not, and if you have in-laws, you've got double the family to contend with.

Family certainly has its benefits. Many of us admit fully to loving our families, even if we don't always like them. Families can offer support, guidance, and encouragement. They're your own personal cheering section. They can stand by you when nobody else will, even if they like to offer the occasional nugget of unsolicited advice. They know you better than anybody else because they have known you longer than anyone else and they have lived with you and loved you for your entire life.

The problem with people who know you so well and with whom you've spent so much of your life is that they know exactly who you are. You can't put on an act for them, convincing them you are smarter, more "together," wealthier, or less neurotic than you really are. Your family knows, and if you try to fool them, they won't let you forget your folly.

You might think such an arrangement is great. People know you so well that you don't have to put on an act—wonderful! What a relief! And often (more often for some families than others), relief is exactly what family provides. But at other times, you don't want to be reminded of all your faults or the kind of person you were in junior high. And especially if your family tends to enjoy dispensing advice or criticism, engages in destructive behavior patterns, or showers you with their continual expectations and assumptions, families can be great sources of stress. Joy, sure. A good time? More often than not, perhaps. But also stress.

So what do you do, short of writing everybody out of your will and arranging for your disappearance?

Leave It to Zen

A Zen approach to family can accomplish a lot and—you guessed it!—nothing at all. People in your family might know just how to push your buttons, but although a Zen attitude toward family won't keep your relatives from pushing those buttons, it can have the curious effect of eliminating your buttons. The next time you are with your family, practice mindfulness and nonattachment. Both are key to a successful Zen attitude, as we've discussed before, and both are just as key when cultivating a Zen attitude toward your family.

Let's say that little brother of yours, who doesn't feel like college is for him and just can't seem to "feel comfortable" with any gainful employment for more than a few weeks, rolls off your couch onto the floor, wakes up, and says, "Hey, I hope you're making something good for breakfast."

What do you do? Do you lecture him about getting a job? Do you explain, in a strained tone, that there is nothing left to eat in the house because he already ate it all? Do you tell him to fix his own *#@! breakfast? Do you bomb him with Cocoa Puffs?

Or do you answer his question in this way, "I did make breakfast two hours ago. I guess you'll have to fend for yourself this morning"? Now, it would be easy to infuse such a comment with sarcasm, mock civility, or blatant anger. But none of these would be leaving the situation to Zen. A Zen response would be one without judgment. It would simply be a response—a true response. Zen means speaking truth, but it certainly doesn't obligate you to cook a second breakfast. If you choose not to, just say so. Simple.

Ah, but it's not so simple! Oh, how you long to lecture that do-nothing brother of yours! Oh, how you long to berate him, to show him the error of his ways, to make him see how he is wasting his youth! Family can stir up intense emotions that can feel impossible to control. But we'd like to remind you of a comment we've made many times before in this book: *You can't control other people.* You can't control your brother, so you have all that energy left over to control your own reactions to your emotions, your own behavior, and your own actions. You could just tell your brother that he is going to have to find somewhere else to stay, you could choose to let him stay with you until he figures out what to do with his life, or you could give him a time frame for pulling himself together. But no matter what you decide to *do*, an awareness of how you *feel* about the situation will help you notice but not engage your emotions, keeping them separate from what you decide to do.

But … but … but … are we really *sure* you can't control your family members? Make them *see?* What you do or say might have an effect on what your family members decide to do or say, but ultimately they will do what they are going to do and say what they are going to say. This is tough to remember when you know people so well that you *know* what is good for them. You *see exactly* what they are doing wrong. You can *precisely predict* when they will repeat their mistakes. But it doesn't matter. If someone asks you for advice, sure, knock yourself out. But if you attach desperately to the notion that you can change your family members, you are in for lots of misery and suffering—*dukkha.*

What about when you are on the other end of the lecture? What about your mother or father or great-aunt or grandfather who keeps telling you what you should have done, what you might have been, or what you could have achieved had you only done X or Y or Z? Do you at least get to tell them off, tell them to mind their own business, explain that they can't control you, or make them or coerce them to adopt your Zen approach so you don't have to listen to it anymore?

Afraid not. Once again, you can't control other people, not even when they are trying to control you. But there is a good side to this one: You can't control them, but *they can't control you, either.*

Whether everyone approves of you or not, all you can control are your own feelings, emotions, thoughts, and reactions to your family. That's plenty to keep you busy. Let Zen help you step back from your family relationships and see them more objectively.

You don't have to do what anybody says, even if you have done what people told you to do in the past. You only did that because of your own thoughts and feelings, but ultimately, as with each of us, what you say and do is up to you. Zen can help you stop, breathe, pause, and consciously and deliberately detach from your emotions, allowing you to gain perspective and act with a clear mind and unclouded compassion.

That's being a good family member and a good person. That's also living Zen.

When You're the Parent

Remember that word *now?* When it comes to parenting, this word is (if possible) even more important than it was before.

Eve's two sons, Angus and Emmett, are 8 (going on 16) and 5 (did you know they still have tantrums at that age?). Polite strangers call them "spirited." The rest just glare or leave the room (or complain to the management). Back when Eve still attempted to take her children to restaurants, she would get seated by the kitchen or in the unused banquet room. Now she thanks the universe for drive-thrus. It isn't that her children don't have rules or discipline, but they are young and, as the nice stranger said, spirited.

On the other hand, Eve's kids are also at that charming age where they throw their arms around her with abandon and shower her with "I love you Mommy" kisses. They haven't yet learned to be embarrassed by shows of affection, and as far as they are concerned, the more Mommy they get, the better.

Leaving parenting to Zen doesn't mean focusing only on the good stuff, just as it doesn't mean focusing only on the challenges. The Zen of parenting just means focus, period. Be there for your kids. Live through the chaos and the joy instead of worrying through it about what chaos might be next—peer pressure, junior high, learning to—*gulp*—drive!—or what joys are left behind—that sweet infant smell, those first baby steps, that belief that Mommy knows *everything*.

People assure Eve that things will get easier, but what Eve tries to remember every day is that things don't get any better than this. Parenting right now means being right here, right now for your kids and your family. How could it get better? There is no future to compare with the wonder of now, of focusing on your family in the moment. The best way to help kids reach their potential is to show them you are with them when you are with them, listening, caring, being together, spending time, and respecting what they say and do. Concentrate on the now, and the future will take care of itself.

One Hand Clapping

A Tibetan story tells of two brothers, one with 1 yak, and one with 99 yaks. The brother with one yak was happy. All he needed was one yak. The brother with 99 yaks always worried about keeping track of and managing his yaks, yet he was obsessed with wanting more. One day he asked his brother, "One yak isn't much different than none. I have 99 yaks, but 100 yaks are really something. Will you give me your yak?" The brother easily gave the yak away, illustrating that the more you have, the more you want, and the less you have, the more easily you can give. What a great lesson for kids.

That doesn't mean that you let your kids monopolize your time or control you. Kids have duties, too, like going to school or the baby-sitter, cleaning up their messes, learning to get along with others. They need to learn that other people have needs, too. They will benefit from lessons in compassion, self-discipline, sharing, and respect. You get to teach your children these things.

Nirvana Notes

Being present for your kids teaches them to be present for others. If you aren't there for them, well, that old Harry Chapin song, "Cat's in the Cradle," comes to mind, in which the distant, workaholic father is eventually ignored by his own grown son. His boy turned out just like him.

When you spend time with your children (and we hope you spend a lot of time with them), spend time with your children, don't do something else at the same time, look over their heads at the television, or worry about other things. How often do you catch yourself in the presence of your children but not really there at all, caught up in some long, complex series of adult worries and plans?

Being present with your family might sound easy, but it isn't. We have so much to do and, it seems, so little time. That's why regular zazen is so important, to help keep your mind clear and in good working order. Just try to remember that time keeps passing. You can plan, you can even imagine, but there is much (and we mean *much*) you can't control about the future. Don't waste your present moment. You know that corny old saying, "Right now is a gift. That's why it's called the 'present'"? Kids enjoy figuring out the trick of this saying, and it's a great motto for them to live by, too.

As with any relationship, if you aren't present for those you love, if you don't wake up and experience your family, you will miss it and them. The years will fly by and you'll wonder what happened. How did the kids get so big, so old, so mature? How did the family drift apart? Where did everybody go, and why don't they ever call?

Being a Family

Families are simply a relationship cluster. Whether you live with your entire immediate family in one place or two places, or whether you are spread out over the world, families have to relate to each other, and often they don't do it all that well. Family counselors get plenty of work these days, and even the most well-adjusted family can get into trouble, in much the same way other relationships get into trouble: We expect.

We expect our children to do what we never did, to make the most of their talents and skills, to follow the rules, to stay safe. They don't always do any of it. We expect our spouses to agree with us when disciplining, making rules, and enforcing rules. We expect them to help us present a united front in the face of conflict. They don't always do any of it, either. We expect ourselves to be good spouses, good parents, good providers, and good nurturers. Sometimes we fail.

Monkey Mind!

Teenagers need lots of attention, too, even if they act like they don't want it. While teens develop their identities, figure out the world, and struggle with issues of self-esteem and peer pressure, they require security, consistency, and support. Don't neglect your teen just because it is easy to do! Be present, even in silence, ready to listen without judgment and with an open mind.

What would happen if parents stopped worrying, obsessing, anticipating, and expecting, and just started living? Being present with your family is an amazing feeling. You might find that when you put down the magazine or the book, turn off the television or the stereo, or stop making dinner for a minute and really pay attention to your kids, they stop acting up. "Wow, I think Mom or Dad is really listening to me!"

Or maybe they won't stop acting up, but you won't feel you are missing your precious time together. Someday you really will miss that boundless energy, enthusiasm, know-it-all attitude, even the tantrums. (Well, maybe not the tantrums …)

Nirvana Notes

Parents can try to stop expecting things from their children, but young children must expect certain things from their parents: food, shelter, protection, and love. Taking on the job of a parent means accepting the task of providing for and supporting the physical, emotional, and spiritual development of another human being. Leave your expectations behind, but let your young children have theirs until they are grown and can be self-sufficient.

These days, parents often work long hours, and time with kids is short. "Quality time" often consists of a group television-watching session, which is certainly the least taxing thing to do together after a long day of work and school. But going the easy route with your kids is not being present with them. Being mindful takes effort, but it is an effort richly rewarded.

Being present with your kids can have a miraculous effect on a stressed-out parent. Your irritation, anger, or frustration can melt away in the delight of a precocious comment, the demonstration of a developmental leap, or a sudden opening-up from a child who hasn't shared much lately.

Even if your irritation remains, you can step back and get a perspective on it. "Wow, I'm feeling really irritated. I think I'll let that go for now so I can concentrate on helping build this block tower." "I still don't like that back-talk, but I think I'll just wait to mention it and see what happens if I keep listening."

Now for expectations: It's easy to expect certain behavior from your kids, such as keeping their rooms clean, showing respect to adults, and following house rules. Yet *expectation* isn't exactly the right word to fit these things. You can and probably should have house rules, jobs for everyone, and certain behavioral guidelines. But rather than *expecting* your kids to follow them, make it very clear what happens when they *decide* to follow them, and what will happen if they *decide* not to. You can release expectation but continue to parent by enacting rewards and consequences. Lack of expectation does not mean lack of structure or discipline.

A Zen Approach to Parenting

Any way you look at it, living with others is difficult. You can't do whatever you want to do whenever you want to do it. Living with small children means you won't often have peace and quiet or much time alone—even to take shower. Living with school-age kids can mean they might not be around a lot, but if they are, attempts at communication can be frustrating. (What parent of a school-age child hasn't asked the question, "What did you do in school today?" only to receive the answer, "Nothing"?) Or you might feel you spend your entire life transporting kids from activity to activity. Friends become more influential on your child, and you may feel you exercise little control over your child's behavior (although you probably influence your child's behavior more than you think you do).

Being a single parent, Eve sometimes feels like life is a whirlwind and she spends most of her time trying to dodge the debris. But when she tries to see the debris, she can't pin down any of it. Little of it is solid. There goes a worry flying by; there goes an expectation. Here comes a flurry of anxieties; now a downpour of assumptions.

What if everything that wasn't concrete just blew away? What would be left? A squabble now and then, a few bills to pay, a teacher conference. Time together. Things to do. Discussions, meals, activities, events, trips, stories, bedtime. Nothing to cause any suffering.

And that's what it means to parent the Zen way. Parents worry. We can't help it. We are responsible for these small (or not-so-small) humans, and we know the world can be a dangerous place. To keep it all together, we have to be organized, we have to plan, we have to have lists, and we have to make rules.

Monkey Mind!

Even if Zen has done great things for you, forcing it on your kids could turn them away from a potentially valuable tool for living. Let Zen appeal to your kids through your own example and by answering their questions, truthfully and with compassion, when they ask.

But all these responsibilities of parenting are jobs, the work of life. Everyone has jobs and duties. What makes it hard is all the worry we tend to drape over and around jobs. "What if people don't like my child?" "What if my child gets hurt?" "What if I can't support my child?" "What if his grades are bad?" "What if she doesn't make the team?" "What if my child can't learn to control himself?" "What if she gets in trouble at school?" "What if I'm a bad parent?" "What are other people thinking of me and my children?"

Anxiety, worry, and even—this is a hard one—attachment to our children are the things we can let go of to be better parents. We are the stewards of our children, but we don't own them. We can teach them how to live, what rules will be most beneficial to follow, how to behave, and how to make good decisions. Then we have to let them be people (they'll be their own people anyway, whether we think we are letting them or not).

Zen doesn't give you a magic method for discipline or any other tricks to turn you into Parent of the Year. But it can help you put the whole business in perspective so you can enjoy the complex and amazing task you are accomplishing right now.

You can get to that place where worries and anxieties are nothing more than things you notice, not giant monsters that control you like a puppet. You can stay focused and centered while raising children, but the best (some would say the only) way to get there is to practice zazen every day, even if you think you don't have time (see Chapter 10 for tips on scheduling your zazen).

Even if you fall asleep 10 minutes after the kids do, that's 10 minutes for zazen. Do it before the dishes, before the laundry, before the vacuuming. Do it before climbing into bed with that overdue report or that book you haven't finished for book club tomorrow. Make zazen a priority, a time to practice just being, and you can step directly into the center of that whirlwind where everything is calm, still, and silent. From this vantage, you can watch the debris circling and see it for what it is: just transitory debris. You'll be a better parent.

One Hand Clapping

I'll tell you what it's like if I go to the movies with my daughter: "Mom, you know your taste in movies is just impossible!" And I say, "Well, you're not remembering the one we went to that you wanted to see! What about that?" So, squabble, squabble, squabble .... We do not lose all our particular, little neurotic quirks from practice. Neither my daughter nor I really cares about the movie; but these little squabbling interchanges are what life is all about. That's just the fun of it .... We don't have to analyze it, pick it apart, or "communicate" about it .... It's perfect in being as it is.

—From *Everyday Zen* by Charlotte Joko Beck

Zen Exercise: Values

Do parents practicing Zen set a good example for their kids? Of course! The practice of Zen establishes important values and virtues for children. Teaching kids the Buddha's Five Precepts (from Chapter 8) is a great way to establish values in your household, no matter what other religion you may or may not practice in your family. Yet even more important than teaching these values is *living* them.

Let's look at them again, with an eye for how parents can live these precepts to set a worthy example for their children. Spend some time talking about this list with your children. This can engender some really interesting discussions:

- The destruction of life causes suffering, so I vow to cultivate compassion and learn how to protect the lives of people, animals, and plants, refusing to kill, to let others kill, or to condone any act of killing in action, thought, and lifestyle.

  What to ask your kids: How do you think you could practice nonviolence in your life? No weapon play? No hitting? What about eating meat? Do you think the practice of nonviolence is important in our world?

- Social injustice causes suffering, so I vow to cultivate loving kindness and work for the well-being of people, animals, and plants, refusing to steal and vowing to share my material resources.

  What to ask your kids: Lots of people, animals, and even the environment have a hard time. Can you think of ways our family might help?

◆ *[Note: Save this one for teens!]* Sexual misconduct causes suffering, so I vow to respect my commitments and not to engage in sexual misconduct, and to work to protect others from sexual abuse and the effects of sexual misconduct.

What to ask your kids: How can you respect the people you are in a relationship with? Are there respectful and disrespectful ways to talk about people when it comes to sex? What kind of guidelines do you think are important for you to practice when it comes to physical relationships?

◆ Words can cause suffering, so I vow to speak only with kindness and love and to listen deeply, never speaking words that could cause division and discord but working to avoid or resolve conflict.

What to ask your kids: In what ways are words powerful? How do they hurt or help people? Think about lying, angry words, criticism, and making fun of people. What about telling the truth, being kind, and being sincere? What effect does that have? What are some good ways you could use words that help others instead of hurt others? Are there ways I could use words to help instead of hurt you?

◆ Unmindful consumption causes suffering, so I vow to cultivate good physical and mental health in myself and in society by only eating, drinking, consuming, and paying attention to things that result in physical, mental, and societal peace and harmony.

What to ask your kids: Do you think we eat, drink, spend, or consume too much in our house? How are ways we can consume less and pay attention to more important things? What do you think about moderation?

Raising a family and nurturing children with these values is an excellent way to give kids a value system to hold on to when faced with peer pressure and other challenges of growing up. Couple that with plenty of open, honest, supportive talk about the importance of mindfulness and being true to yourself, and your kids will have powerful tools for living.

Teaching Kids How to Sit in Zazen

As kids get older and aren't completely reliant on their parents to fulfill all their needs, zazen can be a valuable practice. Kids can learn to recognize and discard expectations and assumptions in favor of living in the present moment.

What do kids expect from us? They except some reasonable things such as consistency and fairness. They also expect some other things that might seem less reasonable such as being just like someone else's parents or being "cool." And at the very least, they expect that we won't embarrass them in front of their friends (which we will, whether we mean to or not).

But parents aren't always consistent. They won't necessarily be who kids wish they are. They certainly won't morph into someone else's parents. Parents, too, are who they are, and kids can't control them. Sometimes parents make mistakes. Sometimes they can be a big help because they have a lot of life experience. If kids can recognize this fact, life will be a lot easier.

Practicing zazen and a Zen attitude can help kids develop a better relationship with their parents. They can learn to listen, to communicate honestly, and to work on discovering who they are and who their parents are. Then they can learn what differences there are between them and where the similarities lie. This work of self-discovery is interesting work for teens and pre-teens and a lot more fun than wasting energy being irritated or angry at parents.

Nirvana Notes

Hey kids, a Zen approach to family means learning to be there in the moment with the people you love, listening, communicating honestly, and experiencing your time together rather than wishing you were somewhere else. Your parents will be so surprised when you actually answer the "How was your day?" question with some real details; it will be worth it just to see the looks on their faces!

Sitting in zazen is just as challenging for kids as it is for adults, and zazen is probably too much to expect for most kids younger than grade-school age. Short periods of zazen each day for school-age kids and longer sessions for teens can provide an oasis of calm, quiet, peace, and independence for kids. If zazen develops into a lifelong habit, your child will cultivate presence of mind, mental discipline, perspective on emotions, and mastery of the self. We're guessing your child will thank you later.

Of course, if your child resists sitting in zazen, this is no time to force the issue. Zazen should be something your child chooses to do, not something you force on him or her. The best way to get your child to want to practice zazen is to let your child see you practicing. (Because that grown-up stuff adults do *must* be something special—and in this case, it is!)

Kids will benefit most from zazen if they understand what it is, but the explanation should be relatively simple and appropriate for the age of your child. The best way to explain zazen to young children depends on your child, but we suggest saying something such as, "Zazen is sitting, breathing slowly and deeply, and paying attention" for very young children. Older children can better understand the concept of mindfulness: paying attention to right now, noticing the thoughts and feelings that come along but letting them pass without holding on to them.

Zen for Adult Children

Those of you who are parents are also somebody's child. Eve's parents are card-carrying members of the sandwich generation, caring for their own aging parents, providing much-needed support to their three children, and logging plenty of hours baby-sitting their grandchildren, too. What would she do without them?

Being an adult child, many of us frequently encounter the child within ourselves. No matter how mature we are, no matter how many of our own children we have, no matter how educated or successful we are in our professions, somewhere deep down is a child who still expects things from Mom and/or Dad. Parents make it all better. Don't they?

Gary's parents are older, and he finds it very difficult to watch his parents age—what a reminder of his own aging. And shouldn't he always be able to rely on them? What business do they have relying on him? Whenever he spends time with his parents, he finds himself encountering all kinds of mixed emotions: compassion and resentment and a fear of aging, of death, and of doing without his parents someday.

Monkey Mind!

When you find your parents, your children, or anyone else in your family utterly exasperating, remember that upon his enlightenment, Siddhartha suddenly recognized that everyone has Buddha nature within. In other words, as different as we all are, we are all part of a larger whole. We are all deserving of compassion, and we are all more alike than we might seem.

As we age, ours parents age, too. This can be difficult and can bring up all kinds of unresolved childhood issues. Some of us might have lost our parents at a younger age and have already worked through much of this, but many of the rest of us are just now encountering the first glimmers of recognition: "Wait a minute. When did Dad go completely gray?" "Why is Mom shuffling like that?" "Retirement, so soon?" "What do you mean you joined AARP?" "What do you mean you are too old? You aren't old! If you're old, that means I have to be a grownup!"

Somewhere deep down, did we really think our parents would never get old or that we ourselves would never age? Aren't our parents supposed to be eternally supportive and unerringly protective? How can we be expected to take care of them, especially when we have such busy lives of our own? Worse yet, how can we be expected to live without them?

Even as we know such feelings are selfish, childish, even irrational, they are also natural and common human feelings. And they also have another side. After taking so much from our parents, we might also feel such gratitude that we feel great about being able to give something back, taking care of certain things and caring for our parents as they age. We might also come to recognize that they are handling aging and the new relationship with us in a way that is surprising, baffling, impressive, instructive, or all of the above.

In dealing with our parents, we probably all feel a mixture of emotions—some that make us proud, others that make us ashamed. But a Zen attitude toward life as an adult child with aging parents means to recognize, acknowledge, and feel the whole range of emotions that will naturally arise as these issues arise.

Acknowledge, but don't attach: "There's a thought about what I might have to give up to care for my parents. Now here's a strong feeling of love for them and a desire to take care of them. And now a feeling a fear—if they age and eventually die, I will, too. Now a feeling of resentment that they are abandoning me. Now I'm thinking I can't imagine being without the feeling of security they provide. And now I think of myself as strong and able to help them. They deserve it."

You can work through a lot of these feelings during zazen, practicing to recognize them without letting them engulf you. See them, define them if you can, sit with them a while, then when they are ready to pass, let them pass. Don't force yourself to think "good" thoughts. Just let your thoughts come and go without hanging on to them like a child to a parent's apron strings. Family life in all its manifestations is complex, full of the pleasant and the unpleasant, courage and fear, love and resentment. That's life. Zen helps you live it.

The Least You Need to Know

- A Zen approach to family means remembering you can't control what your family members do or say—no matter how much you want to try!

- A Zen approach to parenting means being present for your children rather than letting worries and anxieties consume your energy.

- The daily practice of zazen will help you maintain a clear head so you can best keep your family running smoothly.

◆ Kids who practice a Zen attitude can learn to be present with their families and even communicate more effectively with their parents.

◆ Adult children of aging parents can learn to recognize and experience mixed emotions of love, compassion, resentment, and fear as their own parents age and require more care.

Desire, Fear, Worry: Tackling Your Personal Dukkha

In This Chapter

◆ You might not really want what you think you want

◆ Master your desires through Zen

◆ Pull the mask off your greatest fears

◆ When worry consumes you

◆ Determining your personal dukkha profile

What do you want? What do you desire? What do you feel you absolutely *have* to have? What about your fears? What scares you? What worries you? What keeps you awake at night? This chapter is all about these questions. In other words, this chapter is all about dukkha, the stuff of human unhappiness, and how Zen can help you dispel the dukkha you call your own.

Consumed by Desire

Desire is a pretty broad term and can apply to many areas of our lives. We desire people. We desire happiness. We desire a half-pound bag of M&Ms or a giant plate of nachos. We desire a hot cup of coffee or a cold beer. Or we desire stuff.

Desire can be an incredibly strong, overriding emotion. You see something and you just *have to have it!* "Oh, that black dress is perfect. *I have to have it!*" "Oh, that double-pepperoni pizza dripping with cheese on that TV commercial looks incredible. *I have to have it!*" "Oh, that incredibly sexy and engaging person at work is irresistible. *I have to have that person!*"

We are a consumerist society in many senses of the word. One might argue that life has, to a high degree, become largely about what we have, what we don't have, and what we are trying to get.

Some would say we are an insidiously consumerist society. What's so bad about having lots of nice products available at reasonable prices? What's so bad about wanting things, wanting people, or wanting happiness?

The problem with consumerism is that its appeal is compelling and its effects on consciousness are subtle but insidious. Since the 1950s, society has gradually become all about advertising and getting things, whether material goods—a classier suit, a cooler car, a larger home, a fancier electronic gadget—or things less tangible but no less real—power, a good feeling, a good buzz, prestige, respect. You could call it lust. We lust for things, people, and feelings. We lust because we think if we only had this or that, things would be better. We desire something better than what we have.

What We Want and What We Think We Want

What exactly do *you* want? More money? More stuff? More prestige? More power? More attention? More time?

Or maybe you want less. Less stress, less anger, less anxiety, less rushing around, less wondering what it all means.

Maybe what you want is noble. World peace. A clean environment. A better future for your kids. A life of dignity. A peaceful passing.

We'd bet just about everybody wants at least some of these things. Is that okay? Is it "attachment" and "desire" to want world peace or a good life for your kids? Sort of.

Being human, we will want things, and we will strive to make things better, whether for noble or ignoble reasons. And wanting things as a part of your life plan is natural.

Even bodhisattvas *want* all humans to experience enlightenment, so they devote their lives to working for that end.

Wanting in itself isn't bad. But your attachment to that wanting makes all the difference. If you are controlled by your desire, then you will suffer. If you put your desires in perspective, if you aren't too attached to them, then you are living Zen. It is unrealistic to expect humans not to want anything. We want, and we want even beyond what we need.

But how badly do you want? How strong are your desires? If you see a brownie in the dessert case and you realize you want it, who's in control, the brownie or you? Are you able to make a controlled decision about whether you will eat that brownie at that moment or not? If you can decide that yes, it's a long way until dinner, you didn't have much lunch, you can afford the extra calories and fat, and that's okay, this time you'll have the brownie. If you decide that no, it's almost time for dinner, you had that big mocha latte for breakfast, and you don't really want to take in all those extra calories and fat *even though the brownie looks really delicious and you want it*, then you are the one in control. No problem. You want, and you recognize it, and you decide what to do about it.

But if you see that brownie and, mocha latte or no mocha latte, dinner or no dinner, you just absolutely have to have it, then the brownie is in control. Or more accurately, your desires are in control.

> **CAUTION**
>
> ## Monkey Mind!
>
> People have become a commodity. Advertisers dress them up and photograph them to sell stuff. The images become a window onto greener pastures (at least the advertisers hope so, and, somehow, perhaps so do we!). Buy this, and you'll be beautiful, rich, accomplished, cool, ahead of the pack—just like the person in the picture. Beware of this attitude! People are people, no matter their circumstance, shape, size, or appearance. Forgetting this is a quick route to a loss of compassion.

For those of you not prone to a sweet tooth, here's another example. When Gary was about 5 years old, he used to go with his mother to her bowling league. Another member of the league had a 4-year-old daughter named Shirley, and in his 5-year-old way, Gary was smitten.

But Shirley didn't want anything to do with Gary. As their mothers bowled, Gary would follow Shirley around the bowling alley, and Shirley would do everything she could to avoid him. He would scoot closer to her, and she would scoot away. He would talk to her, and she would ignore him. Poor Gary's heart was broken. He wanted Shirley's attention. He wanted her adoration.

He got nothin'!

Sometimes you can want something so badly that you can feel yourself becoming somewhat of a stalker or at least obsessed. Have you ever expected an important phone call or e-mail message and called home to check your messages or hit that "check mail" button on your computer again and again and again, oblivious to that old adage that "a watched pot never boils"? We know we have. Maybe it's a job you want, a person you hope is interested in you, or some news about someone you love. When you can't control your impulse to keep checking that e-mail or driving by that person's house "just to see if anybody's home," when you just can't help pulling out your credit card, or when you can't control your urge to keep following little Shirley around the bowling alley despite her obvious lack of interest, your desires are in control.

If you want something, you can steer your boat in that direction. You can lay the groundwork for a promotion or a new relationship or the good fortune of a loved one. You can save your money for a purchase, or you can have a light salad for lunch in expectation of the chocolate brownie. Then you have to relax and remember what you do and don't control.

Nirvana Notes _____

A simple mindfulness trick that works wonders for some people is to write down (1) every penny you spend and (2) every single bite you eat. The awareness this inspires can bring amazing control and clarity to your life. You might find you decide not to buy that gadget *because you'll have to write it down,* or not to eat that extra helping *because you'll have to write it down.* However, recognize if you are beginning to obsess about writing it all down. That's attachment, too.

Let the seeds you've planted come to fruition. Maybe they will; maybe they won't. If you are too attached to the end result and too obsessed with the object of your desire, you just might destroy your chances. Or if things just don't happen to work out the way you had planned, you'll be in for an awful disappointment.

Or if things *do* work out the way you planned, you might find that things aren't as good as you thought they would be (Shirley might have been cute, but who knows whether she would have been a good friend to young Gary). Maybe you'll find you didn't really want what you thought you wanted because you were seduced into thinking you wanted it through cultural pressure or the efforts of others (such as clever advertisers with multimillion-dollar budgets).

Or maybe you'll be so obsessed with the *next* thing you think you want that you won't be able to enjoy the *last* thing you wanted when you finally get it.

See how desire leads only to suffering? Nothing is ever as good as intense obsession leads us to believe it will be. But if you wait patiently, go with the flow, do your best, and let things happen the way they will, when good things happen, you'll be in for a lovely time.

A Zazen Cold Shower

Oh, but it is so hard not to desire in a society like this, with so much available, with chocolate brownies and sexy people and lovely clothes and cool cars and spacious houses and amazing gadgets everywhere! How does a desire addict get through the day with so much temptation around?

Think of zazen as your cold shower. Sitting in zazen every day can help break the spell of desire. Train your mind to sit and focus, not on stuff, not on what you want, but on the unadorned you. By focusing on the blank wall in front of you, on the breath (which doesn't cost a thing), and on your own perfect self that doesn't need anything else, you can beat desire.

Remember the Buddha's third noble truth? Suffering can be eliminated by eliminating desire. It's true. Let go of the stuff. Let go of the grasping and the wanting and the *absolutely-have-to-having*, and you'll feel an amazing, uplifting sense of freedom.

But you have to do it every day! Otherwise, your desires can get a stronger foothold. Remind yourself through your daily zazen how fulfilled you already are, and you'll have a clearer, easier perspective about all those things out there you think you want. You'll see how much you don't really need it. You'll learn to feel good about what you have and even enjoy finding ways to get by on less. And we're guessing you'll start feeling much more content. (We certainly do!)

One Hand Clapping

In Eve's favorite simplicity book, *The Simplicity Reader*, Elaine St. James suggests a great technique for stopping indiscriminate buying: the 30-day list. If you find yourself experiencing that irresistible urge to buy something, pull out your list (keep it in your wallet) and write down the date and the item you think you want. Put it away. Walk out of the store. One month later, take the list out and look at the item. Do you still want it? Do you still think you need it? If you do, consider buying it. Chances are, you'll wonder why you ever thought you needed that whatcha-ma-giggy, and you won't have wasted your hard-earned cash.

Things That Go Bump in the Night

Desires aren't the only things we attach to. Many of us also attach—cling with white knuckles—to our fears. We don't just mean phobias. Plenty of people have a slight fear of heights or spiders or small spaces or public speaking, but these fears usually don't interfere with their lives.

Other fears might be easily repressed, hidden, or even socially acceptable but are more insidious: fear of failure, fear of success, fear of embarrassment, fear of gaining weight, fear of growing old, fear of losing a loved one. If you've ever sabotaged your own success without exactly knowing why, avoided a social event you know would probably be fun, or found yourself wide-eyed in bed at night at 3 A.M. imagining all the horrible things that could possibly happen to your children or your partner or your parents or friends or even yourself, you know what we mean.

Fear is a natural instinct that, like the craving for high-fat foods, has always played an important role in survival for humans (and for any animals). If none of our ancestors were afraid of saber-toothed tigers or grizzly bears or their large, angry, cave-dwelling neighbors with clubs, humans probably wouldn't have survived into the twenty-first century. But here we are, due in part to a healthy dose of fear instinct.

We teach our kids to fear things at an early age: cars, strangers, drugs, and guns. We do this to protect them. Children also have plenty of fears of their own. Remember your childhood nightmares? Children typically have more nightmares than adults do, and these scary dreams are often very intense and memorable into adulthood: falling; being chased; or being attacked by wild animals, monsters, bogeymen, or ghosts.

Instinct aside, why do we fear things that have no apparent benefit to our survival? Sure, the world is full of danger. But we aren't going to die if we have to stand up in front of a group of people and say a few words. We aren't going to be injured by a promotion or even by getting fired. Chances are good that none of the bizarre things you imagine might happen to your children or grandchildren or parents will actually happen.

And what about natural disasters and random violence? Sure, these things do happen sometimes and always have. These things might be more widely publicized today and broadcast again and again in the media, and yes, they can frighten us and even hurt us and those we love. Yet there isn't much you can do about them. Such things have always been a part of life, even if they change in character from decade to decade, century to century.

As a result of the World Trade Center disaster on September 11, 2000, New Yorkers, along with the rest of America, are now aware of potential dangers that we never expected we would face in our own country. We have all been educated about the potential for terrorism, not only in tall buildings, but in airports and in the air, in stadiums, on public transportation … in virtually any situation where people are gathering in groups. Does this mean we must stay in our homes, well-stocked with candles and water and a cell phone? If we listen to the media, especially when an "orange alert" has been issued, we certainly might assume that living is all about isolation and fear.

Living paralyzed by fear of random violence or natural disaster is no way to live. Maybe you fear death. Death is an unknown, of course, but you certainly can't prevent it. If it isn't happening to you right now, focus instead on your "right now." You are alive right now. Let yourself live in that precious present moment, and you won't ever feel you've wasted the life you have.

Yet such an attitude is difficult, and many of us persist in our fears. What do we do when our fears actually impede our functioning? How can Zen help?

The Source of Fear

Fears can come from many places. Perhaps a traumatic childhood event has sparked certain fears. Maybe knowing you are responsible for others makes you afraid. Maybe those who were once responsible for you failed in their job of keeping you safe, and now you fear you will make the same mistake. The failure or success of a parent or friend might influence your fears about your own career or life.

Zen can offer you a helping hand. You might not like the Zen method for fear management, but it works:

You need to feel your fear.

Just as you need to sit and experience other strong feelings that come your way, so, too, do you need to sit and experience your fear. Step into it instead of running away from it. It just might deflate and reveal itself for exactly what it is.

Sometimes fears are really excuses for not facing other issues. Maybe you get caught up in some intrigue at work, such as a terrible fear that others are plotting against you. Maybe you are obsessed with the safety of your children and are filled with fear because you are convinced they won't be safe unless you are with them all the time. Maybe you are terrified that the person you love will cheat on you or won't love you back.

What is really going on? You can gain insight by sitting and experiencing your feelings. Maybe you want more responsibility at work but are afraid to face success so you distract yourself with fear. Maybe you are afraid you aren't an adequate parent, so you obsess about your fears for your children. Maybe you are afraid to face the fact that you are no longer in love with your partner, so you concentrate instead on fears that your partner is no longer in love with you. Or maybe you never faced the breakup of your own parents, so instead, you fear the imagined breakup of your own relationship or fear even taking the risk of getting into a relationship at all.

> **CAUTION**
>
> **Monkey Mind!**
>
> Only you can uncover the source of your fears, but you might not be able to do it alone. If your fears are seriously hindering your happiness, success, or daily existence, we strongly encourage you to talk to your primary care physician or seek out a licensed mental health professional. You *can* overcome your fears.

The possibilities, of course, are as limitless as there are fears on the face of the earth. But considering that your fear might be masking something that is emotionally risky for you can open doors to self-realization. It means facing the unfamiliar, the repressed, the stuff you really, really don't want to face.

But choosing to sink into unwarranted fear rather than face truth is like paddling against the flow. You're stuck midstream, when the current could be taking you to a new and better destination. Sit with your fear. Look at it. Stand back from it. Think about it. Imagine you are a bystander. Analyze it. Where might it come from? Then open yourself to the greater lesson, the truth about yourself. If you stop clinging so tightly to your fears, they might just float away. If you look your fear in the eye, you might find there isn't much to it.

Pull Off the Mask

The key to a Zen approach to fear is to step into your fear and sit with it until you reveal it for what it really is. Most things aren't quite as scary as you imagine they will be when they are unmasked. Like Fred or Velma at the end of a *Scooby Doo* episode, you can pull the mask off what scares you and see it for what it really is. Why, it's just Old Man Jenkins, masquerading as a zombie!

Eve remembers several recurring nightmares in childhood when she was suddenly able to turn around, look the monster in the eye, and say, "Hey! You're just a dream!" Naturally, the monster, so recently fearsome, slunk away, utterly abashed. Eve also had a recurring dream about being stuck in a car that was rolling down a hill. One day (when she wasn't dreaming), 6-year-old Eve asked her father where the brake pedal was. He showed her. The next time she had the dream, she knew just what to do. She pressed the brake pedal, the car stopped, and the dream never returned.

Remember, you are the master of yourself. Your fears are just thoughts and feelings. They aren't you. They don't define you. Just like all your other thoughts and feelings, they are simply something you have, possessions. You don't have to let them own you. You can put them in their place. You can recognize them, and with a calm but firm demeanor, tell them they are no longer allowed to disrupt your inner household. Eventually, unfed by your energy, your fears will leave you. What will be left? You, unafraid.

That's not so scary.

One Hand Clapping
According to James H. Austin, M.D., in his book *Zen and the Brain,* feelings of fear are based in the brain's almond-shape amygdala, located near the inside tip of the temporal lobe. This area of the brain influences learning based on negative results such as behavior resulting in physical or verbal punishment, and to a lesser extent, learning from positive experiences such as behavior rewarded with a treat. In other words, dramatic, stressful events and negative experiences generate fear because of the amygdala. Injuries to or injections of drugs into this area of the brain can result in a total loss of fear.

Worry: The Real Ball and Chain

Worry, worry, worry. We all do it. We have so much to do, but like a car stuck in the mud, we spin our wheels with worry. Worry is the real ball and chain we drag around with us, as we wonder why we aren't moving very fast or getting anywhere.

Why do we worry? Maybe we think that worrying about something proves we care. Or maybe we think if we worry about things, we can somehow prevent them from happening. How? By the little vibrations our worries surely make in the atmosphere? Of course not.

Worry might be an intense and prevalent part of your life, but the Zen approach to worry is simple:

Let it go.

That's easier said than done, of course. What, not worry? Not worry that I won't have enough money to pay the bills this month? Not worry that my child might get a D in social studies? Not worry that my boss might not like my latest analysis? Not worry that I might not get accepted to the college of my choice? Not worry that my car might break down on the trip to Disney World? Not worry that I might get a nasty cold just before the holidays and be unable to keep up with all the necessary hoopla? Not worry that my mother is starting to forget things, that my father is losing interest in his job after 40 years, or that my grandmother isn't feeling well? Not worry that my dog is scratching her ear a little too often and might have fleas that will infest the whole house? Not worry that if I call the exterminator, he'll spray pesticides everywhere and we'll all die of some horrible chemical-induced disease nobody has discovered yet?

Stop the madness! Worry might be worth the effort—and that's a big *might*—if worry actually helped. But pay attention:

Worry doesn't help.

Worry will have no effect on the outcome. Worry won't bring in more money this month. It won't keep the car from breaking down. It won't keep you from getting a cold. (In fact, the immune-suppressing effect of worry may actually make you more susceptible to cold germs.) It won't be therapeutic for your aging parents. It certainly won't prevent a flea infestation.

Monkey Mind!

Worry raises your blood pressure, induces the production of stress hormones, knots your muscles, and makes you feel lousy in general. Chronic worry is stressful. It depresses your immune system, which could have a wide range of negative effects on your physical, emotional, and mental health. In other words, worry isn't good for you.

We don't expect you to just stop worrying, because that's not so easy. But we are saying that you can see your worries when they just get started, recognize them as worries, label them, and let them go. Attention feeds worry until it grows so out of control that it takes over your life. So cut it out! Quit hanging on to those worries. Look at them, say hello, then bid them *adieu*. You might not even realize how often you worry, but if you practice zazen every day, you'll be able to see your worries more clearly. You'll get to watch them rattle and bounce around inside your head. This is the time to step back and really watch them. How kinetic they are, like little bugs buzzing around and bumping into each other. What a frenzied chaos it is. Why would anybody want to hang out in that place?

When you begin to see your worries from a more objective place and see that they don't actually help, you can learn to let them go. But it takes time. Chronic worrying is an addictive habit.

One way to quit worrying is to become more solution-oriented. Work on things you can actually do to resolve situations that worry you. Organize your finances. Have the car serviced. Go to bed earlier and eat better so you will be less likely to catch a cold. Use preventive pest control on your dog.

Of course, you can't control most worries, and letting go is the hard part. But we've talked a lot about how little we actually control. Remember your river. Go with the flow, and leave your worries behind, like one of those little clouds of bugs that buzz around together in one spot during the summer. That cloud won't follow you down the river. Leave your worries back there over the rapids. Just steer your boat in the right direction, and pay attention. It's really all you can do, and yet, it's a lot.

Worry Myths

We can tell you to stop worrying all day long, but again, we recognize how difficult it is. So let's look at some worry myths to help inspire you to break your worry habit:

- If I worry about something, it won't happen. *Wrong!*
- If I worry about something, I'll cause it to happen. *Wrong!*
- Worry shows I care. *Wrong!*
- Worry helps. *Wrong!*
- Worry is productive. *Wrong!*
- Worry equals love. *Wrong!*
- Worry will keep me better organized. *Wrong!*
- Worry will increase my awareness of danger. *Wrong!*
- Worry makes me a conscientious person. *Wrong!*
- Worry makes me a person. *Wrong!*
- If I don't worry, I'm heartless. *Wrong!*
- If I don't worry, I'm not a good parent/child/sibling/friend. *Wrong!*
- If I don't worry, bad things will automatically happen. *Wrong!*
- If I don't worry, others will have to worry. *Wrong!*
- If I don't worry, I won't get the job done. *Wrong!*
- If I don't worry, I'll be out of the loop. *Wrong!*
- If I don't worry, my whole life will fall apart. *Wrong!*
- You mean … worry is a waste of precious life energy? *Right!*

Monkey Mind! _____

> Do you worry obsessively about something you actually *could* do something about—disorganized finances, an extra 5 pounds, a failure to exercise, a disobedient toddler—but don't do anything about it because you are too exhausted from worrying? If so, you are letting your worries control you. You need to take the reins. Don't waste your energy on worrying. Spend it on things you can actually do something about.

If worry is ruling you, then despite knowing these myths are just that—myths—you aren't living that knowledge. If you rule your worry—if you recognize it for what it is, acknowledge it, put it in perspective, and refuse to let it control you—then you are cultivating a Zen perspective on worry.

Your Zen Bolt-Cutter, Bug-Swatter, Worry-Buster

The regular practice of zazen and the mindful cultivation of a Zen attitude are all you need to cut yourself free from the worry ball and chain, swat that cloud of worry bugs, and deflate the worry monster. You might need to do it time and time again, but that's the business of being human. When worry overcomes you, learn to recognize the signs: distraction, obsession, repetitive thoughts, insomnia, compulsive eating, and nervous behavior. If you recognize yourself doing these things, step back, sit down, and watch what is going on inside your own head.

Like materialism and compulsive buying, worry is a habit. You can break the habit, even if it seems that today, worry largely defines who you are. It isn't true. You are uniquely you, and worry has nothing to do with who you are. Worry is distracting you from your true self. Your true self is much more worthy of your energy than a lot of little worry bugs. You can master your worries, it just takes practice. Let zazen rid you of that ball and chain. Life will be much easier.

Zen Exercise: Name Your Dukkha

Everyone has an individual dukkha profile. Some people don't worry much, but they have a nasty habit of spending, buying, and acquiring things they don't really need but think they want. Others are good at avoiding materialism, but they are plagued by fear. Others seem patently unafraid but are ruled by lust—for power, for sex, or for wealth.

What are your particular attachments? You can tackle your dukkha more easily if you know where it hides. Answer the following questions to determine your personal dukkha profile. Each question asks about certain triggers for desire, fear, and worry. Explore your own personal feelings about each issue. Some you might not care about, and others you might find yourself writing furiously about, so don't be constrained to these few lines. Copy the questions into your journal or onto your computer, and go for it. Look for where your passions lie. Therein, chances are, your dukkha lies, too:

◆ This is how I feel about money:

_____

_____

_____

◆ This is how I feel about my partner:

_____

_____

_____

◆ This is how I feel about sex:

_____

_____

_____

◆ This is how I feel about having nice things:

_____

_____

_____

◆ This is how I feel about power and influence:

_____

_____

_____

◆ This is how I feel about my social status:

_____

_____

_____

◆ This is how I feel about my friends:

_____

_____

_____

◆ This is how I feel about my children:

_____

_____

_____

◆ This is how I feel about food:

_____

_____

_____

◆ Everybody knows I am afraid of …

_____

_____

_____

◆ I don't like to admit it, but I am also afraid of …

_____

_____

_____

◆ My biggest sources of worry are …

_____

_____

_____

Enlightening? We hope so. Now, go back over your list and circle the keywords—the words that spark your most intense feelings of desire, fear, or worry. Where does your dukkha lie? Make a short list, and keep it for reference. If you know where your dukkha lies, if you have named it, you can be on the lookout for it. This is what stands between you and a happier, more serene, more fulfilling life. Now you can be ready to foil your dukkha with your Zen attitude.

By now, you should have a more personal picture of how Zen can work in your life. In Part 5, we'll start to apply Zen to an area of life that is important for most of us. Whether we call it a job, career, profession, trade, or great big burden, it is that thing we do during the day to earn a living.

The Least You Need to Know

- ◆ Desire is the source of suffering, but Zen can deflate your desires.

- ◆ Desire can make us want things, even when we know we don't really want them!

- ◆ Fear can debilitate our functioning, but Zen can help pull the mask off the things that scare you most.

- ◆ We are a society of worriers, but worry is an unproductive expenditure of energy.

- ◆ Once you determine your personal sources of dukkha, you can master your desires, fears, and worries with the regular practice of zazen and a Zen attitude.

Part 5

Zen in the Workplace

Who are you at work? Are you the same person you are at home with your family or alone in meditation? Work is a major part of most of our lives, and in Part 5, we'll help you make your job your own with a Zen approach. Make your work meaningful, or find work that is meaningful. Learn how to be a great employee or a great boss. Zen can help you maintain effective work relationships, too.

Even for those who adore their jobs, most work is stressful, at least some of the time. A Zen approach to job stress, time management, and putting your work life in perspective can make all the difference. We'll end by discussing your career path. Can you be ambitious and still practice Zen? Are you doomed to a static career path, or can you be a mover and shaker between zazen sessions? (Hint: Let go of that career ladder and ascend anyway!)

Chapter 17

Buddha in Your Cubicle

In This Chapter

- ◆ You aren't your job
- ◆ Lose your mind (and your ego) for career success
- ◆ Detach and see more clearly
- ◆ Practice desk zazen

Americans tend to define themselves by what they do. Whether CEO, small business owner, or work-at-home mom, the primary way many of us define ourselves, no matter our gender, no matter our profession or job, no matter whether our occupations make us proud or ashamed or excited or weary, is through our work. "What do you do?" is still one of the first questions we ask people we meet.

But are we really *what we do?* Considering how much time most Americans spend at work—about 2,000 hours a year, more than most of us spend sleeping—it sure can seem like we are what we do. That might seem fine to us if we love our work and depressing if we don't, but either way, is it true? Are we what we do?

Of course not. Financial concerns aside, you can quit your job any time. You can decide to change professions. You can even be unemployed, but you can't quit or change or get rid of who you are inside, that essential you. Who you are might influence which profession you choose, but your job isn't you.

Why is it important to remember that you aren't your job? And what can Zen do for you on the job? Zen can help you make the most of your skills, get the deepest level of satisfaction from your work life, and, perhaps most important, put your chosen employment in perspective. You do your job. You aren't defined by it. And yet, in Zen, doing and being ultimately merge. Where does that leave us? Is this another Zen paradox? Let's consider.

Get Out of the Box

Whether we love our job or complain about it constantly (or both), work is a big part of life for many of us. Some of us have jobs that keep us busy, fulfilled, and satisfied, even if they aren't the jobs we once envisioned ourselves having. Some of us don't care much for our jobs but hold them because we need to make a living. Some of us have multiple jobs: jobs at an office or at a home computer coupled with a job as a parent, caregiver, volunteer, writer, artist, actor, consultant, or any number of other duties.

Most of us have also experienced times when we become one with the work we do. We become so focused and immersed in our work that time seems to pass without our notice, and when we come out of that "zone," we find we've done something really great. This kind of Zenlike immersion is a productive way to work, but it still doesn't mean we are our jobs. We can be our doing, but not what we do.

What's wrong with defining ourselves by our work? Is Gary a psychologist? Is Eve a writer? Are you what you do? Yes … and no. No matter how much we immerse our-selves in our job, defining our self by our job puts us in a box. It sets up preconceived notions about personality, values, interests, social status, financial status, and level of education. A doctor? Oh, she must be smart. A lawyer? He must be rich! A kinder-garten teacher? She probably doesn't make much money, but I bet she is patient and gentle. A construction worker? He must not be educated, but he is probably pretty strong.

As much as we try not to assume things about people based on their jobs or anything else, the cultural pressure to make such assumptions is compelling. Labeling people—even ourselves—by what we do sets us up to start expecting, assuming, and all those other things that keep us from living in the present moment.

But how do we get out of that box? Most of us already live in there, rattling around with our ideas of who we are and who others are. Can Zen help us open the lid and jump out to see the box for what it is? Sure it can. Zen can help us step back and dis-engage from our dearly head notions about work, so we can see them for what they are: notions, only notions.

We will continue to recommend daily zazen as a good way to practice disengaging from expectations and assumptions, but let's consider some other ways, too. One way to foil our own tendencies to make assumptions is to recognize them. Dissect them.

To help you uncover your own tendencies to assume things about work, try the following exercise. After each profession, write a few words about what you would assume about someone were you to meet him and find out he had each of the following jobs. Avoid stereotypes if you don't really believe them. For best results, be honest with yourself.

- Doctor: _____
- Lawyer: _____
- Teacher: _____
- Secretary: _____
- CEO: _____
- Day-care provider: _____
- Insurance agent: _____
- Artist: _____
- Car salesperson: _____
- Fast-food restaurant manager: _____
- Scientist: _____
- Psychiatrist: _____
- Writer: _____
- Telemarketer: _____
- Accountant: _____
- Factory worker: _____
- Stockbroker: _____
- Waitperson: _____
- Minister, priest, or rabbi: _____

◆ Work-at-home parent: _____

◆ Unemployed person: _____

Now, look carefully at each of your assumptions. Don't skip a single one. Where do your preconceptions come from? Are you influenced by someone you know who has that particular job? Stereotypes you've seen on television or in the movies? Things you've heard other people say?

Think about what each of your assumptions about the professions listed says about you, and also think about what effect your assumptions will have on how you treat someone who has any of those jobs. Are you more dismissive to a waitperson than to a CEO? Is that the right way to act? Are you more willing to strike up a conversation with an artist than with an accountant? Think about the ways your preconceptions could limit your relationships with others and also how your assumptions could limit your perception of truth in your daily life.

Nirvana Notes

Next time you meet someone, try not to ask what he or she does for a living so you can remain unbiased. Find out other things about the person first. You might find the person is so surprised you haven't asked about his or her occupation that he or she feels compelled to volunteer the information!

Finally, go back through each statement and ask yourself: What if this isn't true? Then what is? What kind of possibilities open up for human connection and understanding?

Everyone is an individual, and we are all human. Why disregard someone or give him a particular reverence because of a profession? Think outside the box. Let each individual be new to you. And also, let each individual be familiar—a fellow spirit, another sentient being, each equally worthy of respect, reverence, compassion; each a little like you in some way; each also fascinating in his or her differences. Live in each moment of learning about your fellow humans, and you will get the most life out of your time … and the most Zen into your life.

Don't Fence Me In!

Just as you might tend to put other people in a box according to their jobs or professions, you might do the same thing to yourself. But you know yourself much better than you know the person you just met this afternoon. How can you make stereotypes about yourself? It might seem silly, but we all do it.

Have you ever heard someone say something self-deprecating such as "I'm only a receptionist" or ego-ful like "I'm the top orthopedic surgeon in the tri-state area"? One job might make more money than the other, but what does that have to do with the internal worth of each individual holding those respective jobs?

Nothing, that's what. Perhaps the receptionist is a warm, caring, compassionate human being who spends her time away from work caring for her family and volunteering her time to help others. Perhaps the orthopedic surgeon spends his spare time on his yacht refusing to make eye contact with the hired help. Who is more immersed in life? Who is living more in the present moment? Who feels more content with who they are?

Perhaps the receptionist is the one who refuses to be compassionate, helpful, or giving, and the orthopedic surgeon spends his spare time volunteering at the free clinic and donating money to worthy causes. You never know. Who each person is has to do with who he is. That's all. A job might reflect the inner person, and the way each person does his or her job probably reflects the inner person, too, but the job doesn't create the inner person. It is the other way around. The inner person manifests itself on the job.

What do you assume about yourself because of your job? Take a few minutes to consider this question. Think about what positive things you assume about yourself because of your job and what negative qualities you think you have *because of your job*. Are you personable because you are a receptionist, or are you a receptionist because you are so personable? Are you dexterous and smart because you are a surgeon, or are you a surgeon because you are so dexterous and smart?

Nirvana Notes

According to the www.betterworkplacenow.com Workplace 2000 Employee Insight survey of 1,105 people in a variety of professions around the country, 89 percent of those surveyed are proud of their jobs and 72 percent say they do important work most or all the time. Only 5 percent report that their jobs are mostly or entirely busywork.

See how looking at these qualities one way means making assumptions, while the other way is a statement of fact? To say you are creative because you are an artist is an assumption about who and what you are. To say that you chose to become an artist because of your inner creativity is simply a statement of fact. Think carefully about how you define yourself in this way and see if you can keep it to "just the facts, ma'am."

Now, imagine someone meets you and doesn't know what your job is. How would he describe you? Do you think his description would change if you told him what you do for a living? Do you feel compelled to tell people what you do, to make sure they get the "right impression"? Or do you try to hide what you do so they won't get the "wrong impression"?

We won't dispute that what we do does have a major impact on our lives, and whether we like it or not, our jobs can impact our personal lives as much as, if not more than, our home life does. But an important first step in embracing a Zen approach to our work lives is to see beyond the job, beyond the label, beyond the preconceptions you put on the people to whom you ask the question, "What do you do?"

And of course, seeing beyond the preconceptions you put on yourself is equally crucial for an accurate and fulfilling sense of self. "I'm a so-and-so, so I guess that makes me this-or-that." Zen corrects this automatic thinking by calling our attention to it: "Oh, there I go, thinking that about myself again." Then, Zen helps us see more clearly: "I do this. That's all. Here I am, being. Doing. That's all."

Having a job doesn't make you anything except employed.

Nirvana Notes

Have you heard the phrase "in the zone," referring to that state of mind when challenging tasks—running a sprint, playing the piano, delivering a speech, sailing through the air to dunk that basketball—appear effortless, even though onlookers know what they witnessed was anything but easy? In these moments, the athlete, the artist, the speaker, the *doer* becomes one with the work. Without distinction, there is no difficulty.

No-Mind Your Own Business

Even though we might come to understand that our work is just what we do, Zen can also help us accomplish this doing with more focus and concentration, making our doing more rewarding and effective and even more skillful. One way Zen helps us with our work is to help us get our minds out of the way.

In books on Zen Buddhism, "no-mind" is a term often applied to an appropriately Zenlike mental state. To have no-mind is to see past the limitations of thinking and feeling. As Dr. James H. Austin observed in his book *Zen and the Brain*, we Westerners tend to believe the phrase (thanks to the French philosopher René Descartes) "I think, therefore I am," or, in other words, that to think is to be. Yet Zen proclaims: To *stop* thinking is to be.

Just Let Go and Focus

What good will that do you from 8 to 5 each day? Not think? What, should you just sit at your desk drooling? No, no, that's not what we mean at all! Having no-mind means letting go of your ego, that part of you that gets between you and your work. When you are completely focused on what you are doing, you become your doing, escaping that fixed picture you have of yourself as a "somebody," not to mention that fixed picture you have of all the other people in your work environment.

When you let go of your preconceptions about yourself, your life, and your work, you'll find that your mind expands. Suddenly you have a lot more room in there! Say you're working on a project. How many ways is your brain moving? As you work on your project, are you thinking about the other projects you haven't finished, the projects you will start next week, and all those other personal projects you have to work on? Or are you completely at one with the task at hand, so much that everything else goes away for a while?

Learning to focus on your work (whether floor mopping or rocket science, it makes no difference) is the best way to do your work better. Learning to focus to the extent that self dissolves and you and the work become one—now that's where Zen comes in. That is no-mind.

In the book *Zen and the Art of Motorcycle Maintenance* by Robert Pirsig, the main character describes how much harder it is to do a job (in this case, climbing a mountain—an apt metaphor for any number of challenging tasks) when your work is based on ego as opposed to losing yourself to the job. Ego-climbing, as Pirsig calls it, is not only less efficient but also far less rewarding:

> The ego-climber is like an instrument that's out of adjustment. He puts his foot down an instant too soon or too late. He's likely to miss a beautiful passage of sunlight through the trees. He goes on when the sloppiness of his step shows he's tired. He rests at odd times. He looks up the trail to see what's ahead even when he knows what's ahead because he just looked a second before. He goes too fast or too slow for the conditions and when he talks his talk is forever about somewhere else, something else. He's here but he's not here. He rejects the here, is unhappy with it, wants to be farther up the trail, but when he gets there, he will be just as unhappy because then it will be "here." What he's looking for, what he wants, is all around him, but he doesn't want that because it is all around him. Every step's an effort, both physically and spiritually, because he imagines his goal to be external and distant.

To learn to focus so completely that you and your work are the same thing erases innumerable barriers and difficulties. If you and your work are one, if you become the work and the work becomes you, there is no conflict, no difficulty, no external distant goal, only this step, that step, this "here."

"But I'm Just a _____"

"Hold on a minute," you might be saying to yourself. "That's all fine for something grand like mountain climbing, but I'm a just a _____ *(fill in the blank)*." Yes, we know what you mean. But listen, becoming absorbed in your work isn't contingent upon the nature of your work. In Zen, any work is worth total absorption, even tying your shoe or reorganizing your filing system.

In some jobs, it can be hard to feel like what you do is worth total absorption. You might find parts of your job tedious, meaningless, or just not all that important. Rather than focusing on what a small cog you are in such a big wheel (or what a small cog you are in such a small wheel), you might shift your perspective and consider your contribution to the whole—not just a whole office or company, but the whole interrelated world. If you invest yourself in every moment and aspect of your work, even if you don't always think the work worthy of your time or you don't exactly know or understand the details of your contribution, you are moving to a more Zenlike space.

One Hand Clapping

An old Zen story tells of a butcher cutting up an ox. People watched in awe as the butcher's knife flashed quickly and effortlessly, never hitting bone or sinew but gliding easily through the meat. The ox seemed to fall apart. An admirer once asked, "How can you cut up the ox so easily? Most butchers expend great effort hacking and sawing the thing apart." The butcher replied, "I have used this same knife since the beginning and it remains sharper today than ever because it moves only through the spaces of no resistance." In other words, find the flow inherent in the work and follow it, rather than imposing your own order upon it. Your knife will glide much more easily.

Of course, getting to that place where you can become totally absorbed in your work, without letting the "Oh this is stupid" or "What a waste of time" or "Why do I have to be here?" get in the way doesn't just happen on command. The more you discipline and train your mind through zazen, the more easily you will be able to access that place where your focus becomes so complete that you and all your "characteristics," "skills," "tendencies," "qualities," and "problems" dissolve.

Zazen is crucial training for the kind of absorption that can really make the difference between job apathy and job satisfaction, as well as the difference between a so-so employee and a really important, talented, and valuable employee. Zazen trains your brain, making concentration and focus easier. In this way, zazen is serious training for your work life, no matter what your job.

One Hand Clapping

A title might not always give you the respect you think it will. A Zen story tells of a Zen teacher who was once visited by the governor of Kyoto. The teacher's attendant presented the Zen teacher with the governor's card, which read: Kitagaki, Governor of Kyoto. The Zen teacher pushed aside the card: "I have no business with such a fellow. Tell him to get out." The attendant returned the card to the governor, who apologized. "My mistake!" said the governor, crossing out the words *Governor of Kyoto* on the card and asking the attendant to try again. This time, the Zen teacher eyed the card and exclaimed, "Oh, my old friend Kitagaki? I want to see that fellow!"

Making Your Job Your Own

Many jobs are designed according to specific requirements. You have a job description, and it is the same or similar to the job descriptions of others with the same title as yours. Each person in each "slot" of a company, whether a factory, hospital, law firm, real estate brokerage, or publishing company, does a certain thing. In some professions such as accounting, a high level of uniformity exists.

But here's something to consider: Learning how to step back and view your work with a certain level of detachment, in terms of its requirements, its various opportunities for expression, its rules, and its overall "shape," can actually help make your job uniquely suited to you.

It sounds contradictory, doesn't it? If we detach from our job, won't it become less personal? Actually, getting caught up in the day-to-day details of a job can, as they say, keep us from seeing the forest for the trees. If you become your job description, you'll probably be a satisfactory employee. But will you be a great employee, a deeply satisfied employee? Probably not.

Detachment means taking the long view, the big view, the view from the top floor. Look at your job from afar. How does it fit into the company as a whole? How do your responsibilities relate to the rest of the company? What are the requirements, and where are the spaces for individual expression? In other words, what do you have to do, and where do you have some wiggle room?

Nirvana Notes

How do you become detached from your job? Imagine someone else has your job. See it from an outside perspective. What kind of a job does this other person have? Does it seem like a worthy job? Is it interesting? Does it have opportunities for creativity or expansion? How is that person (you) performing the job? Is that person (you) a good employee? A great employee?

From this detached vantage point, you can learn how to approach your job in a new way, as if for the first time, but with a more realistic perspective. You can discover places for creativity, and you can determine where creativity might be inappropriate. You can better understand your relationships with co-workers. You can even see into the past and future of your job—without attaching to them, of course.

You might also be able to see, from this elevated place, how you don't necessarily fit into your job. Maybe your dissatisfaction with your job is based on a bad fit. You didn't realize it when you were too busy to think. But when you sit back and let go of your attachments to your daily tasks—sending out those memos, meeting with those clients, transcribing those tapes or notes, hammering out those press releases or advertising copy—you see how this particular job doesn't give you the space for the creativity you need, doesn't use your intellectual capacity the way you would like, or doesn't let you move around enough.

Maybe the solution is right in front of you: a promotion or a move to a different area. Maybe the answer is a job change. It took both Gary and Eve a long time to recognize that they would be happier being self-employed—a sometimes scary and difficult but ultimately much more suitable and rewarding switch for both!

Of course, ideally, any job you do, whether you "like it" or "hate it," can simply be performed for the sake of the job itself, beyond likes and dislikes, preferences and tendencies. But just as zazen provides an easier forum for learning to clear your mind and simply observe, minimizing distractions, and providing an ideal environment, so finding a job that makes sense to you and matches your individual personality can make job success (meaning the expression of skill through becoming one with your work) much easier to come by. Finding a job that contributes in a positive way to the world is also more in conjunction with the Buddhist idea of "right living."

Monkey Mind!

You might be worried that career dissatisfaction isn't Zenlike. Shouldn't you be happy with whatever work you do? Mindfulness in any activity is great, but that doesn't mean you can't decide what your activities are. Finding a job you feel good about and in which you can make a difference is worth the effort.

To help you get a handle on how to make your job more *yours*, let's look at your job description. Maybe your job matches a printed job description you have in your personnel file. Maybe what you do and what that piece of paper says you do are worlds apart. Or maybe you don't have a written job description. No matter which situation matches yours, forget that preprinted job description or your preconceptions about what you do, and spend a few minutes considering what you *really* do. Answering the following questions will help you get a focus on your true job description:

◆ The first thing I do each day at my job is ...

_____

◆ The last thing I do each day at my job is ...

_____

◆ I spend more time than anything else on ...

_____

◆ The duties or tasks I enjoy most are ...

_____

◆ The percentage of time I spend on the tasks I enjoy most each day is ...

_____

◆ The duties or tasks I enjoy the least are ...

_____

◆ The percentage of time I spend on the tasks I enjoy least each day is ...

_____

◆ The part of my job that seems to be best suited to my particular talents is ...

_____

◆ The percentage of time I spend on the part of my job best suited to my particular talents is ...

_____

◆ The part of my job that seems to be least suited to my particular talents is ...

_____

◆ The percentage of time I spend on the part of my job least suited to my particular talents is ...

_____

◆ If I could change things about my job, they would include …

_____

◆ The things I wouldn't want to change about my job include …

_____

◆ This is how I feel about my relationships with my co-workers (if applicable):

_____

◆ This is how I feel about my relationships to my supervisors (if applicable):

_____

◆ This is how I feel about being a supervisor (if applicable):

_____

◆ This is how I feel about the goals of the organization I work in:

_____

◆ In 1 year, I hope my job situation is different in the following ways:

_____

◆ In 5 years, I hope my job situation is different in the following ways:

_____

◆ This is what I might do to improve my job situation or to move toward my goals:

_____

The last question is really the key to the whole puzzle. Zen is about living in the moment, but it is also about living actively and mindfully in the moment, not nursing grudges and hating life because you don't feel able to make yourself happy. Now go back over your list and look for clues to the ways you can make your job more your own. Circle them. Then, go back again and look for the ways your job is already quite satisfactorily your own. Highlight these.

Now you are beginning to get a realistic picture of where you stand. And only in seeing the truth can you make your job your own. Maybe you have realized how happy you are in your job. Maybe you are beginning to suspect you are ready for a move. In either case, keep your eye on the truth, free from assumptions. Happiness will appear more easily within your grasp if you aren't grasping for things you don't really need or don't really want. Maybe happiness is right there in front of you.

Meditating at Your Desk

Speaking of happiness right there in front of you, how better to maintain it, remember it, keep hold of it, and bask in it, than meditating on the job? We aren't saying you should ignore your work and meditate all day. Your supervisors probably won't appreciate that particular effort toward job satisfaction.

But even in a cubicle, there are moments during the day—even if only two or three—when you can stop what you are doing and focus inwardly. These little breaks can make you more productive and more content.

You might consider coming in a few minutes early in the morning, if you won't be tempted to jump into work early, especially if the early morning work environment is more peaceful than your hectic home life. Sit and take a few deep breaths at your desk. Relax, sit with your spine straight, and quietly focus on your breath moving in and out, in and out. Count your breaths if you find it hard to focus in the office environment. Focus on a single item on your desk and contemplate it to the exclusion of all else. Or listen to the sounds of the room around you. Work on being acutely aware, totally mindful, without judging, attaching, or mentally wandering away. And you have desk zazen!

There are plenty of meditation techniques you could try at your desk during short breaks throughout the day, but we find the most effective is simple zazen. Be aware of the right now, not of your overflowing in-basket, the blinking message light on your phone, the "you've got mail" icon on your computer—all of which signal the future or the past. See the basket, the blinking light, and the icon, but don't engage them. Be in the building. Be at your desk. Be in yourself. Be.

Then, it's back to work with a fresher, newer, recharged mind.

> ### One Hand Clapping
>
> Ordinarily, it's hard to forget that we exist. We constantly reinforce this sense of self. We answer the ever-ringing telephone, hear ourselves speak, see how other people react to us socially, keep looking at the clock …. Each like and dislike generates a sticky web of thoughts. As renunciation and zazen cut back on these desires and aversions, the meditator is less often entrapped in their net. Zazen now becomes less distracted, plumbing deeper levels of no-thought, remaining there longer and more effectively.
>
> —From *Zen and the Brain* by James H. Austin, M.D.

The Daily Work of Letting Go

Zazen can feel great the first few times you do it at your desk. Then the novelty wears off. It can be a revelation to remind yourself to step back and approach your position in a more detached manner or to learn how to become totally absorbed in a project. Then the novelty wears off. Zen isn't about a one-time experience after which you can go back to your old habits. It is about a gradual evolution of consciousness from here-there-everywhere, from I-me-mine, from help-I'm-drowning-in-stress, to the great, daily, universal, personal, eternal pulse of now, now, now.

Bringing Zen into your work life is daily work. It isn't a magic bullet, and it isn't easy. But it can change your attitude about your job, yourself, and the way you choose to spend your days and earn your living. That daily work, unglamorous as it is, is the stuff that can change your life.

The Least You Need to Know

- Assuming you know about a person because of that person's job is limiting and can result in unfair stereotypes about your fellow human beings.

- Assuming you are a product of your job, rather than that your job is simply something you, the individual, choose to do, limits your own perceptions of yourself.

- You can excel at your job without letting your job define who you are by putting aside the distraction of thought to immerse yourself in the doing of your work.

- Cultivating a degree of detachment and perspective on your job can help you find ways to perform your job better. It can also make it clear when it is time for you to move on.

- Zazen breaks at your desk during the day can help keep your day and your duties in perspective.

Chapter 18

Relationships on the Job

In This Chapter

- ◆ Are you the big-company type, the small-company type, or the freelancer type?
- ◆ Are they all out to get you? It doesn't matter
- ◆ Dealing with your boss
- ◆ Being the boss
- ◆ Working alone

No job exists in a vacuum. If you work and somebody pays you for your work or the product of your work, you have a relationship. Most people have work colleagues, office mates, managers, or employees. Even Gary and Eve, who both now work from their home offices, are in constant contact with clients, editors, publishers, interview subjects, co-authors, other writers, and everyone else involved in the various work they do.

That means if you work, you have a whole set of work-based relationships to contend with. Work relationships are simpler than personal relationships in some ways, but in other ways they are more complicated.

How Working Relationships Work

Working relationships have certain unique qualities. In a work environment, a much more clearly defined hierarchy usually exists than in personal relationships.

Everyone who has worked in a group environment knows about office politics—something that exists whether you work in an actual office or somewhere else. People might take out their job dissatisfaction on their colleagues or behave in a way that is based not on the other person but on any number of complex motivations having to do with the competition, jealousy, resentment, and stress that often come with a job.

In small companies or subgroups of large companies, offices can turn into dysfunctional families. The owner or manager becomes a parent figure. Employees might engage in behavior that looks a whole lot like sibling rivalry. Sooner or later, employees begin to play out the roles they held in their own families: the domineering older sibling, the indulged younger sibling, the rebellious middle child, and so on.

Nirvana Notes

What happens when a work relationship becomes personal (such as with an on-the-job romance) or a personal relationship becomes a working one (such as when a husband and wife start a company)? The rules still apply. Make no assumptions, focus on your job, and treat each other with compassion. You'll avoid all kinds of problems.

Sometimes the line between work relationship and personal relationship blurs or disappears completely.

But we aren't saying you should quit your job and go live in a cave. Working for a living provides many opportunities for growth, not to mention a steady paycheck. Large and small companies have their various benefits beyond health insurance and a 401(k). And those who learn how to approach employment with a Zen attitude will find a way to avoid getting caught in the middle of the politics, nastiness, and fierce competition that exist in many work environments.

What Working Environment Works for You?

The first step in taking a Zen approach to work relationships is to optimize your work situation. Are you in the kind of working environment that works for you? Job dissatisfaction might depend more on where you work and with whom you work than on the work itself.

Gary has a bright, hard-working, incredibly conscientious friend who ceases to function in an office setting. She gets bored to the point of falling asleep at her desk. She doesn't interact well with her co-workers. She finds office rules so ridiculous that she can't hide her disdain. Clearly, this woman needs to work alone. Alone, she thrives.

For Eve, working alone is also more productive, but for different reasons. Eve loves to gab, loves to interact with people, and gets fascinated with what everyone else is doing. "So tell me about your job. And what is your job? And what do you do?" (It's the writer inside her.) In an office setting, she finds it very hard to focus because there is so much around her that is so interesting, so much to know! At home, she can sit down in her familiar office and get to work. She gets plenty of time on the phone with people, but when it comes time to work, she can hang up and get it done. For Eve, freelancing from home is a little like zazen: an environment that makes work easier because it contains fewer distractions.

Gary tried the freelance writing thing. But it didn't work for him at all because he was unmotivated and lonely. What should have taken him 1 hour took 3. He worried all the time about work not coming in. Yet when he worked for larger companies, he was equally unhappy. Office politics bored him; the largeness felt stifling; and he felt like he was on a treadmill.

Gary works best on his own, but also with a lot of people contact and a lot of stimulation. He likes the energy of working with clients, even though they can be demanding and he is continuously faced with the uncertainties of where the next client or project is coming from. His clients range from individuals to large companies, so each day has the potential of presenting a whole new set of challenges and skills. The hours are longer and the risks much greater. He certainly can't call a boss to handle things when he's faced with a new client or a situation. Yet he is energized by the constant change and the excitement of having control over his own destiny. For Gary, arriving at this point in his career is the result of following a steady path while acknowledging his own age-related stages of development, being mindful of the lessons of life experience, and listening to his own inner voice. And he remains open to where life will take him next. It is a process after all, isn't it?

What about you?

Where does your path lie? Consider some of the following questions to help focus on your own personal preferences. Perhaps you will discover a job change is in order. Or perhaps you will discover that you are right where you belong after all.

◆ How do you feel about large companies? If you work in one (or if you think you would like to), do you enjoy the excitement of a large company with many levels, opportunities to advance or change responsibilities, and all the accompanying hierarchy and levels of relationships?

What in your personality do you think responds so well to this environment? Or what about you doesn't enjoy this environment? What specifically don't you like? Does a large company make you feel overwhelmed, frustrated, or unchallenged? Is it too impersonal?

◆ How do you feel about smaller companies? If you work in one (or if you think you would like to), do you enjoy the familylike relationship where everyone does a little of everything and everyone grows together? Do you feel a small company is better suited to your personal and career growth?

What in your personality do you think responds so well to this environment? Or what about you doesn't enjoy this environment? What specifically don't you like? Does a small company make you feel bored, edgy, or unchallenged, as if you have limited options for growth or change?

◆ How do you feel about working alone, either telecommuting from your job or freelancing? If you work alone (or if you think you would like to), do you find it stimulating, freeing, and exhilarating? Do you love being your own boss without having to worry about anyone else?

What in your personality do you think responds so well to this environment? Or what about you doesn't enjoy this environment? What specifically don't you like? Do you feel unmotivated, bored, and unstimulated without other people in your working environment? Do you think it isn't worth it to be your own boss if you don't have anybody to manage?

No matter your situation, these questions might shed some light on your feelings about your current employment situation, even if they are only feelings you have right now. Remember, too, that every job is a mixed bag. You'll like some things about it, and you probably won't like other things about it. The question is, do your likes outweigh your dislikes?

Also consider how realistic your perceptions are if you are dissatisfied with your current situation and think a different working environment would be better for you. You know the old cliché about the grass always being greener on the other side of the fence? It is easy to complain about a job and think you know a different working environment would be better, but are you seriously considering your own temperament?

Some people think they would love to freelance, when in reality, they find it incredibly difficult to motivate themselves without colleagues and supervisors around. Others long for the excitement of a large corporate environment but in reality have difficulty dealing with authority and having to be a team player. What you think you want might not be suited to your individual personality.

On the other hand, maybe a move will be the key to finding employment happiness. Eve thought she might like freelancing better than working for a "boss," but for years she was afraid to make the leap. When she did, she finally found job satisfaction. Only you can answer the question for yourself, and it might take a few job changes before you know the answer.

The Sharks You Think You're Swimming with Are Only in Your Head

The world has an uncanny way of reflecting what we believe it to be. Of course, all that reflecting happens in our own heads.

If we see corporate intrigue all around us, that is probably the environment we will find ourselves in. If we are more likely to assume a spirit of openness and cooperation, our environment is more likely to take on that shape. The latter is preferable, of course (unless you are researching your screenplay for the next big blockbuster movie about corporate corruption!).

If your world is what you make it, a positive attitude and compassion toward co-workers will surely optimize your environment, won't it? But Zen has an even better option:

See the world for what it is.

For what it is? If the world is what we make it, is there an objective reality to see? Of course, there is. Just let go, and let the world be what it is. Objective reality is out there, but we tend to cover it up, dress it up, disguise it with our own ideas of what reality should be or must be or probably is. We become so removed from it, we can scarcely recognize it anymore.

Not trying, striving, or straining to alter our job situation in favor of simply seeing it might not be the method promoted in books about career achievement or personal happiness. But it is certainly the Zen way, and we think it is even more conducive to both job success and personal satisfaction.

Think about it: If you aren't responsible for "making" your world into something that works for you, but instead are only responsible for getting out of the way of the world, stepping back, and seeing it for what it is, you'll find your perception increases dramatically. You can see how un-seeing you were! How deluded! So *this* is how things really are!

Refusing to force your job environment into some preconceived mold you've made in your head can open dramatic new possibilities. You might feel you are seeing your work environment clearly for the first time. You'll see how one person can influence an entire work environment with a positive, focused, nonjudgmental spirit, while another can be just as influential radiating negativity, pessimism, and suspicion. You'll also see that although people influence each other, no one can force another to be happy or productive or content.

You'll also see what can happen when you stop assuming the worst—or even the best—about your co-workers and supervisors. Everyone pops into focus as exactly who they are, doing exactly what they do. And where does that leave you? With your own job to do. Your job will certainly include interactions with people, but these interactions can become entirely free of assumptions. When they do break free of the heavy load you've been attaching to them, you might be surprised at how easy they become. You aren't responsible for that comment someone made. You don't have to fume about your supervisor's botched handling of a situation or the bid your team didn't get. All you have to do is your best possible job at whatever you are doing. All you have to do is interact honestly and productively with others, without resentment, anger, or even awe. Just be, and allow others to be, too. If they don't, if they insist on assuming things about you, carrying grudges, acting dishonestly, getting angry, or holding you up on a pedestal—well, notice it, but don't attach to it. And never forget the cardinal rule:

You can't control what anyone else thinks or does.

You only control the job you do, the reactions you have, the thoughts you think, the emotions you feel—and even these you can only control to an extent. Your reactions, thoughts, and emotions will come as they will. You just get to decide whether to engage them or not. And that's plenty.

One Hand Clapping

Because we are human, we judge one another. Someone does something that seems to us rude or unkind or thoughtless, and we can't help noticing it. Many times a day, we see people doing things that seem lacking in some way. It's not that everyone always acts appropriately. People often do just what we are objecting to. When they do what they do, however, it's not necessary for us to judge them …. No person should be reduced to a label.

—From *Nothing Special: Living Zen* by Charlotte Joko Beck

Of course, remaining detached in the face of office politics is far from easy. How many of us go home at night and recreate scenes from the office? We remember an incident where we were "disrespected" or when we failed to gain the upper hand in an exchange when we feel we should have prevailed, and we revisit it again and again in our minds. What do we do with these thoughts?

These are sharks, all right, but they are sharks of our own making, mind sharks.

Perhaps we work with other mind-shark-makers. Eve used to work in an office full of them. Everyone loved to guess and second-guess what everyone else was doing and thinking and saying behind each other's backs. Warfare developed. Enemy camps formed. Rumors ran rampant. Nobody knew what was true and what wasn't. Everyone suspected everyone else. People started getting fired. It was all very dramatic but not much work got done.

What a waste of energy it all was. Because our livelihood often depends on making money, our jobs are critical to us, so it is easy to read too much into them. We are attached to our jobs; we make them so important that they cause us to suffer. It's the same old story of dukkha. We attach and then we suffer.

Even assuming good things about people can get you into trouble. What if someone really is trying to unseat you? Assuming everyone is sweet and nice and friendly can be naive. The Pollyanna approach isn't any more realistic than imagining you are surrounded by sharks.

Nirvana Notes

To quote ourselves from Chapter 2: "Right thought means thinking kindly and refusing to engage in cruel, mean, covetous, or otherwise nasty thoughts. What you think is what you are." Living by the precept of right thought and refusing to assume anything about anyone are the keys to heading off relationship trouble on the job.

Choosing not to assume at all, but taking everything for what it is—and being so mindful that you don't miss anything—is the best way to know what is really going on, to react appropriately, and to be in the best position to stay uninvolved with the things that squander life energy in any work environment.

Just don't assume at all. Or when you catch yourself doing it, recognize it; notice it; then let the assumption go. Go by what you know right now, not what you expect. And don't worry about the rest. Besides, aren't you too busy doing your job to waste all that time?

That's not to say you won't have productive, successful, or antagonistic relationships with the people you share an office, a floor, or a company with. You certainly can't just ignore your co-workers. Some of these people may turn out to be important on your life path. Others may not. That's fine. Living Zen means relating to the world—a world full of people you do not own or control.

People are who they are and will do what they will do. Accept it or suffer. End of story.

The Zen Approach to Having a Boss

Your relationship with your boss is unique, unlike your relationship with anyone else at work or at home although it might be a little like a relationship to a parent. It is human nature to turn a boss into an authority figure. Depending on your individual background, emotional baggage, and past experience with employers, you might automatically fear your boss and/or want to please him or her no matter what, even at the expense of your co-workers—even at the expense of yourself!

Or you might automatically resent your boss, assuming he or she is out to hurt you or at least keep you under their thumb. (Maybe they are; maybe they aren't.) Maybe you resist authority in all its guises. Or maybe you are naturally independent and simply don't like somebody else telling you what to do.

Nirvana Notes _____

The Zen approach to having a boss means recognizing rather than resisting your feelings and assumptions about authority. What is your knee-jerk reaction to your boss? Does it injure your ego to have someone in charge of you? Do you wish you were the boss? Are you afraid your boss won't like you? Are you afraid you'll be unfairly treated because you have been in the past? Engage in a little self-examination.

Having a boss is a particular challenge to those of us with ready-made authority issues. We might end up behaving confrontationally or passive-aggressively for no reason our boss can discern.

Are you letting feelings and thoughts from the past control your behavior in the present? Your initial reaction to an authority figure generally has nothing to do with who the person is. Instead, your ideas about authority are coming into play. If you resist the feelings and don't acknowledge them, the tension will build. You will become more and more convinced of their reality. You might even start to act on them.

Don't let your feelings fool you! Look at them. Examine them. See them for what they are. Don't hide them or hide from them. That's how they get control over you. Look them straight in the eye and call them "feelings," and you'll deflate them.

Nirvana Notes _____

Maybe all those work issues aren't about you. Maybe they are what they are. Your boss is just a person. In your job, in this place, that person called your boss makes or enforces certain rules. It doesn't mean anybody is better than anybody else. It just means that's the way things are set up right now. It isn't a reflection on you, so don't let it be. Just do your work.

Working with a boss means taking time to understand your boss as an individual, with compassion and detachment. How might things look from your boss's perspective? What does your boss have at stake? What authority issues might your boss have to contend with?

The Zen concept of losing your ego is relevant here. Working relationships aren't all about you. The corporation doesn't revolve around your feelings and behaviors. Even if you are self-employed, you aren't working in a vacuum. Everyone you interact with has his or her own job to do; his or her own preconceptions and assumptions they may or may not fight to quell; his or her own agendas, plans, career paths, and relationship issues. And that goes for bosses as well. Transcending your own ego to see your work relationships from a more detached place can illuminate what is really happening and can snap you back to reality.

Monkey Mind! _____

Accepting the behavior of others and the rules of the office doesn't mean being a passive employee or submitting to the abuse of others. Living Zen doesn't mean being a mindful doormat. If someone is abusing his or her power, you can and should do what you can to stop it. Buddhism promotes not only nonviolence but also the active protection—physical, emotional, and spiritual—of all sentient beings (yourself included).

So your boss prefers e-mails to phone calls or would rather have you stop in her office to talk out things in person. So your boss likes reports done a certain way, doesn't want employees to make personal calls, or rambles in staff meetings. So you don't agree with everything your boss says or does.

So what? It doesn't have anything to do with you. It doesn't have anything to do with anything. It just is. You work in a place that has certain rules. Follow them and get on with it. Or make moves to change the rules you think are wrong. Having a boss sometimes requires adjusting to someone else's rhythms and not resisting every little wave that rocks your boat a little (you'll get seasick for sure).

When you can find a way to make peace with that, you will be living—and working—your Zen.

The Zen Approach to Being the Boss

Being the boss can bring out all kinds of insecurities, self-doubt, and emotional baggage from the past. Will you turn out to be just like that domineering parent, that pushover older sibling, that brilliant but naive teacher, or that horribly materialistic boss you once had?

Gary used to manage a small group of people, and he personally had to learn to contend with a basic Zen concept we've mentioned time and again: You can't control other people. Even if you are the boss, even if your job description says you have authority, you can't control what other people do, not really. You can make and enforce rules, sure. But everyone is responsible for his or her own actions. Recognizing this can take a large burden off a supervisor. And it can take a large burden off employees who often respond to controlling bosses by figuring out how to exert their own control through manipulation.

Now, Gary works with managers and their employees to help them work better with each other, and he encourages both groups to listen to and understand each other—in other words, to let go of the need to control.

Nirvana Notes

A boss who doesn't control the employees? Isn't that a sign of weakness? On the contrary, understanding what you actually do and don't control will make you a more effective manager.

Gary has always been just a little uncomfortable with authority because he doesn't like other people trying to control him. That sometimes boomeranged back to him in his job as a manager. Gary used to give orders, then obsess about whether he was being respected and whether his employees were doing his bidding in exactly the way he had directed. Maybe Gary was afraid his staff was as resistant to control as he was. The whole group ended up pushing against each other, rather than pushing together toward a common goal.

Gary also has a tendency to be impatient and overly demanding with himself. And guess what? He can get equally impatient and demanding with his staff if he thinks they haven't done their best.

If they didn't do something perfectly, they must not have listened, or they are being lazy and disrespectful, right?

Sometimes Gary had to catch himself and remember that he was creating scenarios again.

At other times, Gary felt the urge to play caregiver to his staff, doing their jobs for them or doing something himself rather than delegating, even if he didn't have the time. "If you want something done right, you'd better do it yourself!" Then he remembered how he often felt as an employee when bosses were too caught up with being "control freaks" to serve as mentors to their own employees. He realized that he was adding undue stress to his own job, denying his employees the opportunity for learning, and ultimately making himself feel resentful because he was doing all the work.

This is what Gary tells both bosses and their employees:

Being the boss ain't easy.

Every individual boss will have a unique management style, and if you don't take the time to have your feelings, recognize them as feelings, take a few deep breaths, and get some distance from your situation, you might not be the best boss you can be. If you manage other people, just remind yourself:

You are not there to control other people. You are there to be part of a team.

Every employee has an individual work style, just as each manager has a management style. It isn't your job to make value judgments about others. If the work is being compromised, it is your job to take action by making everyone's job clear. It comes down to making sure jobs get done, not that people get controlled.

Take the time to recognize, accept, and even appreciate each individual employee's talents and work style. Let your ego get out of the way. If you find you are mistreated by someone, have to listen to complaints and ranting, or generally have people behaving in a troublesome way, listen. Just listen. See what happens. Don't react immediately. Get that ego out of the way first.

Find ways to make work a positive experience for everyone, rather than trying to force all your employees into the mold of an ideal employee you have in your mind. Work with your team to use their inherent talents so each person is a distinctive member of the group.

If you force your authority, you'll meet with resistance, which leads to more forcing and more resistance. This creates an unproductive working environment, one ripe for inertia and instability, and office politics run amok.

To be a great manager, a great team player, or a Zen boss, facilitate a working environment in which everyone's skills are optimized and everyone can do his or her best possible job.

If You Work Alone

Here is the Zen key to work-alone success: Success is in the doing, right now, sitting down and doing your work with such focus and concentration that nothing else exists.

When the work and the worker are one, none of the other stuff matters.

Not the politics, the relationships (in person or electronic), the hierarchy, the rules, the resistance to the rules, not even those checks that were supposed to be in the mail 3 weeks ago and still haven't come (the bane of a freelancer's financial life!). Immersion in the doing is what keeps you in love with your job.

No matter where you work, what size the office, and with how many other people, it all comes down to the work, right here, right now. Focus on the present moment, and do your job. Let your relationships be what they are, not what you think they are or think they should be. Let the rest go.

And you might find you are a lot better at your job than you ever thought you could be. You might find that your work has value, not only to yourself, but to your co-workers and all the people in the bigger world who benefit from the product or service you and your company create together.

The Least You Need to Know

- ◆ Different people are better suited for work in different types of environments: large corporations, small companies, or freelancing. Finding the right environment for you can improve your working relationships.

- ◆ People tend to assume a lot about their work colleagues. Letting go of your assumptions deflates their power over you.

- ◆ Having a boss means recognizing your feelings about authority and refusing to let them compromise your performance.

- ◆ Being the boss means recognizing your feelings about having authority and refusing to let them compromise your performance.

- ◆ The key to work, whether alone or in a group, is to focus on the work itself.

Chapter 19

Managing Stress on the Job

In This Chapter

- ◆ Are you always employee of the month?
- ◆ Go with the flow, and let stress go
- ◆ Pay attention to you
- ◆ Your job or your life: Can you have both?

You've got your job. You've got the people with whom you work. And you've got that dark cloud hovering over the whole thing. You can't put your finger on it, but there it is. What is it?

Stress.

We all experience stress now and then. Some of us experience it every day. You say you feel it every minute? You've got company.

Sometimes stress is good. It revs us up, readies us for action, and helps us respond more quickly. But we aren't built to withstand chronic stress, and when we are under stress all the time, our physical, mental, and emotional health suffers.

So how can Zen help you manage stress on the job? As you might expect, the Zen approach to stress is characteristically both simple and complex:

Let it go.

What's Your Kryptonite?

Even if we are Superman or Superwoman, Superdad or Supermom, or Super-career-overachiever, we all have our kryptonite: that weakness that gets to us every time and foils our efforts to do it all.

Do you expect a lot from yourself? We know we do. Gary and Eve both tend to expect more from themselves than any human could realistically deliver. We both take on way too much work, partly because we secretly (or not so secretly) think that if we don't overperform, we will fail, be unpopular, suffer a diminished reputation, "never work in this town again," and so on.

We also both get a lot of ego gratification from what we do. Being the expert, the hero, the one who can do it all, or hearing people say, "I just don't know how you do it!" with admiration and respect … well, that's pretty gratifying.

And with a lot of that kind of attitude, our work changes. It isn't about service, even if it looks that way on the surface. It's about being the best, about getting more accolades than anyone else. It becomes about distinguishing oneself. It becomes ego. And we both have to work on that. Maybe you do, too.

Think of your ego as kryptonite, that extraterrestrial substance that neutralizes Superman's super powers. Working from a desire to stroke the ego is stressful and exhausting. Eventually we make mistakes, fall down, and suffer. But the bigger you are, as they say, the harder you fall. When Superman (or Superwoman!) gets knocked down, everybody knows it.

Stop attaching to the things that cause you stress. Do your job. Do what needs to be done. If your job isn't you, then job failures won't be personal failures. They'll be job failures. Job successes won't be personal successes, either, but by now you've got plenty of personal gratification to keep you going. You're getting in touch with the inner you, and that's a lot more rewarding than channeling all your energy into saying the right thing in front of your supervisor so you can get a pat on the back. Do your job without letting your ego interfere, and you'll probably get more than a pat on the back, anyway. You'll be a valuable employee.

Nirvana Notes

In your own mind, if it wasn't all about you when the job was done well, it won't be all about you when something goes wrong. It won't be personal. It will just be another experience.

Expectations: Yours, Theirs, and the Ones That Don't Exist

You aren't doing your job alone, and you aren't doing your job without expectations. They exist, there is no denying that. Other people expect certain things of you, and you expect certain things of yourself.

But expectations aren't always clearly communicated in the workplace, and when something isn't clear, our human tendency is to fill in the blanks. Have some of the following thoughts buzzed through your head when thinking about your job?

- What did she mean by that?

- Is he trying to suggest something about my performance?

- Is that a threat about what will happen if I don't do this right?

- Is she partnering me with someone because she thinks I can't do it alone?

- How can he expect me to do all that?

- How can she suggest I should work on this one alone?

- The last time I did this alone, I messed it up.

- The last time I did this with someone, I messed it up.

- What if I don't do what my boss expects?

- What if I don't live up to what my employees expect?

- What if I don't live up to what I expect?

One Hand Clapping

It is sometimes the case that beings with actively hostile intentions can help us to the highest realizations. Enemies are very important, because it is only in relation to them that we can develop patience. Only they give us the opportunity to test and practice our patience. Not your spiritual master, your friends, or your relatives give you such a great opportunity. The enemy's antagonism would normally arouse your anger, but by changing your attitude you can transform it into an opportunity …. This is why the enemy is sometimes described as the greatest spiritual friend, because he affords us not only the opportunity to practice patience, but also to develop compassion.

—From *Awakening the Mind, Lightening the Heart* by His Holiness the Dalai Lama

---

It isn't easy to simply see your current duties and job situation for what they are. Gary often finds himself recounting situations in which he has been treated unfairly and expecting them to happen again, but that is an expectation he can control. We set traps for ourselves and others by overinterpreting any sign that might point to something that reminds us of a negative past experience. Or we create scenarios of things that haven't happened and convince ourselves they are reality—or at least imminent reality. "It happened before. Surely it will happen this time! It must be me, doomed to repeat the same mistakes. Uh-oh, my supervisor hesitated before he answered. It's happening all over again! He must hate my idea. He's probably thinking of replacing me!"

Of course, you can and probably should learn from your mistakes, as well as proceed in a work environment with both eyes open. Yet that doesn't mean assigning expectations and assumptions on everything anybody says. Be quiet, mindfully pay attention, and you'll learn a lot more than if you expend mental energy creating scenarios you are just sure will happen.

Gary admits that one of his greatest fears is not being perfect. To complicate matters, Gary tends to be an introvert, and his own high standards necessitate (or so he thinks) that he be perfect not only on the outside but also in his own eyes. Gary doesn't always care what anyone else thinks, even if someone tells him he is doing a great job. At the least indication that he has let himself down, Gary falls on his own sword.

Gary used to think the internal need to exceed all human expectations was a guy thing but has since learned that it is just as common with women in the workplace. So what did Gary (and so many others of us) used to do? He said "yes" to everything.

He would take on more than he knew he should then race around trying to get it all done. At the first whisper that something might possibly work better a different way, Gary panicked, interpreted the comment as criticism, and decided he had messed up completely. He would announce his screw-up and fall on that old sword again.

This kind of behavior ultimately leads to two feelings: resentment at being underappreciated or misunderstood (even when nobody has suggested any such thing) and self-flagellation for letting the proverbial ball drop.

You might be amazed at how much Gary used to suffer during this process. Or maybe you're finding it sounds all too familiar.

Gary could carry these feelings around for days, reliving them and agonizing over how he might have handled things differently. "If only I hadn't …." "If only I would have …."

And then, at last—and luckily before he exploded—Gary began to discover a better way to handle these feelings. He learned to sit with them.

Sitting with his work stress, allowing himself to experience it completely, was incredibly enlightening. He began to ask himself, "When have I felt this feeling before? It is strangely familiar."

Inevitably, Gary's mind drifted to childhood situations during which he had felt a similar kind of stress. He remembered times when he had disappointed his parents or teachers. His stressful feelings weren't so new and perhaps not so immediately linked to the present as Gary had thought!

Feelings of stress can come out of childhood, linked in our minds to old experiences we continue to conjure up and relive well into adulthood. Unfortunately, this baggage, although heavy and burdensome, is also familiar and, therefore, to some degree comfortable—or at least, more comfortable than dealing with the unfamiliar: change, growth, and personal evolution.

Go With the Flow

When you sit with your stress, you might find that just sitting is pretty difficult at first. Focus on, even visualize, that river we've mentioned so often throughout this book. Imagine going with the flow, living in the moment, and being just exactly where you are right now in life. You are a grownup now. You live in a fast-paced work world. You have responsibilities. But you also have experience under your belt and lots of resources to help you. You are never alone, even when you are by yourself. You have a universe of resources within you.

Also recognize that you might not always make decisions that work out the way you want them to work out. Other times, things will go just the way you envision. But envisioning outcomes is a matter of expectations again, so don't attach to what you envision. Let yourself merge with the river. Hold the helm with a loose hand.

Reliving something over and over, regretting, or wallowing in disappointment or anger is like trying to stand still in the middle of a river. It certainly isn't easy, and eventually the water is going to win. Standing still in the middle of the river takes a lot of effort. You're fighting, kicking, and paddling upstream but going nowhere. And eventually, chances are good that you'll sink. Remember Jay Gatsby in F. Scott Fitzgerald's classic novel, *The Great Gatsby?* In the last sentence of the novel, Fitzgerald encapsulates Gatsby's passion to control the course of his destiny and his failure to achieve it with these words: "So we beat on, boats against the current, borne back ceaselessly into the past."

Why not go with the flow of your life and your life's work? Work *with* the river and not against it. Look for the big lessons: Where is the bank? Where are the boulders to avoid? Don't waste your energy in futile struggling or efforts to maintain strict control against every little buck of current.

In life, it all comes down to balance. Gary finds he is most susceptible to overwork and overreacting on the job when he has allowed his life to get out of balance. For Gary, that means not spending enough quality time with friends, not getting to the gym, not reading a good novel, not spending time with his personal writing on the weekend, or not meditating.

Remember the big picture. Look at the whole scope of yourself and your life. Then you'll begin to have the power to put your stress in perspective.

Zap Your Stress with Zen

A Zen attitude toward job stress means giving up your expectations no matter what anyone else does. Acknowledge your fears, your anger, your whatever. But if you can learn not to let these feelings affect what you actually do and say to others, you have learned an important Zen lesson. If someone expects something of you, acknowledge it. Do your job to the best of your ability, with total concentration and attention. If someone gets angry with you, fairly or unfairly, recognize it: "My boss is really angry. She doesn't like the way I did this project."

But don't let it affect your feelings about yourself because the anger of another person or the irritation or criticism is not a reflection of you. It is a reflection of that person, and to a greater or lesser degree, of the situation itself.

Interactions are complicated, but when it comes right down to it, we all act and react out of our own heads. To recognize this is to be set free from the bondage of other people's attitudes and reactions.

 **Nirvana Notes** _____

Much research points to the stress-relieving and mood-boosting qualities of regular exercise. In one study, regular exercise was just as effective as antidepressants in relieving depression. Exercise is physical maintenance, just as zazen is maintenance for your mind. The repetition of regular exercise can be soothing, and total focus and concentration on your exercise is zazen in motion. Even if you think you are too tired, 30 minutes of daily exercise will energize you.

That doesn't mean you should ignore other people, of course. That would really make them mad. But with full recognition of the emotions that flit in and out of you, see if you can react from a place that is untouched by emotion, that relies only on the situation itself and nothing else. This isn't easy, but it's extremely important for managing stress. This is now, not the last time, not the next time, not the same as always. Only now.

If you don't expect, assume, project, or attach to your emotions, you will see the situation more clearly, and chances are, you'll react appropriately. It might not fix the problem, but it is all you can do.

Did you hear that?

If you don't expect, assume, or attach to your emotions on the job, you are doing all you can do to act and react appropriately.

Bad things still might happen. Your boss might get really angry. You might even get fired. But you can't control that. All you can control is the way you do your job and the way you act and react to the way people act and react to you. Even if you made a mistake, it is made now and all you can control is the way you act and react. Right now.

You are human, and, just like the rest of us, you have physical, emotional, and intellectual limitations as well as abilities. That's just fine. You are only responsible for yourself. That's one expectation you can have: "I can be responsible for my own attitude."

Of course, as with everything else in this book, telling you not to attach to your expectations is a lot easier than your doing it. So how do you train your brain to do it? You guessed it. Stick with zazen. Practice, practice, practice. Sit with your feelings, your stress, your dilemmas, and your problems. Look at them. Feel them. Examine them. Then practice, practice, practice letting them go. See them for what they are— ideas, feelings, and thoughts that are not you but that pass over you like clouds on a breezy day.

You don't have to be subject to these things. You created them in your own head. No, you didn't create the situations, but you did create the stress that arises from the situations. Why be a slave to something you created in your own brain? See it for what it is. You own the thought. You own the feeling. The thoughts and feelings are products of your mind. That's all. If you can make them up, you can decide to let them go. Zazen will teach you how, if you let it. Give yourself the time you need to see things the way they are. You can do it. You have it in you. But if you don't take the time to sit down and look for it, you won't find it.

In other words, if you do nothing else for stress management, practice zazen. Allow zazen to let the air out of that giant balloon you've overinflated. You'll find there isn't much to it, once it's deflated. And you'll find you've zapped your stress with Zen.

A Zen Approach to Time Management

"I don't have time! I don't have time! I don't have time!" How much time do we spend each day procrastinating or wasting time? How much time do we waste telling ourselves we don't have time? Eve's father always used to say, "Not having time is always an excuse, never a reason." Eve has yet to really examine a situation and find this to be untrue.

We say we have no time to exercise, yet we find time to watch television at night. We say we have no time to balance the checkbook, but we have plenty of time to spend money at the mall, writing checks out of that same checkbook. We say we don't have time to keep the house clean or the bills paid, that we don't have time to coach the fourth-grade soccer team or bake cookies for the charity bake sale or do any number of things, worthy or unworthy of our time. What we really mean is *we don't want to take the time away from something else.*

Eve's dad was right. Time is relative.

Gary is amazed by how much time he can waste simply resisting doing something he doesn't want to do. Maybe he finds out he has 2 hours' worth of work he will need to do over the weekend. He can spend Friday evening being angry about it and Saturday trying to start it but not feeling like it. He won't do anything else, because he is supposed to be doing the work. But he can't get himself to do it.

 Monkey Mind! _____

> You just can't get yourself to do something? That article or report or presentation or chore is just too daunting, too horrible, too much? Sometimes recognizing the exact origin of your resistance can diffuse its power. Are you trying to be a hero or a martyr again? Are you resentful because you think someone else should be doing this work? Do you resent the extra work or feel it is beyond your job description? Is your

He can spend the whole day on Sunday going through the same thing:

Should do it.

Don't wanna do it.

Sound familiar? Gary inevitably spends the tail end of his Sunday evening resentfully completing the work, which inevitably takes 4 hours instead of the 2 it should have taken if he hadn't wasted so much time resisting. Why does the job take longer now?

Frustrated sighs, eye rolling, pencil tapping, pacing, and getting up for a snack, to stretch, or to get some fresh air—that all takes time.

Resistance Is Futile (So Just Do It)

Resistance is insidious. It is self-indulgent because it is letting your inner child (the bratty one) whine and mope and complain. It is also self-destructive because all that negativity takes its toll, unbalancing your life. Hey, when did you turn into such a pessimist?

The more Gary works with a Zen attitude, the more he learns to view all his responsibilities as opportunities. Sometimes he even gets that weekend project finished on Friday! It's a process, of course. That inner child doesn't mature in a day or a week or even a month. But a weekend project or any other chore you think you don't want to do is just what you make it. It can be something interesting to spend a little time on in addition to the other interesting things on the agenda or a great big horrible annoying pain in the *derrière*. Your pick.

Nirvana Notes

If you've ever visited the ocean, you might know what it is like to stand in knee- or shoulder-deep water while the waves rush past you to the shore. It isn't easy to stand when the waves are high, but it's easy to float or swim because you aren't resisting the water. You are working with it, moving with it; it is lifting your anchor.

If you dive in without paying attention to all those reasons floating around in your head that tell you why you don't want to do something, you'll get it done. That is the Zen approach. Go with the flow and do your job. Resisting life's currents is a lot more exhausting.

Knowing When and How to Relax and Rejuvenate

We all have our own rhythms. If we are paying attention, we know when we are tired, when we are frustrated, and when we feel overworked. If we learn to recognize our own rhythms and respect them, we'll find that taking work for what it is will be much easier. We'll be better able to sidestep stress, rather than tripping all over it.

Gary knows mornings aren't his best time, so he doesn't volunteer for morning meetings. He also knows that when he is on the road too much or has booked too many meetings, he will feel exhausted. With exhaustion comes unclear thinking, feelings of resentment, anger, depression, loneliness, and so on.

We all go through this. We all know that when stress gets to us, everything seems worse, less manageable, more dramatic, and way out of control. When we've gotten enough sleep (if we can remember what that feels like) and enough exercise and have been eating healthful foods and practicing zazen—in other words, when we have made an effort to approach our life with a Zen attitude—things seem a lot easier.

The only way to get to this place is to pay attention. Mindfulness will give you the key to your own limits and the clearheaded state you need to be able to respect them.

You won't always be able to stay within your own limits, of course. Sometimes work or your personal life will make demands you have to meet. You might have to push yourself a little harder than you would like to be a part of the team, contribute to the goal, and still maintain your own performance.

Nirvana Notes

Yoga is a great way to keep your physical body healthy, flexible, and strong while it keeps your mind clear and focused. If you're familiar with yoga, consider taking a class or working regular practice into your schedule. If you don't know much about yoga, you might read *The Complete Idiot's Guide to Yoga, Third Edition,* by Joan Budilovsky and Eve Adamson.

But take care of yourself as you do it all. Pay attention. Listen to your inner rhythms and needs. Go to bed early that night or the next night. Let the household chores go until tomorrow. Eat a really healthful meal (no, not a cup of coffee and a doughnut, and no, not a diet soda and a bag of chips). Balance, weigh your options, and make your list of priorities. With this kind of self-care comes a heightened ability to stay grounded in reality, free from all the extra stuff that stress eventually generates: creating hysterical scenarios, total exhaustion, and an inability to be productive at all.

Even as our culture reminds us that it is surely self-indulgent and unnecessary to take vacations, take an afternoon off, or miss that must-see TV in favor of a hot bath and an early bedtime, a Zen approach to stress can supercede those cultural influences. Just as it is your responsibility to do your job well, it is also your responsibility to take care of yourself. Buddha's Middle Way means refusing to let your work take over your life.

To Be or Not To Be ... Your Job

It's one thing to become totally absorbed with a given task; it's quite another to let your job take over your life. A Zen attitude toward work means both doing your job as completely and "rightly" as possible and balancing your work life with the rest of your life.

Moderation in all things means keeping your life in balance. If you become too consumed with your job at the expense of your personal life, home life, social life, and so on, your life will become unbalanced. You won't be able to see as clearly. The influence of work will distort your perspective.

Our culture has many reasons for encouraging us to be workaholics. Such an attitude is convenient because if we are completely immersed in our jobs, we can avoid uncomfortable feelings of loneliness, anger, boredom, or unhappiness. If we stay in a constant state of overdrive, we can bury those feelings so far under a load of paperwork that they might never see the light of day.

We have all worked with people who are job-obsessed. (Maybe it's you.) These people live and breathe their work, leave work at night with a full briefcase, send e-mails at midnight or 5 A.M. so everyone knows they are still focused on their jobs, even at home. Telling yourself how very, very busy you are sure can feel safe. "Boy, I'm up to my ears in work tonight! Don't have time for anything else! I guess I'll be burning the midnight oil!" How dedicated that sounds, how committed.

And we do want to be committed to our jobs, don't we? An attitude of nonresistance to responsibilities, integrity, absorption, meeting our promises, fulfilling our obligations—these are all demonstrations of a Zen attitude, aren't they? If we want to keep our jobs, we can't sit and meditate at our desks all day or be completely oblivious to office emergencies because we are too absorbed in typing a memo. We have to live in the world. Where is the balance?

The balance comes back to this: mindfulness.

The key to balance is to look at our job for what it is—a way to make a living, contribute to the world, and express ourselves creatively. A job is not a way to get a personality or an identity; it is not a way of life. And our whole being, our very self, does not depend on our job (even if it feels that way sometimes). If we think we are defined by our job, we will begin to lose our focus.

> **Monkey Mind!**
>
> Are you overworked? Overwhelmed? Feeling like you can't control it? Increase your time in zazen. The discipline, perspective, and clarity zazen brings to your life can help you get your life under control and your work in balance. Yes, you do have time for it.

> **Nirvana Notes**
>
> The Buddhist concept of right livelihood means working in a job that is nonviolent and doesn't compromise the life or quality of life of other sentient beings. Does your job qualify? Could you alter your job to make it more in line with right livelihood? If not, does this bother you? Is it worth working toward a different line of work? These are questions only you can answer for yourself.

Maybe you have noticed that those employees who are able to concentrate and focus but who nevertheless remain somewhat detached tend to be more successful. They approach their work with dedication, even passion, but they don't let their work define them. A job crisis isn't an identity crisis for people who have things in perspective.

Make other commitments. Cultivate friends other than work colleagues. Schedule "unbreakable appointments" for weekend activities that have nothing to do with your job. You can build balance into your life through proactive discipline and a commitment to yourself first and your work-self second.

The Least You Need to Know

- ◆ Separating your job from your ego is difficult but crucial for stress management.

- ◆ Letting go of your expectations can put stress into perspective, even when you are the victim of other people's expectations (which you can't control).

- ◆ Learning to go with the flow rather than resist what you have to do can help you be more productive and enjoy your work more.

- ◆ Take care of yourself and pay attention to your own needs for less stress and better job performance.

- ◆ You don't have to choose between your job and your life. Both will be more enjoyable and productive if they are balanced.

20

Manage Your Career by Not Managing Your Career

In This Chapter

◆ Your career path: yours or someone else's?

◆ Stop grasping and start working

◆ Setting the course with an open mind

◆ Your money or your life … or can you have both?

◆ You've already made it!

Some of you may still be struggling with the seemingly contradictory ideas of living in the present and planning ahead for the future. Maybe you've been planning your career since your teenage years. Maybe you love your job, but you'd like to go farther with it. Maybe you feel you can't help being the ambitious type, or you know a bigger and better position would make the best use of your talents and skills.

These days, careers come and go faster than we can say "What's your web address?" Who knew 10 years ago that people would be building careers around the Internet? Job-hopping is even considered by some to be a valid approach to high-speed advancement.

Can you manage your career and still have a Zen attitude? Can you plan for the future while living in the present moment? Can you live Zen and be ambitious at the same time? That depends on what you mean by being ambitious …. To be Zen in your career doesn't mean to stop planning or managing your career. It doesn't mean to stand still. Zen is fully compatible with go-go-go. But it also requires another important principle:

Let go.

Let Go? I'll Fall Off the Ladder!

If you work for a living, it is easy to slip into a mode centered around getting ahead. Climb the ladder, get paid more, get a better title, and so on. The thought of actually letting go of that effort, that striving, is pretty intimidating. Won't you fall right off the corporate ladder and land back in the mailroom? To do your job is to get ahead, right?

No, not if you want to live (and work) Zen. Letting go of your striving and your constant, frantic forward-looking doesn't mean compromising your job performance in any way. It doesn't mean you'll stop succeeding. When you stop focusing on what comes next, you can focus more completely on what you are doing right now. What you are doing right now might be planning next week's project, collaborating on next year's big deal, or drafting your company's 10-year plan.

Focusing on right now means taking the necessary measures to do your job well, which often involves a broader view. Where do you want to be in 10 years? What steps can you take right now to make it happen? That is Zen. But living 10 years from now, mindlessly rushing through the now so you can get to the then—that's a waste of a life.

What do you think gets a person promoted? What gets people better titles? What engenders job satisfaction? We'll tell you: doing a job really, really well.

The cynical among you might be snickering. "Oh, poor naive Gary and Eve, thinking that doing a good job gets you ahead. How simplistic. Don't they realize it's all about who you know, who you schmooze, being in the right place at the right time, and getting the competitive edge?"

The edge of what? The edge of your sanity? The edge over your friends and loved ones? Right up close to the edge of a heart attack? And what are you getting ahead to? What is up there that you don't have back here? More money? More stuff? Friends with more expensive clothes? Anything that really matters or lasts?

We aren't saying people don't get ahead (in a materialistic sense) through less than noble means. But is that what you want for yourself? If it is, you probably wouldn't be reading this book. The employee with the good work ethic, with the ability to take responsibility for his or her actions, with the focus to get a job done in all its complexity with thoroughness, with integrity and a good attitude—that's a valuable employee. If you can do that and be those things, you'll float right up to the top without that ladder.

Focusing on being your best you in the present moment of your career keeps you from splitting your energy, fragmenting your attention, and torturing yourself about what kind of comment or move you should have made and how you can best butter up your superiors so you'll be first in line for the next quarter-step up the ladder.

It might be hard to let go. It will be hard if you are used to clinging tightly to that ladder. The important thing to remember is that you don't control others. You don't control life. You can only control what you do. You might as well spend your energy where it will make a difference.

One Hand Clapping

In an old Zen story, a student approached a Zen master and asked him, "Master, how long will it take me to achieve enlightenment?" The master looked the student up and down, then pronounced, "I'd say 15 years." "Fifteen years!" the student protested. "I'm sorry, I'm mistaken. It will take 20 years," the Zen master replied. "Twenty? Surely not 20!" the student protested again. "Oh my, you are right. Not 20. It will take 30 years," the Zen master answered. "Thirty?" the student cried in horror. "No, no, I am wrong again. It will probably take 50 years." … You get the picture. The more you strive, the more you keep your eye on the future, the farther from "now" that future becomes. The student present in the now gives no thought to some future state.

A Time for Effort, a Time to Sit Back and Wait

This whole "focus on the now" thing seems simple, but when it comes to work, we understand how complicated things can get. How do you know when to do your job, oblivious to the corporate machinations around you, and how do you know when to put in your bid, suggest that raise, present that proposal, or pitch your great idea to your boss?

Few jobs are simple, and we can't give you a simple way to succeed. No one can. However, it helps to remember that sometimes in your work life, a focused and concerted effort is the best thing you can do. And sometimes, you are best off sitting back and waiting.

Nirvana Notes

Every day while you are at work, take a breathing break. Stop what you are doing, sit back, and breathe. Listen to the environment around you. Look. Feel. Smell. Sense what is going on, but don't get sucked in. Let yourself see the work environment around you as if you didn't work there. You might gain some interesting insights.

Waiting for what? For the right moment, for the ebb and flow, those currents and rapids and doldrums of life, to become apparent. How will you know when your right moment is before you, for making any kind of move in your job, presenting something, asking for something, even quitting? There is only one way to know: by being mindful.

Mindfulness can take you far in your career, and it means more than focusing on the task at hand. It means remaining fully aware of everything going on around you, all the time. Mindfulness requires a certain detachment, and it is this very detachment that can lift you just slightly above the chaos so you can get a perspective.

Without that perspective, you'll be stumbling blindly around the forest, hopelessly lost, with no knowledge that you keep passing and missing the path straight out into the sunlight. From above, you can see the forest, not just the tall trees. (You know the saying about not seeing the forest ….) You can see the size of the forest and the paths in and out. You can see what you need to do to get to where you want to go.

We can't tell you "If you have this job, you need to do X or Y," but you can tell yourself exactly what you need to do and when you need to do it if you practice mindfulness. Regular zazen each morning and evening will cultivate that mindful attitude in a way that will hone and refine your ability to have a perspective at work, to know when to dive in, and when to sit back and let the currents of life go where they will.

Monkey Mind!

As you consider ways in which you try to control others, also consider ways in which you might be swayed by a compliment, a gift, a favor, or, conversely, by rudeness, disrespect, or an insult. How often do you let yourself be affected by the behavior of others so dramatically that you do things you wouldn't normally do had you maintained a clearer perspective?

What You Control, and What You Don't

It is so hard to believe that you don't really control others, even just a little bit. If you schmooze your boss, he might be more inclined to give you that account. Maybe that's true in your workplace. Maybe treating people a certain way will help them be more favorably inclined toward you. So taking that client out for dinner and being extra complimentary lands you the account. So helping your co-worker with a tedious job will get you some future help.

We remember an episode of Michael Moore's now-defunct television show *The Awful Truth*. Moore was unable to get anyone at a major corporation to talk to him or meet with him. When he sent three supermodels in their lingerie to do the job, the CEO of the company wound up in the lobby and happily promised the girls a meeting. Unfair? Sure. Real life? Of course.

We aren't so out of touch with reality to think what we do doesn't have an effect on others. (And in fact, practicing Zen puts us in *better* touch with reality!) Our work lives are filled with relationships, and with relationships come the dynamics of interaction. What's the difference between interacting with a specific result in mind and controlling other people?

Interacting with a specific result in mind is doing your job. Working with a Zen attitude means having the results in mind but not being attached to them. You can only do what you can do: your best work, right effort, preparation, a good attitude, and honest, friendly interaction with others. You can do things that will probably have a certain result. But they might not. Remember chaos theory? There is much we can't predict. Maybe things will go the way you would like them to, but maybe not. All you can do is what you can do.

And sometimes, when you think you are controlling people, you are having the opposite effect. Once, in college, Gary applied for a job he really wanted. He had a good interview. The guy said he would call Gary in a few days. When Gary thought a sufficient number of days had passed, he called the man, making an excuse to "check in." The man said he was "still talking to people." Gary waited a couple more days, then called again. And again. Finally, the potential employer got irritated, and Gary knew he had destroyed his opportunity.

Gary's father used to call this "casting bread upon the water." You do what you think is right, what you think will work, then you let it go. If Gary had just given the best job interview he could give and then left the situation alone, he might have won the job. Or he might not have. Either way, it was beyond his control. If you obsess over what you can't control, you will at best drive yourself to distraction; at worst, you could shoot yourself in the foot and mess up a great opportunity. At some point, your effort is over, and all you have left is your patience. Zen is about being patient. It is also about learning to lose.

 Nirvana Notes

When the Buddha attained enlightenment, he is said to have proclaimed his wonder at the sudden recognition that all living beings are Buddhas but they don't recognize their perfection because of delusion. Remember this when dealing with others along your career path. Everyone (the competitor, the irritable co-worker, the guy who just fired you) has perfection within and deserves compassion, respect, even reverence.

Learning to Lose

Sometimes things won't go the way you want. You might lose the account. You might not get the job. You might get a reprimand. You might get embarrassed. You might even lose your job.

What will you do? Rage? Scream? Sob? Quit? Fire somebody? Or will you move on to the next thing?

Long ago, Gary was working for a substance abuse program and was ready, for a number of reasons, to move on to something else. He interviewed with a hospital in-patient program. They liked him. They called him back for a second interview. They liked him even more. He waited two more weeks for that final letter, the letter he knew would begin, "Congratulations …" or, "Welcome …" or, "We can't wait to begin working with you …."

Then Gary got the letter. You guessed it. No job.

Gary was incredibly disappointed. It was a tragedy. He thought it was the only job opportunity he would ever have. At the tender age of 27, Gary thought it was all over. He was a failure at everything. Nothing good would ever come his way. He was doomed to suffer.

He sat with his feelings for another two weeks, sulking, and grieving his loss of face because he had told everyone within earshot that he was going to get that job. How humiliating, that he might have been wrong in his belief that hard work and being a good person—a good person by his own standards—would get him whatever he wanted. How could this have happened?

Finally, Gary got tired of sitting around and moping. The sadness was out of his system. He had acknowledged the feelings and was ready to let them go. He went to the gym. He went out with friends. He looked around to see what else was interesting out in the world. He began to consider that maybe the job wasn't the right one for him. Maybe someone else deserved it more or fit the position better. Maybe it was just something that had happened.

Gary began to broaden his job search beyond substance abuse programs. Could it possibly be time to think beyond the box he had put himself in? He looked at educational settings. He looked at business. Ah, business. Now that was something fascinating he hadn't even considered.

So Gary began contacting people in the business world to see what was out there. His resumé reached someone who was looking for an individual just like Gary to teach people from third-world countries how to use software. This employer just happened to have begun his search when Gary's resumé fell into his hands.

A few weeks later, Gary moved to a new state and started a new career. He had moved on to something that would throw his life in a new, exciting direction. But it only happened after he let go of his expectations and allowed himself to move on.

One Hand Clapping

They call this making a living? How many people have you seen who are more alive at the end of the workday than they were at the beginning? Do we come home from our "making a living" activity with more life? Do we bound through the door, refreshed and energized, ready for a great evening with the family? Where's all the life we supposedly made at work? For many of us, isn't the truth of it closer to "making a dying"? Aren't we killing ourselves—our health, our relationships, our sense of joy and wonder—for our jobs? We are sacrificing our lives for money—but it's happening so slowly that we barely notice.

—From *Your Money or Your Life* by Joe Dominguez and Vicki Robin

---

In your job, in any job, things happen for a range of reasons. When Gary worked in advertising, his team might stay up all night doing great creative work on a new account they were trying to win. They would give it their all and do their best. But sometimes they would lose the account.

How could it happen? Sometimes another agency had a presentation the prospective client liked better. Sometimes the personal chemistry between the agency and the client was stronger with one of the competitors. Sometimes somebody knew somebody who knew somebody else, a call was made, and a favor was called in. And sometimes, of course, Gary's team got the job.

But Gary and his colleagues couldn't possibly control all the variables. They could only do their best job. They could hope to win, they could even expect to win, but hoping and expecting won't affect the outcome.

We all have our expectations, some of them unrealistic or unreasonable. Sometimes we fail to remain detached, to step back and put things in perspective. It is a long process. After years of steady work, we are getting there, and you can, too. If you do your job with all possible skill and focus, without focusing on expectations that might or might not happen, you'll be a better employee and better able to take full advantage of the way your career path unfolds.

Nirvana Notes _____

If you are a manager, you have to set certain standards, rules, and goals for those you supervise. You expect certain things. But the best managers aren't attached to those expectations. They can take anything that happens and make the best of it, even when it foils all expectations. Rather than wasting energy on blame, anger, or punishment, Zenlike managers focus only on what they can actually control.

Where Is It Getting You?

We have all heard the cliché about what we would want our tombstones to say. Would yours say "Worked himself/herself to death"? Although in Zen we don't focus on a goal beyond the present moment, let's just look ahead for a moment. We all have one final ending, don't we? Our lives all have one thing in common: They will end.

So if that's the goal, the real goal, why are we in such a hurry to get there? Why are we killing ourselves doing things we don't enjoy or find fulfilling or worthwhile, that don't improve life on this earth while we've got it?

Wouldn't it make more sense to spend our precious present moments balanced, interested, productive, relaxed, loving, and joyful? Of course it would. So what can you do right now to be that way in your present moment?

Being Zen means finding the balance that will make right now worth our total attention. As many of us have learned the hard way, working smartly and productively doesn't necessarily mean working the longest hours of anyone in the office, jockeying ourselves from promotion to promotion, or stabbing other people in the back (metaphorically or otherwise). Working in a spirit of openness, joy, integrity, commitment, concentration, and focus while keeping other areas of our life in balance with our work is a much more pleasant path to career—and life—satisfaction.

Monkey Mind! _____

If you don't enjoy your work as much as you enjoy doing other things, you are either in the wrong line of work or you are forgetting how important it is to be present and make the most of every moment, whether you are working, playing, eating, or relaxing. It all counts. It is all your life.

What we learn and create in our lives outside work can certainly influence what we bring to our job. After all, it is all connected. Balance means letting those connections happen organically, rather than forcing this much work, this much play, or this much sleep into our days.

A life dedicated to work isn't a recipe for career success. It is a recipe for burnout. We prefer a Zen recipe:

A life dedicated to life.

You've Already Made It!

Remember the line from the *Mary Tyler Moore* theme song (are we showing our age?): "You might just make it after all!" That's a nice, optimistic sentiment, but Zen has a different version: You've already made it!

If you can't attach yourself to some nebulous end result you can't control, you can only do what you can do, right now. You can only immerse yourself in the process: on a small scale, the process of an individual project; on a larger scale, the process of your entire career.

Do what you enjoy. Think about things that interest you. Work and be with people you like. Focus your energy on that being, that work, that camaraderie, that effort that grows out of a real love and affinity for what you do. That is your reward. That is your success. If you can be the culmination of your career goals right now, you are a success.

Nirvana Notes

Being your career goals doesn't mean pretending to be the CEO when you aren't. ("What's wrong with Joe? Why is he in the boss's office with his feet on the desk? I think he's finally lost it!") It means being the best you, right now. If you expend all your energy projecting yourself into the job, the mansion, or the friends you'll have someday, you'll miss it all—the job, the home, or the friends you have *right now*.

Perhaps you protest that the current moment is mere drudgery—a job you don't like, a stepping-stone for something better, all you could get at the moment, you have to make a living, etc. How can that be success? If that's how you see the work you do, you will find it drudgery and full of suffering. Is your goal clear, or are you just grasping at whatever you can to make this month's rent?

Let's take a look at your long-range perspective. Remember, this isn't at odds with mindfulness or "now-ness." This is being mindful of your big picture. Every moment is worth living, but as they come along, moment by moment, it helps to have a plan—a flexible plan, a plan you are ready to change when necessary, but a plan nevertheless.

If you haven't set out a career plan, or what we like to call a happiness plan, perhaps this is the time to do it. Consider the following questions as completely as possible, giving each some serious thought. You might come up with some surprising answers:

◆ How would you describe your job right now?

_____

_____

◆ Is your job right now the job you want to have, a step toward something else, or just whatever you could get?

_____

_____

◆ If your job isn't what you want, why do you think you have this job?

_____

_____

◆ What could you do today to make your work life more satisfying?

_____

_____

◆ What could you do tomorrow to make your work life more satisfying?

_____

_____

◆ Where do you want to be in your work life one year from today?

_____

_____

◆ What can you do this year to move in the direction of your goal?

_____

_____

◆ Where do you want to be in your work life five years from today?

_____

_____

◆ What can you do in each of the next five years to move in the direction of your goal?

_____

_____

◆ How would you feel if you knew you would never reach your goal?

_____

_____

◆ Consider other interesting career goals. What else might you like to do?

_____

_____

◆ What things you might do today or this year to move in a different direction (even if you don't plan to do so)?

_____

_____

◆ What is your personal satisfaction with your work life today?

_____

_____

◆ How attached are you to your career plan?

_____

_____

◆ What is holding you back from career satisfaction right now?

_____

_____

Giving serious consideration to these questions means being mindful of your life plan. But remember, attaching to your plan will set you up for disappointment. If your job is truly part of a process, then your success is in the right now, no matter where along the continuum of your career path right now happens to be. So you are "just" a secretary or an assistant or a clerk or an apprentice or the person who runs someone's errands? If you are on your own path, you can find everything you need in the present.

That doesn't mean you won't keep moving, but the moving won't be toward a future, exactly. It will be a series of nows, each with a plan and each with a direction, but not so attached to a destination that the present moment is lost. Let each moment be as fulfilling and miraculous and ordinary as the next, and you'll be managing your career in a way that will bring you job satisfaction.

The Least You Need to Know

◆ Many of us choose career paths based on false assumptions, what other people want, or on our own unfulfilled needs rather than on where our abilities lie.

◆ Striving to get ahead implies the future is somehow preferable to the now and more worthy of your attention. It also tends to backfire. Being the best you can be right now will take you farther.

◆ You can't control how life might impact your career-related circumstances. You can only control what you do.

◆ Put your energy where your life is by focusing on your wholeness, no matter where along your career path your present moment happens to be.

Part 6

Home Is Where the Zen Is

In Part 6, we'll help you integrate everything you've discovered into your daily life. Can you make your environment more Zenlike? Sure! Does a Zenlike home mean you're going to have to do some serious decluttering? Afraid so! We'll also talk about Zen and your creativity, whether you express that through drawing, writing, poetry, music, art appreciation, or sports. We'll finish with a discussion about loving kindness, that "step two" of Zen that happens when you wake up, look around you, and discover what it means to be mindful. Compassion and kindness surface as you learn how to do and be without attachment and desire, and we'll talk about what that means, both for you as an individual and for the world as a whole collection of individual waves in the great sea of being. Zen is what you make it. It is your life, your self-discovery, your present moment. Let it resonate, and you'll be living life to your fullest potential. And that feels great. You'll wonder what took you so long!

Chapter 21

A Zendo to Call Your Own

In This Chapter

◆ Transforming your home into your own personal zendo

◆ Controlling clutter the Zen way

◆ Cleanliness is next to Zenliness

◆ Really living in your house

◆ What does feng shui have to do with Zen?

While a Zenlike attitude encourages us not to be too attached to the things in our possession, it also encourages us to be fully present in the moment and fully immersed in our duties. Having a home uniquely suited to our lives can help encourage this effort. We might devote a room to zazen or to writing or painting. Maybe fly-fishing, knitting, or walking on the electrical treadmill are meditative pursuits for us.

Zen means waking up to our daily life, and what is more representative of our daily life than our home? Of course, Zen isn't about something representing something else. In Zen, our home is just our home. But we can make our home more conducive to the practice of Zen, and that doesn't mean selling all our stuff and sitting on a pillow in the middle of an empty apartment chanting in some exotic foreign language. It means adjusting our environment to be more conducive to mindfulness and to the business of our life, whatever that might involve.

Home Is Where the Zen Is

How do you bring Zen into your home? We would suggest a four-pronged approach:

- ◆ Keep it simple.
- ◆ Keep it clean.
- ◆ Keep it useful.
- ◆ Keep it in perspective.

Each of these points isn't important in itself. Cultivating these qualities in your home is simply a way to remind yourself how to be mindful. Living simply helps counteract materialistic impulses. Cleanliness can help you feel more clearheaded and less overwhelmed, and getting your house clean provides plenty of opportunities for mindfulness practice (remember all that talk about washing the dishes?).

The point of a Zen home is to help you keep a perspective on what is important in your life: the being and the doing, not the having and the holding.

Transforming Your Space

If you're looking around at your living space while you're reading this, you might be feeling a little discouraged. "What, transform this disorganized mess into an example of Zen simplicity and function?" Getting from here to there isn't the point. Don't let some future goal discourage you. Transformation happens moment by moment, now by now. The work of creating and maintaining a home is your work. Right now, let's just look around and see what you can do.

Define Your Goals

Make a comprehensive list of everything you think you want to do. Do you really want to learn to paint, sculpt, master kick-boxing, read the complete works of Shakespeare, take a course on public speaking, write more letters, learn French, and take up the saxophone? Maybe you believe someday you will do all these things, but imagine how much simpler your life would be if you were to narrow your list to your top five priorities? Perhaps your top five are to spend more time with your family, entertain friends more often, have space and time to meditate, become a really knowledgeable and skilled cook, and work on your own personal writing. Remember, in Zen, even your priorities and goals are held lightly because life is changeable.

One Hand Clapping

Life is full of so-called conveniences: computers, laptops, PDAs, DVD players, CD burners, caller ID, and remote controls. In the kitchen, we have bread machines, food processors, juicers, and pasta makers. Our cars have individual climate control and onboard GPS systems so we can drive to convenience marts, pay-at-the-pump gas stations, and ATMs. Some of these things really will simplify our lives, and others will actually complicate them. In *The Simplicity Reader*, Elaine St. James suggests asking this question to determine what to add to our life and what to keep out of it (or what to get rid of): Ask yourself, "Will this really simplify my life?" If the answer is no, then forget about it!

Okay, so get ruthless (lightheartedly ruthless). Cross off everything on the list but five items. These five things are serious priorities in your life today. They are things on which you really do plan to spend your time, things around which you can adjust your home (and also, things you can change at any time when your priorities change, so don't get hung up on this, either) …

My five life priorities right now are:

1. _____

2. _____

3. _____

4. _____

5. _____

This top-five list will give you a focus and an anchor point for your home. If meditation or writing are goals, you might transform a guest room or unused office into a meditation room or a workspace for your writing. If you are serious about cooking, you might reorganize your kitchen to match your cooking goals. If entertaining is fulfilling to you, you might add more seating in your family room to accommodate guests.

Monkey Mind!

Are you a pack rat? If you have trouble throwing away anything, you might have a problem with attachment to material things. This can be an area for personal contemplation. Why are you afraid to let go of material possessions? Do they enhance your life or complicate it?

Your home is yours, and you can choose to cling to, attach to, or obsess about it. Or you can live in it and make it workable, individual, useful, and conducive to your own personal happiness. Note that we don't say your own personal *desires*. We mean happiness, free from desires.

Living in the Doing

Making your house more utilitarian is another way to encourage mindfulness and concentration on the work you do, whether that work is your job, a hobby, or the creation of art. A room devoted to possessions that require maintenance or worry is much less conducive to a Zen attitude than a room devoted to something you have to do. Again, doing is the focus, not having.

If you are serious about your zazen, you might find that an area devoted to zazen helps you commit to your practice even more firmly. We hope this is one of your priorities! Although many people don't have the luxury of a spare room, you might be able to claim a corner of a bedroom, living room, or office space for meditation.

Furnish your zazen area with a mat, a cushion or meditation bench, and if you like, other appropriate tools such as an object to focus on or a source for meditative music, a candle, incense—whatever helps you relax and concentrate on being mindful.

Of course, you don't need any tools for zazen, and you might find you are more successful in your zazen without any "props." It's completely up to you.

Other ways to make your house more focused on usefulness is to make the tools of living—cookware; cleaning products and appliances; clothing; tools for your job, your hobby, or your art; etc.—organized and easily accessible. Remember your five-item list? Keep it in mind whenever you make a change to your living environment. Live in the doing, and know what you are doing.

Making your home more conducive to the work of daily living is a highly individual matter, so let's get personal with some strategies. You won't attach too obsessively to these strategies, of course, but they will give you somewhere to begin:

◆ In addition to my five priorities, I would like my home to be a place where I can …

_____

◆ First, I will declutter, clean, and organize these areas …

_____

◆ Next, I will make each area more useful by …

_____

◆ I can promote my five priorities for living by making these changes in my home …

_____

◆ Some other ideas I have for creating a more Zenlike home are …

_____

And remember, Zen is in the doing, in the work of getting there, not in the looking ahead to the goal. Your home will never be perfectly clean, perfectly organized, or perfectly focused on what you need. That doesn't matter. The future never happens. Make now count by giving your home attention and care in the same way you give yourself attention and care through the work of zazen.

And where will you get the space for such changes? That's where clutter control comes in. _Clutter control_ might not be a classic Zen term, but perhaps it should be. Clutter is stuff, and stuff just hangs around encouraging us to get attached to it.

Clutter vs. Simplicity

If your home is cluttered, you are in good company. Very few of us (especially if we live with others) can escape the clutter monster, and hundreds of books, articles, even professional organizers exist to help us conquer it.

But you can do it yourself. You might remember us saying earlier that a messy desk might be a nice metaphor for a cluttered mind, but it doesn't actually mean you have a cluttered mind. True. In Zen, things are what they are. They don't represent other things.

However, because your home is so integrated into your life, a very cluttered, disorganized, or messy home can actually have a cluttering, disorganizing, or messying effect on your life. Every bit of clutter in your house is there because you acquired it in one way or another, and now you are more or less attached to it. If your house is burgeoning with stuff, that's a lot of attachments to drag around with you. How incredibly freeing it would be to dump some of it!

Streamlining the stuff in your life can help you focus on more important things, such as people, your own personal development, and the work you do—including your list of your top priorities. Why spend your whole life maintaining and worrying about stuff? Stuff doesn't last. Stuff doesn't contribute to _you_.

You can work toward a simpler existence by getting control of the clutter in your life and by consuming less so you generate less. Consuming less is a process you can grow into in ways that make sense to you. It might mean growing more of your own food, biking more and driving less, or questioning your own shopping habits to try to buy less stuff by asking yourself what you really need to live comfortably.

Clutter control is a more immediate process. There's the clutter, all around. Don't you wish you could just zap it away? If you try to conquer your clutter all at once, you'll probably throw in the towel when you realize it's too much. Clutter is best managed bit by bit. To begin clearing out the clutter in your life, make a list of areas to tackle, maybe something such as: bedroom closet, hall closet, junk drawer, garage, pantry, playroom, desk, files, or clothing.

Once you've clarified where your clutter lingers, give each item on the list some time. Spend one afternoon a week on each area. When you've got your time set aside, you can begin to process. Work through your clutter and give each item the test:

- Is this useful to me?

- If not, why do I want to keep it?

Nirvana Notes

A Zen approach to clutter control doesn't focus on the goal of a clutter-free house. The goal does exist, but it isn't the impetus because it is in the future. Instead, your goal for the moment is eliminating the clutter. As you clean, discard, and organize, concentrate on the task. Experience the process for the sake of the process.

If you can't think of a good reason to keep something, give it away or toss it. ("I might need it someday" isn't a good reason. "I just love this" can be a fine reason.) You've probably heard all these suggestions before, but a Zen approach is a little different. The clean house isn't the goal. The goal is instead the process of cleaning.

As you move through the process, you might find yourself coming up against attachment time or emotional barriers. You just can't face that messy office. You really aren't ready to go through that box of personal things that belonged to your deceased grandfather. You know you just might wear that pantsuit some day.

If you really aren't ready for something, don't force it. As you declutter and simplify, little by little, you'll get to a place where you can conquer the bigger (or emotionally bigger) projects. Start with what is easy: the junk drawer in the kitchen, the hall closet, or maybe the toys in the backyard.

You won't conquer clutter in a day. And you'll probably keep accumulating more. But being mindful of the clutter in your life and working, bit by bit, with concentration and purpose, to simplify your life by minimizing the stuff can be good practice that parallels your work in zazen to eliminate the clutter in your mind.

It's Just Stuff

Throughout all the cleaning, discarding, organizing, and refocusing, remember also to keep it all in perspective. One of the challenges of clutter control is deciding what to discard. Many of our possessions evoke memories or represent future things we want to do: a souvenir from a memorable vacation, a stack of unfilled photo albums, love letters, that rock-polishing kit you haven't opened in 10 years.

We aren't saying you need to get rid of everything that doesn't represent the present moment. But how important is that souvenir? Maybe you decide the love letters are important to you, but you'll remember the trip to Florida without the inflatable pink flamingo you never look at.

Having memories or future plans isn't anti-Zen. Attaching to them, letting them consume you, or living with them at the expense of living in the now is what will impede your efforts to live your Zen. It's all just stuff. Sure, you like some of it. Some of it, you love. But it isn't yours—not really, not in a universal sense. You can like it, but if you can let go of your perception of your need for it, your desire for it, you'll be living Zen.

> **One Hand Clapping**
>
> An old Zen story tells of a traveling monk who came to a monastery one chilly evening. He was cold, so he took one of the wooden statues of the Buddha and used it to make a fire. The head monk caught him in the act and cried out in horror, "What are you doing? Why are you burning the statue?" "To get the holy essence," replied the crafty monk. "Why would you get holy essence from a statue?" asked the head monk. "If it isn't there, then why shouldn't I burn the statue?" replied the monk. The point of this story is that there is no reality or ultimate value in things. They represent nothing. How things can be used is much more valuable.

Clean Up Your Act

Beyond clutter is cleanliness. Maybe you can keep everything picked up, but you can't seem to get yourself to mop the floor every weekend or scrub out the bathtub. Yet as we've mentioned before, household chores are an excellent opportunity to practice mindfulness. Keeping a clean house is also a good way to practice self-discipline, and living in a clean house is not only more sanitary but also much more pleasant. It just feels better.

As long as you are going to be mindful and really notice and experience where you are, isn't it nicer to experience a clean environment? And like clutter control, working to keep your home clean can serve as an appropriate reminder of the work you are doing in zazen: that spring-cleaning of your mind.

Conscious Living

We'd like to stress once again (because this is important) that living Zen is not about fixing up your house. Buying those little Zen gardens or fountains, little Buddha or Kuan Yin statues, silk kimonos, or other things that suggest Asia or Buddhism might please you. You might like the Japanese decorating style or the feeling such objects impart. But that isn't Zen. That is attachment to an idea about Zen. And it's more stuff.

British Zen scholar R. H. Blyth once wrote, "Zen is the unsymbolisation of the world and all the things in it." No object, no thing in your house makes your house Zenlike. Your experience of living in your home and doing your work there is Zen. Nothing else. We certainly don't mind if you have an attractive, bubbling desk fountain that's labeled "Zen Fountain" on the box. We just hope you won't mistake that for living Zen.

Living Zen is living consciously, with full awareness, wherever you live and wherever you are—a mansion, a one-room trailer, or under the stars. Zen is the perception of the eternal you and your part in the universe. What does that have to do with a house?

Only this: you, in a house, right now.

Is Zen Good Feng Shui?

These days, everybody's talking about feng shui, the ancient Chinese art of place-ment. In most cities, you can hire a feng shui master to come to your home and tell you how to arrange things according to who you are, where your home is, which direction it faces, and so on. A feng shui master can also tell you where and in what orientation to build a new home, depending on the landscape.

Feng shui as it exists in China is a highly complicated process akin to astrology, and its Western incarnation is often diluted, oversimplified, even completely

misinterpreted. But even in its most
authentic form, does it have anything to
do with Zen? They were both developed
in the same place, weren't they?

Feng shui seeks to take full advantage of
the flow of life-force energy in an environment to maximize the health, wealth, and
potential of the inhabitants of that environment. We would say feng shui contains similar
ideas as yoga, tai chi, acupuncture, or Chinese
medicine—areas that all seek to facilitate and
optimize the flow of life-force energy.

Nirvana Notes

Zen doesn't mean doing without possessions, knowledge,
hobbies, or the daily trappings
of life. But it does mean we
could do without these things,
that we are just as whole without
these things, and that we refuse
to be trapped by the trappings.

But in Zen, the distinctions between the inhabitants and the environment begin to
blur. What is energy, either flowing or stagnant, in Zen? Zen is just awareness. Maybe
your awareness will lead you to perceive something that seems to you like life-force
energy. Zen doesn't say these other disciplines are wrong or untrue or invalid. Not at
all. But in a sense, Zen transcends them. Zen means awareness to such an extent that
all becomes one. When all is one, when you have tapped into the great oneness of all
things and perceived it, what does it matter in which corner of the living room you've
decided to put your sofa?

But many of us won't necessarily get that far with our Zen. We work on mindfulness,
awareness, and living simply to be more in touch with our inner selves. We might
find feng shui interesting and even choose to study it. Great! Why not? We're all for
gaining knowledge about anything. But the point of a Zen approach, of course, is not
to attach to what you learn. To get you going on feng shui, check out *The Complete
Idiot's Guide to Feng Shui, Second Edition.*

Learn. Find the world interesting, but don't think it defines you, changes you, or even
affects you very much. To live Zen is to experience without holding. Learn and do
with complete attention, but without attachment. That goes for feng shui as much as
it does for fly-fishing.

The Least You Need to Know

◆ You can make your home more conducive to Zen living by refocusing your environment on simplicity, cleanliness, and usefulness.

◆ A special area for zazen can encourage practice.

◆ What you do to your house isn't Zen. Experiencing the process of maintaining a house and being aware while in your house is Zen.

◆ The ancient Chinese art of feng shui seeks to arrange an environment to optimize the flow of life-force energy.

◆ The ancient Chinese art of Zen transcends environment, inhabitants, and energy channels with total awareness of the unity of all things.

Chapter **22**

Zen-Powered Creativity

In This Chapter

- ◆ Your creative side is your only side
- ◆ Drawing the Zen way
- ◆ Zen writing and the Zen of poetry
- ◆ Musical Zen
- ◆ The Zen way to experience art

Whether you think you aren't creative at all or are weighted toward the creative side, this chapter can give you new insight into what it means to create the Zen way.

Historically, creativity has been like a cousin to Zen. Zen poets, Zen artists, Zen practitioners of the tea ceremony, Zen flower arrangers—all bring Zen and art together into a unified expression of the true self.

Zen can help you bring out your inner creativity as well, whether you like to draw or write or sing or just tell fantastic stories to your kids. The Zen path to your creative side is short and simple. You're already on it. In fact, you already *are* it.

There is no difference between you and the creative force. You are a physical incarnation of creative energy.

The Zen Drawing Diary

So you think you can't draw? Perhaps you haven't tried drawing the Zen way. Even though she is a writer, Eve has a horrible time keeping a journal. Writing overkill, perhaps. Instead, Eve keeps a drawing diary.

Drawing is an excellent way to train yourself to see without the intermediary of language coming between you and what you observe. Zen drawing trains your eye to meet the subject head-on, merge with it, and become it. In his excellent book on the subject, *Zen Seeing, Zen Drawing: Meditation in Action*, Frederick Franck suggests that learning to draw means learning to see:

> When the eye wakes up to see again, it suddenly stops taking anything for granted. The thing I draw, be it leaf, rosebush, woman, or child, is no longer a thing, no longer my "object" over and against which I am the supercilious "subject." The split is healed. When I am drawing leaf or caterpillar or human face, it is at once de-thingified. I say yes to its existence. By drawing it, I dignify it, I declare it worthy of total attention, as worthy of attention as I am myself, for sheer existence is the awesome mystery and miracle we share.

What a wonderful expression of the creative process! Zen drawing isn't about using techniques of perspective or proportion. It is a meditation on life, energy, and love.

Nirvana Notes

Although sitting meditation provides the fewest distractions during which to practice mindfulness, other forms of meditation can be just as effective for practicing mindfulness. Try zazen through drawing, writing, playing music, crocheting, cooking, refinishing furniture, or tending to your beautiful rose garden. Total absorption in the task is the ticket.

Just because your eighth-grade art teacher made some offhand comment about how you wouldn't ever have to endure the burdens of creative genius doesn't mean you can't draw. Anyone can draw. *Anyone.* You don't have to be "good" (whatever that means) because the drawing isn't for display. Zen drawing is a meditation. "Talent" (whatever that is) has nothing to do with it.

How do you do it? Let's take a mini-lesson in Zen drawing. You'll need a piece of paper, a pencil, and an object to draw. Any object will do, but to start, try something with simple lines. Perhaps, as Franck suggests, a leaf, a piece of fruit, or a green pepper cut in half. Or maybe you have something else in mind.

Once you've chosen your object, get comfortable in a quiet place where you won't be distracted. Put your object in front of you. Gaze at it; focus your total attention on it. Then, take your drawing pencil in hand and move your pencil over the paper to trace what your eye sees.

Imagine your pencil stroking the object's contours and curves, but keep looking at your subject. Don't look at your drawing. If you look at your drawing, you might start judging it. Always look at your subject, the focus of your meditation. Look at it deeply and fully until you feel you have become it or at least know it intimately. Keep tracing it, examining every contour, every change in texture, every surface and angle, every line and curve.

A drawing diary lets you practice and practice this kind of seeing. Draw the things in your house, the stuff piled on your bed, family members eating or watching television (if they don't mind!), friends and neighbors, pets and plants. Draw the beautiful things in your life and the ugly things, too (in Zen, they are all just what they are, neither beautiful nor ugly).

Recording your day through drawings is a profound way of meditating on your environment. It is zazen with a pencil, a response to the experience of mindfulness.

Zen and the Pen

Some people prefer writing as a kind of meditation. Like drawing, language can also be a direct response to mindfulness. In Zen writing, the rules of grammar, usage, and style aren't important. Only a direct response to your experience is a worthy subject for your writing efforts. And of course, that includes anything at all, because your daily life is made of experience.

You might call Zen writing a form of free-writing. Sit down with a paper and pen (or your computer) and begin to follow your breathing, as if beginning zazen (because that is what this is). Then begin to write. Don't plan it. Don't worry about it. Don't attach to your words ("This is horrible!" or, "Hey, I'm pretty good at this!"). You don't even need to have a subject in mind. Just let the words come out, a direct flow from within, a response to mindfulness.

What does that look like? Here is an example of a passage of Zen free-writing. It doesn't have to be good or interesting or meaningful. It just has to come from you, a sort of meditative transcription:

Sun in the window. Air through vents, the carpet rough under my knees. The dog licking her paw, serene, in a square of sun. Hmm hmm la la la. The rectangles of the bookshelf, up and down. Books like soldiers, or not like anything. Books like books. Am I judging my metaphors? So I am. What to write? I don't know. I don't know. True, how true, I really don't know anything! Pictures above and below. Photographs of people I love. Round frames and oval, square, rectangular. A pile of magazines, will I ever read them? What could it be about? Swirls of color, imagined, dust motes floating in the light, I really should vacuum up all that dust. Too quiet. Oh for the phone to ring. Here I sit. Za-za-za-za-za-za-zenning by hand. Mind standing still, but churning. A car going by. Someone shouting. A dog barks, my dog looks up, ears pricked. Shadows on the walls. My house. Whose house? A house. With doors and windows, air and light, movement and stillness, sound and silence. And me in the middle. Writing. Being. Wishing the phone would ring. Noticing that I'm wishing the phone would ring.

Or maybe you'll choose to pick a subject. You might decide to write about a problem that has been bothering you, to help you experience it, feel it, and move through it. Maybe you will choose to describe an object or a scene in front of you. Maybe you will decide to write about a person, a past event, or a dream you had. You can write about anything you want to write about! The point is to immerse yourself in the writing process, to let it be an expression of your mindfulness and your focus—or even your lack of mindfulness or focus! In expressing your lack of focus, you might find you gain focus.

What you write won't always be representative of pure mindfulness. Sometimes your attachments, assumptions, worries, fears, thoughts, and emotions will come pouring out, too. Writing them is a way to recognize them: "*A-ha!* There's an assumption! Look how attached to it I was, writing about it for two pages!" Writing that stuff you are trying to release can help you release it. And when it goes, what is left? Pure mind—your mind—and its translation onto the page.

A Zen writing diary is a great way to practice this type of meditation. But a writing diary (like a drawing diary) can also become a source of attachment, worry, even fear if you attach to what you've written, drawn, or otherwise created. You might often enjoy looking back on what you have written or drawn, but resist the urge if you will begin to judge your efforts. Just as you needn't judge your own zazen or reprimand yourself for a wandering mind or for having

Nirvana Notes

Is it less Zenlike to use a computer than to write by hand? Of course not. Computer, printer, pen, paper, hand—it's all the same thing in Zen. What matters is your true self. The tools you use are irrelevant.

Monkey Mind!

Are you discouraged because you can't think of anything to write? Remember, the key is to stop thinking and just write. What comes out doesn't matter. Focus on the process, the right now, the pen to paper or the fingers to keyboard. Your mind holds your work at arm's length. Only in releasing your mental hold on the task can you become one with it.

too many chaotic thoughts, you also needn't judge your own writing or drawing. Just let it be what it is. There is no good or bad.

If you practice it every day and learn to let it be, you might be surprised how great it makes you feel.

The Poet Within

As a student in school, you were probably forced to learn about poetry. Maybe you haven't thought much about it since. But maybe a few terms come to mind: metaphor, simile, rhyme, meter, assonance, or alliteration.

Forget it all! Or don't forget it, but don't let it concern you. Zen poetry is an ancient art and not one that is easy to master, for Zen poetry is a direct expression of the world—no metaphors, no figurative language at all, no tricks, no layers or levels of meaning—just direct expression.

There is an old Zen story about the famous Zen poet Basho. Basho was very educated and a master of the *haiku*, a form of Japanese poetry containing 3 lines totaling 17 syllables.

Zen-Speak

A **haiku** is a form of Japanese poetry traditionally containing three lines of five, seven, and five syllables each. Haikus are meant to be direct expressions of experience with little, if any, reliance on literary devices such as similes and metaphors (comparing something to something else).

Basho was visiting the Zen master Takuan one day, and as they talked, Basho referenced and quoted endlessly from many complex works of Buddhist thought to support his points. At last, the Zen master said to Basho, "You are a great Buddhist with much understanding, but all you have been saying to me are the words of others, the Buddha's words and the words of scholars and teachers. What are your own words? What are the words of your true self? Give me a sentence that comes from you, that is all your own."

Basho was stunned into silence. He had no idea what to say. Words from his true self? Words not quoted from some famous, time-tested manuscript? Basho remained silent. He was humiliated. His true self? He felt frozen to the spot. The Zen master commented, "What, you, the great Basho, so learned and you can't give me one word from your true self?"

Suddenly, Basho heard a sound of water splashing from the garden—a frog had plummeted into the pond. Without thinking (that's the important part), Basho turned to the Zen master and said:

Still pond
A frog jumps in
Splash!

The Zen master laughed with delight. "Now that is an expression of your true self!"

This story shows how we can only respond to mindfulness directly, without ideas, thoughts, the words of others, and our preconceived notions getting in the way. If we filter experience through all these other things, we have created something that, although possibly very interesting or beautiful or admirable or impressive, is nevertheless compromised by our delusions.

When Basho heard the sound of the frog, he responded directly, using no fancy poetic devices, no quotes, no literary references. Just pure experience. That is Zen poetry.

> ## One Hand Clapping
>
> When you understand yourself, it is very easy to paint or write poems or do calligraphy or tea ceremony or karate. You paint effortlessly; you write effortlessly. Why? When you are painting or writing or doing any action, you become totally absorbed in that action. You are only painting; you are only writing. No thinking gets between you and the action. There is only not-thinking action. This is freedom.
>
> —From *Dropping Ashes on the Buddha: The Teaching of Zen Master Seung Sahn* compiled by Stephen Mitchell

You and Haiku

Anyone can write a haiku, but haiku, although short, are difficult to write well. Just follow the rules: three lines containing five, seven, and five syllables, respectively, and for subject matter: pure experience. The translation of Basho's haiku doesn't actually fit the syllable requirement ("splash" obviously doesn't have five syllables), and even this "rule" is less important than the pure experience part.

Haikus are good practice for the work of avoiding comparisons, assumptions, and judgments. Basho's haiku about the frog wouldn't be haiku if it went more like:

A still pond
A frog like a beam of sunlight
Bothers the surface

In this version, the frog is compared to something, and the judgment is made that the frog's jumping has compromised or somehow irritated the pond. This last line also personifies the pond, as if it were a person who could be bothered.

This version might sound Zenlike or interesting or even beautiful to some, but a Zen master would see right through it. It might be poetry, but it isn't Zen. The mind is elsewhere, not with the pond, the frog, or the sound of the splash.

Without worrying about how Zenlike or perfect your haiku will be, let's try a few. Sit mindfully in zazen for a few minutes. Look around you. Listen. Breathe. Feel with awareness. What is contributing to the experience of your present moment? Recognize that and start writing. Here's an example:

> The wristwatch ticking.
> Across the street, a mower.
> Afternoon sunbeam.

Here's another one, for inspiration:

> A man sits alone
> On a bench under pale sky
> Looking at a cloud.

And one more for good measure:

> Gray squirrel, perched, trembling,
> Eyeing the striped cat below.
> The cat's tail twitches.

One Hand Clapping

Many ancient haiku are famous in the West as being classic representations of Japanese poetry, but haiku isn't the only form of Japanese poetry, and many other poetic forms exist in other Far Eastern countries, too.

Now you try it. Remember, use five syllables in the first line, seven syllables in the second line, five syllables in the third line. Stick only with the experience. Don't judge. Don't assume. Don't compare. Don't create a scenario. Stick with your actual experience. Let your eye, your ear, and your mindfulness find worthy haiku subjects (everything real is a worthy haiku subject).

Musical Zen

Among Eve's other creative pursuits (she is one of those people who may be a little too in touch with her creative side), she is also a jazz singer. Her father is a jazz pianist, and she sings for his band. Singing has always come naturally to Eve. She learns songs quickly and remembers lyrics easily. She doesn't usually have to think about it; it just happens. She merges with the song, and it sings itself. She considers singing a form of zazen.

Nirvana Notes _____

Singing in the shower or the car is often more Zenlike than singing in a performance. In the shower, you aren't thinking. You are singing as a pure expression of your experience (even if you are singing something silly). In a performance, you might be more attached to the result, to the reactions of others, and to a flawless product rather than on the "now" of your expression.

But one night she was singing a song by special request, a song a friend had asked that she learn. It was a fast song with a lot of quick words, and Eve kept forgetting them. All day before the performance, Eve obsessed about the lyrics, singing them until the kids couldn't stand it anymore ("Mommy, will you please stop singing that song!"), going over them silently in her head, worrying, and projecting ahead to what might happen if she forgot them on stage. What would happen? How might she cover it up?

Even as she did this, Eve remembers thinking to herself, "This isn't a very Zenlike approach. I am attaching to the idea of remembering the lyrics of this song." The recognition wasn't enough to stop her, however. She didn't trust the song to sing itself this time. And it didn't.

Sure enough, right around verse two, the lyrics went completely out of her head, and Eve had to stutter a little, make something up, then resort to repeating the first verse. Not many people noticed, but Eve noticed, and so did her friend who had asked her to sing the song.

Even during the performance, Eve kept thinking ahead. As she sang each word, she was thinking ahead to the next line. She was not being mindful. She was existing in the future of the song, and she paid for it—not a high price (it's not like there were record producers in the audience), but a price.

Of course, the local cable access company was taping the show, and replayed her error over and over on cable access television during the next few months. All her friends *said* they didn't notice. Uh-huh.

Later, when Eve found herself singing the song at home one day, completely without thought, she got through the whole thing without a hitch. And that's just one more reminder about how effortless experience can be when thought doesn't get in the way.

The Zen of music is just like the Zen of the other creative pursuits. Whether you are playing, singing, or listening to the music, immersing yourself completely in the music is the Zen way to experience music mindfully. Only then can you fully appreciate the beauty and truth in a great song, whether it is an aria, a jazz standard, Rachmaninoff, or an off-the-cuff rap session.

A Zen Lesson in Art Appreciation

Zen can be a way to understand, firsthand, what makes great art. Whether someone calls it Zen or not, a Zen approach to understanding art means experiencing art or receiving art, with total mindfulness. Let your preconceptions go. Let your assumptions go. Let go of your urge to compare what you experience to anything else.

When you listen or observe with total mindfulness, it should be apparent when the composer or painter or writer or musician created his art with total mindfulness. You will feel a connection. You will be in the presence of art, which is to be in the presence of humanity, which is to be in the presence of truth.

It's a lot of fun to exercise the Zen of art appreciation. Every opportunity becomes a delightful exercise in mindfulness. The possibilities, fortunately, are endless. Here are some ideas:

♦ Visit an art museum and spend a full 10 minutes in front of at least one piece of art. Really look at it. Focus on it until you feel you are beginning to understand it, even become one with it.

♦ Bring your drawing diary to the art museum, to an outdoor sculpture, or even to the pages of a book about art. See what happens when you practice your Zen drawing meditation using a piece of great art as your subject. Draw what you perceive. Take your time.

♦ As long as you are in that museum, write haiku about different works of art you find particularly inspiring. Let the haiku speak of your direct experience of the art, rather than trying to understand it, analyze it, or compare it to anything.

♦ Alone in a room with the lights off and your eyes closed, sitting in zazen, listen to some music you consider truly great or music known to be great that you've never heard before. Let the music be your meditation focus. Listen with complete mindfulness.

♦ Draw or write in response to a piece of music. Let one art medium inspire your creativity in another medium.

◆ Go alone to the theater, ballet, opera, or even a great movie. Let yourself become completely immersed in the experience. Notice when you feel the need to say something to someone, and direct your thoughts inward instead. Practice mindfulness and concentrated focus. Realize your experience of the performance needn't be validated by anybody else.

Nirvana Notes _____

Are you wondering what makes a piece of art, music, or writing "good"? Just experience the art mindfully without judging or labeling it, and you'll find that eventually the answer floats to the top of your consciousness. Mindfulness allows you to perceive what is quality and what isn't. Maybe some people won't agree with your perception, but you will know that it is true for you.

Certain works of art, whether a painting, a poem, or a symphony, are clearly "good," but often what makes art "good" is subjective. Yet applying the Zen test to a work of art can be a good indicator of quality. Does this piece of art speak directly of the creator's experience, and does it translate that direct experience to you? Does it speak to you? Does it tell you something about life? If it does, you are in the presence of great art.

Or instead, you might see yourself in the presence of the expression of creativity that came from a fellow sentient being. Such a success is your success! We are all one, all part of the magnificent flow of creative energy in the universe. We can all tap into it, and we can all rejoice when our fellow humans tap into it, too. That's art appreciation!

The Least You Need to Know

◆ Creativity isn't some aspect of you. It *is* you. You are an expression of creative energy.

◆ Drawing, writing, or playing music as zazen are effective and illuminating forms of meditation.

◆ Zen poetry is an ancient art in which the poet expresses through language, as directly as possible, the experience of the present moment.

◆ A Zen approach to art appreciation means experiencing art directly, without thinking about it, comparing it to anything, or judging it. Such experiencing makes the difference between great art and lesser art more apparent.

Chapter 23

Loving Kindness: What the World Needs Now

In This Chapter

- *Psst* … wanna know the meaning of life?
- Why we need loving kindness right here, right now
- Healing the world
- Strength, power, and unity through loving kindness

Have you ever wondered about the meaning of life? "What does it all mean? Why are we here? What is the purpose of existence?" These questions have haunted humankind since we were evolved enough to come up with them. We wonder about meaning and if there is some guiding purpose for the existence of life on Earth.

The funny thing is, the meaning of life isn't all that complicated. In fact, it's even obvious. Yet most of us don't see it. The meaning of life stares us in the face, clamors from within us to be heard, and struggles to rise up out of our hearts and overcome us; yet we resist, all the while looking for it, searching for it, even calling its name.

And what is it? Buddha knew. Jesus knew. Many others since—famous or not, leaders or not, remembered or not—have known. Yet even when someone tells us the meaning of life, we might not believe it, see it, or really find ourselves able to understand it. But there it is, waiting for us to open our eyes, wake up, and see it. The answer to all our searching is simply this: love.

The Zen Path Leads to Love

In Buddhism, love, or "loving kindness" (*metta*), is a guiding principle. This concept can be tricky to understand, because throughout this book, we have talked about Zen as a process of total awareness, mindfulness, and nonattachment. If Zen is all about letting go and living in a state of noninvolved awareness, then (in the immortal words of Tina Turner) what's love got to do with it? Stepping back and seeing, moving with the currents of life, watching it all happen without judging, without labeling things "good" and "bad"—how does that fit in with love, with kindness, with the Buddhist concept of "loving kindness"? Zen is about letting go of striving, releasing desire, but don't we strive for love? Don't we desire it, almost desperately?

Zen-Speak

In Pali, the scriptural language of Buddhism and the language in which the Buddha's sutras (or *suttas*, the written record of what the Buddha said—basically, his speeches or teachings) were written, **metta** is the word for "love." The Buddha's sutra on loving kindness is called the *Metta Sutta*.

Letting Go and Loving

Being human, living in our natural state of nonseeing, of delusion, we all desire love. But that's not the fault of love; that's the fault of our faulty vision. Here's how it works: Zen teaches us that desire causes suffering. Desire, attachment, and striving delude us and distract us from our true nature and the true nature of the world. The practice of Zen—zazen, mindfulness, awareness, nonattachment, etc.—helps us let go of desire and attachment, thereby releasing us from suffering. But then what? What do we see? What's left? A big blank nothing?

Certainly not! What we see when we wake up and look at our real selves, the other sentient beings around us, the real world, is love: love is like a great current flowing through all life, animating it and driving it from within. Remember the 10 Bulls we talked about, those illustrations that represent the search for enlightenment? (See Appendix C for illustrations of the 10 Bulls.) At the end, the seeker of the bull doesn't just float off into some blissful heaven. The enlightened one returns to the world and, no longer plagued by delusion, is driven by one purpose: love.

When we finally see the love that flows through us and around us and through and around other living things, suddenly hate and pettiness and separation seem irrelevant and absurd. Why would we hate anyone or anything when they are filled with the same love that fills each of us? Recognizing the love within us leads to the recognition that this great river of love unifies all life. It is the essence of our true nature—ours and everyone else's.

There's No Place Like Home—and You Are Already There

Remember when Dorothy woke up at the end of *The Wizard of Oz* with the recognition that all she had been searching for was within her all the time? She realized that the fantastical world she had created in her own mind was just an illusion, a convoluted and seductive and sometimes frightening dream of a journey outward to look for meaning, for love, for her true home. That movie isn't a classic by coincidence. Judy Garland's voice and Ray Bolger's physical comedy and all those fantastic Technicolor effects aside, *The Wizard of Oz* sets forth an eternal truth: We already have love within us.

We have everything we need already. "And if I ever go looking for my heart's desire again, I won't look any further than my own backyard," Dorothy realized. There is, indeed, no place like home, and home is within your own heart. It doesn't matter where you are, who you are with, or what is going on around you. Click the heels of your ruby slippers, and you are already home. Open your heart and step inside, set up your house, and settle in and live there. *You are home.* This is what we mean when we keep telling you that you are already perfect. You have all the tools, all the ingredients. Sit. Be still. Listen. Wake up. You'll see it. It's love.

As Dorothy learned with a click of her ruby slipper heels, we already have all we need within us.

And once you see it, there it is: everywhere. And then what? Seeing love everywhere, seeing how we are all connected, finally seeing the meaning of it all, the completed puzzle, the great beauty and rightness of it, we finally recognize that as long as we live on this Earth, immersed in love, a being made of love, there is only one way to behave, only one way to act: with kindness.

One Hand Clapping
The difference between misery and happiness depends on what we do with our attention. Do we, in the mist of water, look for something elsewhere to drink? Transformation comes from looking deeply within, to a state that exists before fear and isolation arise, the state in which we are inviolably whole just as we are. We connect to ourselves, to our own true experience, and discover there that to be alive means to be whole.
—From *Loving-Kindness: The Revolutionary Art of Happiness* by Sharon Salzberg

Loving Kindness: Ring Any Bells?

Gary will never forget the time when he was loaded with luggage on a business trip to London and had forgotten to grab a luggage cart at the gate. As he struggled to make his way out of the Heathrow Airport, an older British woman called out to him and told him to add his luggage to the cart she and her husband were using. Gary was so tired and so grateful for this kindness. He thinks of that woman sometimes. She helped him, purely out of loving kindness. She didn't gain anything except the gratitude of a stranger from another country. Or did she?

Kindness. Hmmm. A kinder, gentler world? A kinder, gentler family? A kinder, gentler partner? A kinder, gentler parent? A kinder, gentler stranger? Kindness almost seems to be a cliché, words we say, almost in jest, but don't really practice. What does it mean, *kindness* or *loving kindness*?

Kindness has a bit of a bad rap these days. Sometimes it almost seems a sign of weakness. Being kind seems hard to do when other people annoy us, get in our way, or behave badly. That whole "do unto others" business, that "love your enemy" business, well … doesn't it all just seem a little old-fashioned?

Kindness: Furthering the Connection

How strange and skewed our value system has become. Being kind doesn't mean being a doormat. Rather, being kind generates an immense source of power: the power that comes from unity rather than separation. When we send out kindness to others, it comes back to us. Barriers fall away. We vibrate with that universal current of love, and others find their way back to it also, just from being in the proximity of its power.

Loving kindness is infectious and generates a ripple effect. When someone offers us kindness, we become more giving and more open. Whether we are consciously aware of it or not, we are all connected and can sense the energy emanating from the people around us. We feel it, and it influences us. Kindness spreads, and so does its opposite.

So what does that mean for Zen living? We can't coerce others to be kind, but we can, nevertheless, spread kindness and love around the world by practicing it ourselves.

Nirvana Notes

Think about a time when someone was kind to you for no apparent reason or benefit to them. How did you feel? How did you react? Write about it.

But what if you don't feel it? Can you force loving kindness? How do you get to the place where you can practice loving kindness with ease and compassion—that place where you want to do it, feel it coming from inside you? We've seen people who spend their lives giving to others and who seem burned out and resentful about it. How do you practice loving kindness and compassion toward humanity in a way that nourishes you and others at the same time?

By not striving for it. Gary and Eve have both noticed that when they feel centered and clear and calm, loving kindness comes naturally, but when they are out of balance and feeling immersed in stress (attachments, desires, *dukkha*), loving kindness isn't so easy. But is forcing kindness the best way? Although acting kind might sometimes help spur the honest feeling of kindness, Zen suggests a better way.

Stop Striving for Loving Kindness, and It Will Come

Remember, when you let go of your attachments and desires, only love remains. Just as the practice of Zen can help us release our attachments, it can also help us release our striving toward kindness! This might seem contradictory—stop striving to be kind? Yes! This is Zen. Let go of all striving, no matter what it consists of. Let go of labels, of "shoulds" and "can'ts" and "good" and "bad." Let it all go, and love will rise up unbidden as the great force it is, and when it does, kindness will be the only course of action. It will come naturally and easily. It will be what feels right, what you simply do. In your doing and being, you will find kindness, compassion, and love.

In the practice of your life, this kindness, love, and compassion can manifest itself in many ways. Perhaps you will step back from the angry reactions of others in your life, returning anger with compassion. Perhaps you will seek out opportunities to relieve the suffering of others because you feel such compassion for the humanity in every soul around you.

Perhaps you will stop eating meat because you can no longer condone the killing of animals. Perhaps you will stop and really see for the first time the people in your city or town who are suffering, who can barely meet their basic needs, and you will feel compelled to help them. How loving kindness happens to you is a highly individual thing—but the fact that it can happen to you, that you can get to that place through the practice of Zen—well, that's universal. That's where unity lives.

In other words, focus on your Zen practice. Focus on mindfulness, on zazen, on being and doing. The loving kindness part will take care of itself because it is an organic part of the reality that you will comprehend through the practice of Zen. When you practice Zen, your being and doing will come out of loving kindness.

How easy is that?

Monkey Mind! _____

It's easy to think we "should" be helping, volunteering, sacrificing, giving to charity, and all those other things that make us feel we are doing our part. But don't force it! Instead, practice. Giving to others flows so naturally out of a Zen practice that it loses its sense of obligation and becomes not only a natural reaction to perceptions of the world, but a source of pure joy.

Zen and the Art of ... International Politics?

It might be one thing to practice Zen and, by extension, loving kindness, but what do you do when others don't practice it—especially others whose decisions affect your world? World leaders in many different countries preach adherence to religious tenets (whichever ones), but sometimes they also act steeped in a deep suspicion of difference. We've all seen this happening in our world—all too often with tragic results.

Somehow, when cultures clash and violence results—violence that affects us and the people we know and love—loving kindness seems a much more urgent matter. How can we "inflict" the power of loving kindness on others? Can't we make others see it, feel it, and enact it in their policy decisions?

No, we can't. You already know you can only control your own reactions, and you can't control others. Yet at the same time, as we mentioned earlier, loving kindness does have a ripple effect. It is indeed infectious in the best way. So maybe we can make a difference after all?

Yes, we can! But making a difference the Zen way isn't about evangelizing or controlling or even arguing with others. It isn't about doing nothing at all, however. Instead, the way to make a difference in the world through Zen living is simple: Practice. Be. Do. Recognize the unity in all life, in all people and cultures. And as you do this and as you make your way through life and through the world, others will see that such a way of thinking is possible. When you perceive unity rather than difference, others will, too—not because you force them to but just because you do it.

Practice Loving Kindness, and Others Will Follow

The practice of Zen opens you to new possibilities for behaving and doing and being because it clears out all the attachments and desires that have been interfering with your ability to really make a difference. Maybe you have been so caught up in your own delusions that you haven't had the energy to look outward and see how others could benefit from interaction with you. Maybe you have forgotten how to listen or how to give of yourself. Maybe you have convinced yourself that some people in the world are essentially different from you and should be at best suspected and at worst despised. You wouldn't be the only one! And if you think this isn't you, are you sure? Are you really sure there are no people you put in a different "category" or "class" than yourself?

Practice, practice, then mindfully look around. What needs doing? What, in your compassionate mindfulness, do you see? Do you see difference? Or do you see the common current of being that ties us together, the energy of love that lives in the hearts of each of us, no matter what we do, where we live, how much money we make, how we look, what we believe, or even how we behave?

Now, chances are, you don't have a huge amount of influence in the international political sphere (we don't, either). But even if you don't have an audience with the president any time soon, how can the simple recognition of the unity of all things influence what goes on in the world? When you practice mindfulness, when you learn how to listen, when you wake up and see what the world is doing around you, you gain a new awareness of the currents and trends of your culture. What world leaders do is often a direct result of how the people they lead react to world events. If a president or other leader of a country, or even of a state or city, knows that a particular decision will be popular, he or she will be more likely to make that decision. On the other hand, if that leader knows that a decision—particularly one based on fear, divisiveness, hate—will cause an outcry of protest, he probably won't make that decision.

Zen-Speak

I believe that every human being has an innate desire for happiness and does not want to suffer. I also believe that the very purpose of life is to experience his happiness. I believe that each of us has the same potential to develop inner peace and thereby achieve happiness and joy. Whether we are rich or poor, educated or uneducated, black or white, from the East or the West, our potential is equal. We are all the same …

—From *An Open Heart: Practicing Compassion in Everyday Life* by The Dalai Lama

Then again, actions in the world that are contradictory to loving kindness might well happen anyway. In fact, we can guarantee they will (witness September 11 and much of the aftermath), and you can't stop that. You can't make things happen or not happen. But you can do, and be, in the best way you know how. Trust us when we say that others will follow your lead.

Monkey Mind!

When someone behaves rudely, aggressively, or otherwise negatively, do you attach to that behavior and let it spur you on to behave the same way to others? Or do you let it bounce off you, pass you by, noticing it and consciously deciding to let it go? Guess which way is the Zen way?

Sometimes (and this is part of being a leader), the leader will choose the unpopular decision, but generally, leading doesn't mean acting in a vacuum. It means leading a group of people who influence the flows and currents of events. A cruel leader might lead passive or fearful or subjugated people. A benevolent leader might lead supportive or contented or loyal people. Of course, exceptions even to these rules exist, but the fact is that the minds and actions—the being and doing—of the people in the world can impact what leaders do.

"Now wait one minute," you might be protesting. "Didn't you just get through saying that we can't control the actions of others?" Yes, yes we did say that, and we are happy you're paying attention! However, what we mean by that is not that your actions don't influence the actions of others. They do! We also said, at the beginning of this chapter, that the practice of loving kindness—the practice that flows naturally out of living

Zen—influences those who experience it in others. That's the ripple effect. Your loving kindness can help generate love and kindness in others. In the same way, rejecting the negative energy that flows from others, repelling it with loving kindness, also has a ripple effect, nipping one sort of energy in the bud and replacing it with another.

None of us lives in a vacuum. We live in a world community, and that's how it works. We are all connected. We are all part of the universal flow of energy, so what comes from one flows through the rest. Seeing this, really recognizing the truth of it, can be a pretty powerful influence after all.

You can't force someone to believe something they don't believe, and you might or might not be able (through rewards, punishments, or coercion) to make somebody do something they don't really want to do. But you can walk the earth peacefully and contentedly, being kind to others, feeling compassion, exuding the loving energy you've tapped into by freeing yourself from attachments and delusions. A wise, enlightened community with an unclouded sense of purpose focused on helping relieve suffering in the world can indeed affect what happens in the world.

Let Go of Others, Let Go of What You Grasp, and Free Yourself

But again, you can't force other people around you to become wise and enlightened. And when what you do doesn't seem to influence what happens around you, part of Zen living is also to let that go. All you can do is work, each day, each moment, toward becoming wiser and more enlightened yourself. Let go of others, let go of what you grasp, and free yourself. Then, without forcing anybody to do anything, your enlightened state will influence others. Turning away anger with kindness, acting out of love, listening deeply to others who are suffering, spending your energy helping rather than hurting, giving rather than taking—these things *do* change the world! And (ironically) they do so the best when you don't struggle but simply let go and do, let go and be.

Sure, it's more Zen paradox: Change people by ceasing your efforts to change people. Change people by recognizing that we are all the same. Change people by looking within yourself. Yet we see it happen every day—the way an act of kindness, a gesture of love, or a compassionate spirit turns anger, hate, frustration and despair into hope.

The Healing Power of Loving Kindness

Casting your loving kindness out into the world can do even more than make people feel good or change their course of action. It can actually heal them. And it can heal you, too. Loving kindness should arise naturally out of a Zen practice, but old habits die hard and we can all use some techniques for reframing our patterns in a more loving way. Here are some suggestions for consciously and purposefully healing the world when you don't feel particularly inspired:

♦ Talk to yourself. Remind yourself that your attitude will influence those around you. Rude store clerk? Catty friend? Critical parent? Remind yourself how you are all connected, and repel that negative energy with a healthy dose of kindness. (It's actually kind of fun to see the looks on their faces.)

♦ Logic can sometimes seem the most sensible course of action. Remember that feelings are only feelings and don't define you or anyone else. Acknowledge yours, and let them pass away. Also, look at your reactions. Are you reacting out of old fears, desires, or attachments? What happens when you let all that go?

Zen-Speak

Most of our suffering is born from our lack of understanding and insight that there is no separate self. The other person is you, you are the other person. If you get in touch with that truth, anger will vanish.

—From *Anger: Wisdom for Cooling the Flames* by Thich Nhat Hanh

♦ Feel their pain. Empathy can help you to reset a negative spiral of thought and feeling. Imagine you are someone else. How would you really feel and react if you were on the other side of that proverbial fence?

♦ Act out of a spirited sense of compassion. What can you do to relieve someone's suffering? Get creative. There is so much dukkha out there, and you have the power to banish some of it! Go for it!

Zen to Unify the Planet

Finally, we want to emphasize one last time how the practice of Zen living helps us all perceive our commonality rather than our differences. In a time when cultures clash, this sense of unity can spell the difference between a world that falls apart and a world that comes together to evolve into something greater than it was before. The whole of humanity can be greater than the sum of its parts. We can spread the word, not by evangelizing but by waking up, one zazen session at a time.

The Least You Need to Know

◆ Love really is the answer. Zen living reveals that loving kindness, compassion, and the desire to relieve the suffering of others emerge naturally from a Zen practice.

◆ As the world experiences struggle, conflict, and pain, Zen living can teach those who practice it how to release fear, hate, and the delusion of difference.

◆ Loving kindness can heal emotional, political, social, and spiritual separation.

◆ We can help spread strength, power, and unity through loving kindness by practicing mindfulness every day.

Chapter 24

Everyday Zen

In This Chapter

◆ You don't have to call it Zen

◆ Making Zen your own

◆ If you could write your own book about your Zen awakening, what would you include?

◆ You are the universe, and you have the universe within you

Zen is just your life, lived fully. But you don't have to call it Zen. Maybe you want to tell people you are "into Zen" or go to a Zen center to practice zazen and talk with other people on a similar path. Or maybe you don't. Maybe you aren't interested in Buddhism, necessarily, or in attaining enlightenment. You just want to make the most of your present moment. You want to find your true self and really live your life. Great! That's Zen, whether you call it that or not—because by now you know that Zen defies labels, categories, comparisons, and anything else separate from you and your universe.

How you practice Zen, what techniques you choose to follow, and which parts of the tradition you choose to embrace—that's all up to you. It's your life. You might not want to go all out with the whole Zen thing—the rituals, koan practice, and finding a Zen master. Those things can be very helpful, but they aren't required. Your Zen is in you. It doesn't really matter how you find it.

Zen resists definitions, and true Zen isn't called anything. So don't worry about it. Just concentrate on being you. The other stuff is neither here nor there.

Making Zen Your Own

People who embark on a spiritual path of any kind, including one seeking self-knowledge, go through a process. Sometimes it seems easy. Sometimes it seems so far from your understanding you can't remember why you are even doing it. Then, all of a sudden, you feel drenched in peace, like it all makes sense and you can imagine letting go of all your attachments without a thought.

This process is yours, and you can drape it over your life in whatever way makes sense to you. No one else can tell you how to find truth, your true self, or enlightenment. As the Buddha is famous for saying: Be a light unto yourself. Teachers, masters, and books can all point the way, but they are all fingers pointing to the moon. You have to lift your own head and look at the moon. Expert guidance can save you some time, but the real work is up to you.

Nirvana Notes

Are you still practicing your zazen every day? Even when it gets boring, zazen is incredibly important for helping to maintain a Zen attitude. And if your zazen is boring, maybe you aren't really paying attention!

Monkey Mind!

Personal dissatisfaction or unhappiness are reasons many people seek out Zen, but they are not sufficient motivation to continue a practice. Finding wonder, serenity, and self-knowledge through mindfulness is the best motivation for continuing a Zen practice.

You might not do the work like anyone ever did it before. But what great person's great life was ever just like anyone else's who came before? Not Buddha's. Not Jesus'. Not Muhammad's. Not Moses'. We could name 100 others, and they all found truth in their own way. You can, too. You don't need anyone's permission.

In Chapter 3, we talked about Zen as the cowboy religion. It's also like the pioneer religion. You are a pioneer, and you are pioneering the vast, uncharted terrain of you. Maybe you'll homestead. Maybe you'll be a wanderer. But the land is yours. You can't trespass on what already belongs to you. You get to make the rules.

And that's the great thing about Zen. We've given you lots of advice and many suggestions in this book, things that have helped both of us and that we thought might make the journey into your own present moment easier for you. But when it comes right down to it, you are ready to write your own book about how you go about living your life. What better subject for a book could there be?

Let's say you do write the book of you. How would you start?

How Does Your Life Look?

Take an honest look at your life. How is it going so far? How happy are you most of the time? How content, how satisfied? How is your job? How are your relationships? How do you feel about yourself?

Where do you feel the need to change?

If you are unhappy or dissatisfied, you are suffering, and if you've read this book, you know what causes that. What are you obsessing over, what are you attaching to, what are you convincing yourself is lasting or important that really isn't? How have you neglected to look inside? And when you do look inside, what do you see? Look deeper. Deeper still. There is a diamond in there. We know it for a fact.

Every Moment Is Now

The next chapter of your book might be about how you have come to see how reality exists only in the present moment. Your past is interesting, or painful, or memorable, but it isn't real anymore. The future never actually comes. It is always ahead of you. Only now matters. What does that mean for you right now? What exists in your present moment? Who are you in the present moment? Who do you love in the present moment? What is your work in the present moment? What surrounds you in the present moment? What do you see and hear, think and feel, know and wonder about? What do you do, and what do you wait for? What do you fear, and what do you love?

And how do you learn to wake up to the present moment? Zazen? Mindfulness in daily life? Contemplation of Zen texts? Talking with friends? More zazen? How did you get there? Or are you getting there still?

All Is One

Then one day you recognize, in your contemplation, your meditation, that all those boundaries and distinctions you made to separate yourself from everyone else and to separate out everything else are all temporary and, in the scheme of things, meaningless. What happened when you recognized the unity of all existence? What happened when you saw your part in it? Did you feel at once more powerful and less? Happier and more detached? Did you feel a nostalgia followed by excitement at the potential of this new way of seeing? How did it happen for you?

One Hand Clapping

The Zen monk Joshu, a character in many Zen koans, is considered one of the greatest Zen masters of the T'ang dynasty in China. When he first began his training, Joshu studied under the Zen master Nansen, and a famous interchange between them goes something like this:

Joshu: What is the Way?

Nansen: Ordinary mind.

Joshu: Should we strive toward it?

Nansen: If you strive toward it, you go away from it.

Joshu: If we don't strive toward it, how can we know it is the Way?

Nansen: The Way does not belong to knowing or not knowing. Knowing is delusion. Not knowing is blankness. To attain the Way without doubt is to attain the vast and boundless void. How can there be right or wrong in there?

Live in the Doing

After your many new perceptions, you finally brought it all back to the things you are doing in your present moment. How did you bring Zen to your relationships, your job, your hobbies, your art, or your favorite sport? How did you bring mindfulness into your daily household chores? How did you bring Zen into your everyday work? What happened that let you finally live fully in your doing?

Your Everlasting Final Chapter

Your personal book about Zen will have a doozy of a final chapter because once you get to the place where you see the truth, the truth is everlasting. You will never cease to be because of what you are made from. Your eternal self, recognized and brought into the light, will endure. It all comes down to you—the real, universal you. You haven't lost anything except your suffering.

And no matter how endless and everlasting and eternal you are, always remember to come back to the world and live in it. Zen master Soyen Shaku offered the following guidelines for life, as quoted in *Zen Flesh, Zen Bones*, compiled by Paul Reps and Nyogen Senzaki, which we think make an apt reminder about living Zen in the world:

In the morning before dressing, light incense and meditate.

Retire at a regular hour. Partake of food at regular intervals. Eat with moderation and never to the point of satisfaction.

Receive a guest with the same attitude you have when alone. When alone, maintain the same attitude you have in receiving guests.

Watch what you say, and whatever you say, practice it.

When an opportunity comes, do not let it pass by, yet always think twice before acting.

Do not regret the past. Look to the future.

Have the fearless attitude of a hero and the loving heart of a child.

Upon retiring, sleep as if you had entered your last sleep. Upon awakening, leave your bed behind you instantly as if you had cast away a pair of old shoes.

The Universe Within

But we don't want to leave things exactly like that, with the "you, you, you" mantra echoing. It's your life, your process, your Zen. But on the other hand, what is in you is in us, in Gary and Eve, in your parents and children and friends, in all the people you know and all the people you don't know, right there in your neighborhood, in your city, your country, and on the other side of the world. What is in you is in the universe, and in everything and everyone in the universe. And the whole universe is within you.

This is the place where Zen extends beyond the boundaries of you and, ideally, blurs those boundaries until they don't seem that important. A lot of Zen literature talks about the illusion of the material world, but it isn't that the world and everything in it doesn't exist. It isn't that the self doesn't exist.

It all exists. Intuitively, you know the couch you are sitting on is real and the friend on the phone with you is real, too. You know you are real because you can feel it.

So if Zen tells you the "self" is an illusion, you aren't really going to believe it. That isn't what Zen is saying. Zen says: The self is real, the world is real, the universe is real, but we are all a part of the same thing. So when you look at it from a more detached perspective, we all look remarkably similar. We are all real, yet we are all one. Our separateness is temporary, and in that it can seem like an illusion, but what is inside us is unity.

> **Monkey Mind!**
> How can you be you without clinging to your ideas about yourself? By remembering that your ideas are only a superficial part of the picture. Are you your blond hair or your people skills or your ability to bench-press 200 pounds? Of course not. You can still be you even when those external things change, as they inevitably will.

Remember the ocean analogy so often used in Zen? Every wave in the ocean, every whirlpool and eddy, is real. But they are transitory. They swell up, foam or swirl, break or sink back down into the great vast ocean, and when they arise, they are very real. That wave is most definitely there, moving through the ocean, rolling onto the beach, breaking on the sand. But then, where is the wave? Yet there is the ocean, always there, never gone. Because the ocean remains, so does the wave. And yet its temporary manifestation as a thing you could see, point to, saying, "There's a wave," that has passed on. And now, other waves have taken its place, and in a moment, they, too, will pass on. And more will come, and some will look different from others, and some will seem similar, but they will all move, roll in, spread out on the shore, sink into the sand, and pull back into the sea.

These are all just ideas for you to consider. Don't get too attached to them! We are all waves, even Zen masters, even world leaders, even movie stars and famous athletes and book authors. Even criminals and saints and babies and elderly people with no one coming to visit them. Even people in pain and people in love. Even the Buddha himself. We come and we go, but the ocean that flows through each of us and is an eternal part of us; it is everlasting. And we have this ocean within us. We are made of it, just like waves are made of it. Imagine a wave saying, "Here I am, but where is the ocean? Deep down inside? I can't find it!" The question is absurd because the wave is made of ocean. The wave is the ocean. But the wave just doesn't see it because it too is caught up in being a wave.

And we, too, are all caught up in the details, when very little of it—some would say none of it—is worth a whole lot of energy. To relish, even rejoice in being a wave, with the recognition that this life on Earth is limited and will end and that's okay because it's just a little fraction of what we are in the present moment—that is Zen.

That curiously self-aware wave we just wrote about will be living Zen if it recognizes every bit of foam, every bubble, every speck of algae, and every fish that passes through it. If it rejoices in the clear or cloudy sky, the fair or turbulent weather, and the whole long rise, swell, and fall of itself in the context of the whole ocean. If it recognizes the other waves, too, and makes room for them. And if it can let go of itself and rejoin the ocean when its time as a wave has come to an end—because how can a wave decide to keep being a wave after it breaks on the shore? It can't. It sinks back into the ocean, no matter what it desires or strives after. That is the nature of reality.

Maybe you've noticed that we keep going back and forth: You are you. But you are the universe! But you are still you. But you are still the universe! That is one of the recognitions of Zen. Can you find your place within that dichotomy, a place that makes sense? You can try.

> ## One Hand Clapping
>
> The aspiration of the Zen student goes further than the wish to be a well-rounded person managing their lives in the world. The Zen practitioner wishes to move on from this plane of firm ego strength to one where the ego and the personal self are transcended. He or she wishes to experience the source from which human consciousness arises and to live out of this very ground of being. The question is now no longer "I" focused but it is instead "Who am I?"
>
> —From *The Elements of Zen* by David Scott and Tony Doubleday

And trying like this is a lot of fun because that means living Zen! And living Zen means living like never before (and like it has always been): being truly alive, not wasting a moment of this transitory time we have on Earth, as humans, with the opportunity to experience, feel, think, love, and make other people's lives better, too.

You can do it. You can make your right now, which is to say your entire life and self, everything it can be. And all you have to do to begin is to pay attention.

> ### Nirvana Notes
>
> Keep a written record of the ways your life has changed from your practice of Zen. You can refer to it during those times when you need inspiration or when one more second of zazen seems impossible.

The Present Embrace

Whatever effect living Zen has on your life, we know it will be a positive one. We believe the human experience—getting to be that wave for a while—is a great, powerful, and ultimately positive experience, so living it mindfully is great, powerful, and ultimately positive, too.

Let the present embrace you and see what happens. Zen living!

The Least You Need to Know

◆ You can live Zen without calling it Zen. You can call it whatever you want to call it, including nothing at all (which would be very Zenlike).

◆ Zen is your life, so you can make it into whatever you want. Search for truth your own way.

◆ Zen means finding your place within the knowledge that you are you, and you are also the whole universe.

◆ Let your present moment embrace you, and you will be living Zen.

Further Reading

Want more Zen living resources? The following should help get you started.

Books

We like to read books as well as write them. Here are a few of our favorites that we find helpful and inspiring:

Austin, James H., M.D. *Zen and the Brain: Toward an Understanding of Meditation and Consciousness.* Cambridge, MA: The MIT Press, 1998.

Beck, Charlotte Joko. *Everyday Zen.* San Francisco, CA: HarperSanFrancisco, 1989.

———. *Nothing Special: Living Zen.* San Francisco, CA: HarperSanFrancisco, 1993.

Budilovsky, Joan, and Eve Adamson. *The Complete Idiot's Guide to Meditation, Second Edition.* Indianapolis, IN: Alpha Books, 2003.

———. *The Complete Idiot's Guide to Yoga, Third Edition.* Indianapolis, IN: Alpha Books, 2003.

Carradine, David, and David Nakahara. *Introduction to Chi Kung.* New York, NY: Henry Holt and Company, 1997.

Chearney, Lee Ann. *Visits: Caring for an Aging Parent*. New York, NY: Three Rivers Press, 1998.

Chih-I. Stopping and Seeing: *A Comprehensive Course in Buddhist Meditation*. Translated by Thomas Cleary. Boston, MA: Shambhala, 1997.

Crompton, Paul. Tai Chi: *A Practical Introduction*. Boston, MA: Element, 1998 (first published as *The Art of Tai Chi* in the U.K. by Element Books, Ltd., 1993).

Dalai Lama. *Awakening the Mind, Lightening the Heart: Core Teachings of Tibetan Buddhism*. San Francisco, CA: HarperSanFrancisco, 1995.

———. *Ethics for the New Millennium*. New York, NY: Riverhead Books, 1999.

———. *An Open Heart: Practicing Compassion in Everyday Life*. Boston, MA: Little Brown and Co., 2001.

Dalai Lama and Howard C. Cutler. *The Art of Happiness: A Handbook for Living*. New York, NY: Riverhead Books, 1998.

Davich, Victor N. *The Best Guide to Meditation*. Los Angeles, CA: Renaissance Books, 1998.

———. *8-Minute Meditation*. New York, NY: Perigee, 2004.

DeMello, Anthony. *Wellsprings: A Book of Spiritual Exercises*. New York, NY: Image Books, 1986 (originally published in India by Gujarat Sahitya Prakash in 1984).

DiSanto, Ronald L., and Thomas J. Steele. *Guidebook to Zen and the Art of Motorcycle Maintenance: An Inquiry into Values by Robert M. Pirsig*. New York, NY: William Morrow and Company, Inc., 1990.

Dominguez, Joe, and Vicki Robin. *Your Money or Your Life, New Edition*. New York, NY: Penguin, 1999 (originally published by Viking Penguin, 1992).

Elgin, Duane. *Voluntary Simplicity, Revised Edition*. New York, NY: Quill, 1993.

Epstein, Mark, M.D. *Going to Pieces Without Falling Apart: A Buddhist Perspective on Wholeness*. New York, NY: Broadway Books, 1998.

Foster, Nelson, and Jack Shoemaker, eds. *The Roaring Stream: A New Zen Reader*. Hopewell, NJ: Ecco Press, 1996.

Franck, Frederick. *Zen and Zen Classics: Selections from R. H. Blyth*. Torrance, CA: Heian International, Inc., 1978.

———. *Zen Seeing, Zen Drawing: Meditation in Action*. New York, NY: Bantam Books, 1993.

Glassman, Bernard, and Rick Fields. *Instructions to the Cook: A Zen Master's Lessons in Living a Life That Matters*. New York, NY: Bell Tower, 1996.

Goddard, Dwight. *A Buddhist Bible*. Boston, MA: Beacon Press, 1970 (first published by E. P. Dutton & Co. in 1938).

Goldberg, Natalie. *Writing Down the Bones: Freeing the Writer Within*. Boston, MA: Shambhala, 1986.

Goleman, Daniel. *Emotional Intelligence*. New York, NY: Bantam Books, 1995.

Hagen, Steve. *Buddhism Plain and Simple*. Boston, MA: Charles E. Tuttle Co., Inc., 1997.

Hanh, Thich Nhat. *Anger: Wisdom for Cooling the Flames*. New York, NY: Riverhead Books, 2001.

———. *Breathe! You Are Alive: Sutra on the Full Awareness of Breathing, Revised Edition*. Berkeley, CA: Parallax Press, 1996.

———. *For a Future to Be Possible: Commentaries on the Five Wonderful Precepts*. Berkeley, CA: Parallax Press, 1993.

———. *The Miracle of Mindfulness*. Boston, MA: Beacon Press, 1975.

———. *Peace Is Every Step: The Path of Mindfulness in Everyday Life*. New York, NY: Bantam Books, 1991.

Humphreys, Christmas. *A Western Approach to Zen*. Wheaton, IL: Quest Books, 1971.

Kabat-Zinn, Jon. *Full Catastrophe Living: Using the Wisdom of Your Body and Mind to Face Stress, Pain, and Illness*. New York, NY: Delta, 1990.

———. *Wherever You Go, There You Are: Mindfulness Meditation in Everyday Life*. New York, NY: Hyperion, 1994.

Kapleau, Philip. *The Three Pillars of Zen, Twenty-Fifth Anniversary Edition*. New York, NY: Anchor Books/Doubleday, 1980 (a revised and expanded edition of the original published by John Weatherhill, Inc., in 1965).

Katagiri, Dainin. *You Have to Say Something: Manifesting Zen Insight*. Edited by Steve Hagen. Boston, MA: Shambhala, 2000.

Kerouac, Jack. *The Dharma Bums*. New York, NY: Penguin Books, 1976 (first published by The Viking Press, 1958).

———. *On the Road*. New York, NY: Penguin Books, 1976 (first published by Viking Press, 1957).

Kornfield, Jack. *A Path with Heart*. New York, NY: Bantam, 1993.

Kubose, Gyomay M. *Zen Koans*. Chicago, IL: Henry Regnery Company, 1973.

Langer, Ellen J. *Mindfulness*. Reading, MA: Addison-Wesley, 1990.

Larkin, Geri. *Stumbling Toward Enlightenment*. Berkeley, CA: Celestial Arts, 1997.

LeVert, Suzanne, and Gary McClain, Ph.D. *The Complete Idiot's Guide to Breaking Bad Habits, Second Edition*. Indianapolis, IN: Alpha Books, 2000.

Luk, Charles (Lu K'uan Yü). *The Secrets of Chinese Meditation*. York Beach, ME: Samuel Weiser, Inc., 1969 (first published in England in 1964).

Mitchell, Stephen, comp. and ed. *Dropping Ashes on the Buddha: The Teaching of Zen Master Seung Sahn*. New York, NY: Grove Press, 1976.

Pirsig, Robert M. *Zen and the Art of Motorcycle Maintenance: An Inquiry into Values*. New York, NY: William Morrow and Company, Inc., 1974.

Reps, Paul, and Nyogen Senzaki. *Zen Flesh, Zen Bones: A Collection of Zen and Pre-Zen Writings*. Boston, MA: Tuttle Publishing, 1957.

Saddhatissa, H. *An Introduction to Buddhism*. London, UK: British Mahabodhi Society (no date).

Salzberg, Sharon. *Loving-Kindness: The Revolutionary Art of Happiness*. Boston, MA: Shambhala, 1997.

Scott, David, and Tony Doubleday. *The Elements of Zen*. Rockport, MA: Element Books, Inc., 1992.

Smith, Jean, ed. *365 Zen*. San Francisco, CA: HarperSanFrancisco, 1999.

———. *The Beginner's Guide to Zen Buddhism*. New York, NY: Bell Tower, 2000.

St. James, Elaine. *The Simplicity Reader*. New York, NY: Smithmark, 1999.

St. Ruth, Diana, and Richard St. Ruth. *The Simple Guide to Zen Buddhism*. Kent, England: Global Books, 1998.

Stryk, Lucien, and Takashi Ikemoto, comp. and trans. *Zen: Poems, Prayers, Sermons, Anecdotes, Interviews, Second Edition*. Chicago, IL: Swallow Press, 1981 (originally published by Doubleday & Co., Inc., in 1963).

Suzuki, Shunryu. *Zen Mind, Beginner's Mind, Revised Edition*. New York, NY: Weatherhill, 1999.

Trungpa, Chögyam. *Meditation in Action*. Boston, MA: Shambhala, 1996.

Watts, Alan. *Zen and the Beat Way*. Boston, MA: Charles E. Tuttle Co., Inc., 1997.

Zen Master Keizan. *Transmission of Light: Zen in the Art of Enlightenment*. Translated by Thomas Cleary. San Francisco, CA: North Point Press, 1990.

Websites

As long as you are surfing, you might as well surf for sites that encourage and inspire you in your quest for Zen living. Here are a few we love:

www.geocities.com/Athens/Parthenon/6469/main.html
This site, As Zen Replaces the Id, is an interesting site dealing with the link between Zen and psychology

www.dailyzen.com
Daily Zen

www.dharmanet.org/infowebz.html
DharmaNet's Zen Buddhist InfoWeb, the Virtual Library of Online Zen Buddhist Associations, Monasteries and Practice Centers

www.ibiblio.org/zen/faq.html
Frequently asked questions (FAQs) from alt.zen

www.frugalfamilynetwork.com
Frugal Family Network

www.simpleliving.net/
The Simple Living Network

glwarner.narrowgate.net/haiku
The Haiku Gateway

www.dalailama.com
His Holiness the Fourteenth Dalai Lama of Tibet's own website

www.verdant.net/
Overcoming consumerism

glwarner.narrowgate.net/haiku/hkuframe.html
The Shiki Internet Haiku Salon of Matsuyama University

www.simpleliving.net
Simple Living Network

www.tricycle.com
Tricycle.com: The Buddhist Review is the website for the most well-known of Buddhist magazines, includes *Buddhist Basics* and *Daily Dharma*

www.ciolek.com/WWWVL-Zen.html
Zen Buddhism WWW Virtual Library

www.rider.edu/users/suler/zenstory/zenstory.html
Zen Stories to Tell Your Neighbor contains many famous Zen koans and anecdotes— you'll probably recognize a few

www.zenko.org
Zenko International, an international kyudo (Zen archery) organization

Glossary

asceticism The practice of self-deprivation, which can include doing without possessions, fasting, going without sleep, begging, and even self-inflicted pain.

Bodhidharma A much-legendized figure who traveled to China from India to spread the word of Buddhism. He is usually represented as a scowling figure with a long, hooked nose and was known as the blue-eyed demon because his Aryan appearance and blue eyes were an oddity in China.

bodhisattva Someone who devotes his or her life to ending the suffering and aiding the enlightenment of all sentient beings. In classical Buddhism, bodhisattvas such as Kuan Yin ("Kannon" in Japanese) are similar to gods and goddesses, appearing occasionally to humans in need. A Buddhist who makes a formal commitment to the life of a bodhisattva will vow to follow certain bodhisattva precepts in a formal ceremony.

bodhisattva precepts These are precepts the long-practicing Zen practitioner formally commits to in an official ceremony. They embody the spirit and values of Buddhism. The precepts are (1) Be one with the Buddha; (2) be one with the dharma; (3) be one with the sangha; (4) don't do evil; (5) do good; (6) do good for others; (7) don't kill; (8) don't steal; (9) don't misuse sex; (10) don't lie; (11) don't become intoxicated; (12) don't put down other people; (13) don't consider yourself above anyone or blame anyone; (14) don't be stingy; (15) don't become angry; (16) don't put down the Buddha, the dharma, or the sangha.

Ch'an The Chinese term for "meditation" and for the type of Buddhism that is "Zen" in Japanese.

chi kung An ancient system of movements and other practices designed to maximize the flow of energy, or chi, in the body for greater physical, mental, and spiritual health.

cosmic mudra The traditional zazen hand position in which the dominant hand cradles the other hand just below the navel with thumbs meeting to form an oval shape.

dharma Truth, or truth as realized by the Buddha, or the Buddha's teachings about this truth (or all three).

dhyana The Sanskrit term for "meditation."

Diamond Sutra One of the teachings of the Buddha (written down many years after the words were actually spoken), expounding upon the diamond-hard edge of emptiness that can finally cut through delusion, leading to enlightenment. In many Zen communities, the Diamond Sutra and other sutras such as the Heart Sutra and the Platform Sutra are recited, chanted, and/or studied and contemplated.

dokusan A private meeting between a student and a Zen teacher, during which the student can ask questions, receive encouragement, or present the answer to a koan.

dukkha Suffering or, more generally, that deep feeling of discomfort, dissatisfaction, restlessness, unfulfilled desire, and want that so often characterizes human existence.

Eightfold Path The substance of Buddhism's fourth noble truth, consisting of guidelines for purposeful living that will help pave the way to the release from suffering: right understanding, right thought, right speech, right action, right livelihood, right effort, right mindfulness, and right concentration.

Five Precepts The Buddha's five guidelines for living a compassionate life: (1) practicing nonviolence; (2) cultivating loving kindness; (3) refusing to engage in sexual misconduct; (4) speaking only words of truth and kindness; (5) and refusing to overindulge in food, drink, or the accumulation of possessions.

Four Noble Truths The heart of the dharma, or the Buddha's teaching, these Four Noble Truths state that: (1) To be human is to experience dukkha, or suffering; (2) suffering is caused by desire for or attachment to impermanent things at the expense of the knowledge of truth; (3) suffering can be eliminated by the elimination of desire; (4) desire can be eliminated through the practice of the Eightfold Path. *See also* Eightfold Path.

haiku A form of Japanese poetry traditionally containing three lines of five, seven, and five syllables each. Haikus are meant to be direct expressions of experience, with little, if any, reliance on literary devices such as similes and metaphors (comparing something to something else).

half-lotus pose A less-advanced meditative sitting position than the lotus pose; you place one foot on top of the opposite thigh and the other foot under its opposite thigh.

Japanese sitting pose The traditional meditation posture in Japan; in this pose, the meditator sits on his or her heels with a cushion between the feet to sit on.

karma Also called *kamma*, karma is a Sanskrit term for the universal law of cause and effect. Everything that happens is balanced by an effect, either in this life or the next. Karma isn't punishment for bad behavior or reward for good behavior. In Buddhism, there is no one to punish or reward you. Instead, karma gives you the power to create and determine your own destiny through your actions.

kensho A Japanese word for an enlightenment experience, or an experience of self-realization, sometimes used interchangeably with the terms *nirvana* and *satori. See* nirvana and satori.

kinhin Walking meditation, which can be practiced individually or, in the context of a zendo, in a group with everyone walking in a circle. Kinhin is often used in alternation with zazen during long periods of meditation. In kinhin, the mind does just what it does in zazen. It is only the body that does something different.

koans Illogical scenarios or questions meant to be considered until the mind makes a leap past logic to understand the koan at a higher level. The most famous koan in the West is the "one hand clapping" koan: You can hear the sound of two hands when they clap together. What is the sound of one hand clapping?

kundalini Psychospiritual energy force in the body that can be released and utilized through certain techniques.

kyudo The ancient Japanese way of the bow and arrow, a spiritual exercise designed to teach the archer that bow, arrow, target, and archer are all one. When this realization is achieved, the arrow will always hit the target.

Lin-chi The Chinese word for the branch of Zen (*Ch'an*) called Rinzai in Japan.

lotus pose An ancient yoga/meditation pose that is meant to mimic the perfection of the lotus flower, providing a stable, solid position for meditation. To sit in lotus pose, sit cross-legged and place each foot on top of the opposite thigh.

mandala   A circular, geometric design that draws the eye to its center, designed as a focus for meditation.

mantra   A sound, word, or words chanted during meditation as a point of focus and to evoke certain energies in the body.

martial arts   A system of combat techniques dating back thousands of years and coming out of many cultures. Some define the martial arts as mental and physical methods for self-defense and offense, unarmed or with weapons. Others claim martial arts are primarily spiritual exercises that also work for combat if necessary. Martial arts popular today include tae kwon do, karate, judo, aikido, and tai chi chuan.

metta   The Pali word for "love," or "loving kindness." The Metta Sutta or Metta Sutra is also called the sutra of loving kindness and is attributed to the Buddha.

nirvana   A Sanskrit word meaning "extinction," referring to enlightenment due to the liberation or release from the cycle of death and rebirth. Nirvana is sometimes used interchangeably with the terms *satori* and *kensho*.

Rinzai   Called *Lin-chi* in Chinese, this branch of Zen Buddhism was brought to Japan by Zen master Eisai and emphasizes the practice of koans.

samsara   A Sanskrit word for everyday life in the phenomenal world. Technically, it refers to the succession of births and rebirths before the release from this cycle that comes out of the attainment of nirvana. Practically, the word is often used to refer to the daily existence on Earth.

samurai   Members of the Japanese warrior class, influential in Japanese culture for more than 1,000 years, samurai were famous for their swordsmanship. The Samurai class disappeared in Japan in the nineteenth century.

sangha   The community of either Buddhists or other like-minded people who practice meditating together, or on a wider scale, of all sentient beings, who are essentially one.

satori   A Japanese word for enlightenment as experienced by the Buddha. It's a comprehension of the unity of all things and is sometimes used interchangeably with the terms *nirvana* and *kensho*.

sesshin   A period of intense practice (typically a week or two), with long sessions of zazen, as one might experience on a Zen retreat.

shavasana   The Sanskrit word for "corpse pose." It is a meditative yoga relaxation pose that involves lying on your back on the floor in total relaxation.

Siddhartha Gautama   Sometimes spelled Siddhattha Gotama, this prince born of India's warrior class about five centuries before the birth of Christ was the man who eventually attained enlightenment and became known as Buddha.

Sixth Patriarch   Named Hui-neng, the Sixth Patriarch was Ch'an Buddhism's final patriarch and the most influential individual on Buddhism's manifestation in China.

Soto Zen   Called *Ts'ao-tung* in Chinese, this branch of Zen Buddhism was brought to Japan by Zen master Dogen and emphasizes silent sitting meditation.

t'so-chuan   The Chinese word for "zazen," or sitting meditation.

tai chi chuan   The ancient art of tai chi chuan, which is based in the even more ancient art of chi kung, consists of combat movements that maximize the flow of energy, or chi, in the body. Today, tai chi chuan (sometimes called tai chi) is widely practiced around the world for its health benefits rather than as a martial art.

Tao   Sometimes translated as "the Way," the Tao is the Chinese word for the universal principle that allows all things to be and thrive, effortlessly and in their natural state.

Taoism   A Chinese philosophy and religious system emphasizing effortless action, simplicity, mindfulness, and following the Tao, and an influential contributor to the Zen branch of Buddhism. Taoism's beginnings are attributed to historical figures Lao-tzu, who wrote the *Tao Te Ching*, and Chuang-tzu, who wrote the *Chuang-tzu*. Both texts explore and explain Taoism and were written around the third century B.C.E.

Three Treasures   The three resources Buddhists have, in which they can take refuge and find relief: the Buddha himself and the notion that everyone has Buddha nature; the Buddha's teachings, or dharma and the recognition that the teachings reflect ultimate truth; and the Buddhist community, or *sangha*.

Ts'ao-tung   The Chinese word for the branch of Zen (*Ch'an*) called Soto in Japan.

zabuton   A rectangular mat or cushion typically used in a meditation hall, at retreats, or if you purchase your own, in an at-home zazen practice. The zabuton goes under the small round zafu, or sitting cushion.

zafu   The full, small round cushion placed on top of the zabuton and used as a seat during meditation.

zazen   The Japanese word for "sitting meditation." *Za* means "to sit," and Zen means "meditation." The Chinese word for "zazen" is *Ts'o-chuan*.

Zen   The Japanese word for "meditation," not in the sense of the contemplation of something, but as a mode of existing (whether sitting, walking, or otherwise going about your day) without any goal or ulterior motive in what Alan Watts, in his *The Way of Zen*, calls "unified or one-pointed awareness." *Dhyana* in Sanskrit and *Ch'an* in Chinese, the term originated in India (with Buddhism).

zendo   A Zen meditation hall. Many larger cities have zendos where people can come to practice zazen together or participate in Zen retreats. Certain rules of etiquette and form are typically practiced in a zendo. These vary according to different Zen traditions.

Ten Bulls

The 10 bull pictures are part of the Zen tradition. Many versions exist, but they all illustrate the Zen process using the bull as a symbol for the truth we seek—or think we need to see—and the mind that eventually perceives truth.

1. First we search for the bull we have lost. Where is it? Where is truth? We feel lost and cannot find what we seek. We know something is missing.

2. We see footprints! A sign! Suddenly we feel we have a direction, a clue to what we seek. We get excited. We feel inspired.

3. We glimpse the bull, just out of reach, running away. But now we know what direction it has gone. We have direction! We feel our search for truth is finally going somewhere.

4. We find the bull and seize it. It fights, and it is strong. But we labor until we have subdued it. At last, we have apprehended what we seek. Mind no longer masters us. We master our own minds.

5. Our efforts have paid off. We tame the bull and secure it with a rope. Once the bull is trained, it won't need a rope any longer. Our minds are controlled, serene, tamed.

6. Now we are master of the bull. We climb on its back and ride it home, triumphant! We feel a sense of joy and pride. Is this truth? Is this enlightenment?

7. Now the bull is put away in its pen, and we sit alone, happy, at home. The rope, bull, and struggle are forgotten. We are content. Mind, now mastered, no longer interferes with the perception of truth. But what is truth? Can we see it now?

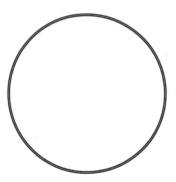

8. Rope, bull, even ourselves are finally transcended. Nothing remains, or everything, because all is one. Truth takes over. It becomes everything, and everything becomes truth. There is no bull, no rope, no struggle, no self.

9. Suddenly we perceive the origin of all things, how we came to be, how the bull and the rope came to be, where it all began. How misled we have been! The bull was never lost! This, at last, is truth.

10. Now we are able to return to the world, mingle with others, back to work, but changed. We are no longer deluded. We are simply happy. We are enlightened.

Index